MUSTAINE

MUSTAINE

A LIFE IN METAL

DAVE MUSTAINE

WITH JOE LAYDEN

HarperCollins*Publishers*

Some names and identifying details have been changed to protect privacy.

HarperCollins*Publishers*
77–85 Fulham Palace Road,
Hammersmith, London W6 8JB

www.harpercollins.co.uk

First published in the USA by itbooks,
an imprint of HarperCollins*Publishers*
This edition 2010

10 9 8 7 6 5 4 3 2 1

Designed by Renato Stanisic
Photograph on pages ii–iii by Rob Shay
All photographs in the book courtesy of
the author unless otherwise stated

Excerpt on p.vii from *A Clockwork Orange* by Anthony Burgess,
published by William Heinemann. Reprinted by permission of
The Random House Group Ltd.

A catalogue record of this book is
available from the British Library

ISBN 978-0-00-732409-5 (hardback)
ISBN 978-0-00-732412-5 (paperback)

Printed and bound in Great Britain by
Clays Ltd, St Ives plc

Mixed Sources
Product group from well-managed
forests and other controlled sources
www.fsc.org Cert no. SW-COC-001806
© 1996 Forest Stewardship Council
FSC

FSC is a non-profit international organisation established to promote the
responsible management of the world's forests. Products carrying the FSC
label are independently certified to assure consumers that they come
from forests that are managed to meet the social, economic and
ecological needs of present and future generations.

Find out more about HarperCollins and the environment at
www.harpercollins.co.uk/green

TO MOM AND DAD,
I PROMISED I WOULD BE GOOD.

THIS BOOK IS DEDICATED
TO ALL OF THE PEOPLE WHO TOLD
ME I WOULD NEVER . . .

COME, COME, COME MY LITTLE DROOGIES. I JUST DON'T GET THIS AT ALL. THE OLD DAYS ARE DEAD AND GONE. FOR WHAT I DID IN THE PAST, I'VE BEEN PUNISHED. I'VE BEEN CURED.

ALEX, A CLOCKWORK ORANGE

REGRETS, I'VE HAD A FEW . . .

SID VICIOUS

CONT

A HORSESHOE UP MY ASS

IF YOU'RE LOOKING FOR BOTTOM, THIS SEEMS TO BE ABOUT AS GOOD A PLACE AS ANY—ALTHOUGH I'D BE THE FIRST TO ADMIT THAT THE BOTTOM HAS BEEN A MOVING TARGET IN MY DARK AND TWISTED, SPEED METAL VERSION OF A DICKENSIAN LIFE. IMPOVERISHED, TRANSIENT CHILDHOOD? CHECK.

ABUSIVE, ALCOHOLIC PARENT? CHECK. MIND-FUCKING RELIGIOUS WEIRDNESS (IN MY CASE THE EXTREMES OF THE JEHOVAH'S WITNESSES AND SATANISM)? CHECK.

ALCOHOLISM, DRUG ADDICTION, HOMELESSNESS? CHECK, CHECK, CHECK.

SOUL-CRUSHING PROFESSIONAL AND ARTISTIC SETBACKS? CHECK.

REHAB? CHECK (SEVENTEEN TIMES, GIVE OR TAKE).

NEAR-DEATH EXPERIENCE? CHECK THAT ONE, TOO.

James Hetfield, who used to be one of my best friends, as close as a brother, once observed with some incredulity that I must have been born with a horseshoe up my ass. That's how lucky I've been, how fortunate I am to be pulling breath after so many close calls. And I must acknowledge that on some level he's right. I have been lucky. I have been blessed. But here's the thing about having a horseshoe lodged in your rectum: it also hurts like hell. And you never forget it's there.

So here I am, staring down the throat of another stint in rehab, at a place called La Hacienda, out in the heart of the pristine Texas Hill Country. It's only about two hundred miles or so from Fort Worth, but it seems a world away, with only cattle ranches and summer camps for neighbors. The focus is on healing . . . on getting better. Physically, spiritually, emotionally. As usual, I've brought only modest expectations and enthusiasm to the proceedings. Ain't my first rodeo, after all.

You see, I've learned more about getting loaded, more about how to get drugs, more about mixing drinks, and more about how to bed the opposite sex in Alcoholics Anonymous than in any other single place in the world. AA—and this holds true for most rehabilitative programs and treatment centers—is a fraternity, and like all fraternity brothers, we like to swap stories. It's a ridiculous glorifying of the experience: *drugalogues* and *drunkalogues*, they're called. One of the things that always bothered me most was the incessant one-upmanship. You'd tell a story, sometimes baring your soul, and the guy next to you would smirk and say, "Ah, man, I spilled more than you ever used."

"Oh, really?"

"Damn right."

"Well, I used a lot, so you must be one clumsy fuckhead."

For some reason, this sort of interaction never did much for me, never made me feel like I was getting better or improving as a human being. Sometimes I got worse. It was at an AA meeting, ironically, that I first learned about the ease of procuring pain medication through the Internet. I didn't have any particular need for pain meds at the time, but the woman telling the story made it sound like a great buzz. Before long the packages were coming to my house and I'd fostered one hell of an addiction. By this time I was a world-famous rock star—founder, front man, singer, songwriter, and guitarist (and de facto CEO) for Megadeth, one of the most popular bands in heavy metal. I had a beautiful wife and two wonderful kids, a nice home, cars, more money than I ever dreamed of. And I was about to throw it all away. You see, behind the façade, I was fucking miserable: tired of the road, the bickering between band members, the unreasonable demands of management and record company executives, the loneliness of the drug-addled life. And, as always, incapable of seeing that what I had was more important than what I didn't have. The joy of writing songs and playing music, which had sustained me through so many lean years, had slowly been siphoned off.

Now I simply felt . . . empty.

And so I went off to Hunt, Texas, hoping this time the change would stick. Or not hoping. Not caring. Not knowing much of anything, really, except that I needed help getting off the pain meds. As for long-term behavior modification? Well, that wasn't high on my list of priorities.

And here's what happens. Early in my stay I wander off to get some rest. I remember slumping into a chair and tossing my left arm over the back, trying to curl up and sleep. The next thing I know, I'm waking up, dragging myself out of the fugue of a twenty-minute nap, and when I try to stand up, something pulls me back, like I'm buckled into the seat or something. And then I realize what's happened: my arm has fallen asleep and it's still hooked over the back of the chair. I laugh, try to withdraw my arm again.

Nothing happens.

Again.

Still nothing.

I repeat this motion (or attempted motion) a few more times before finally using my right arm to lift my left arm off the chair. The moment I let go, it falls to my side, dangling uselessly, pins and needles shooting from shoulder to fingertips. After a few minutes, some of the feeling returns to my upper arm and then to part of my forearm. But my hand remains dead, as if shot full of Novocain. I keep shaking it out, rubbing it, whacking it against the chair. But the hand is numb. Ten minutes pass. Fifteen. I try to make a fist, but my fingers do not respond.

Out the door, down the hall. My breathing is labored, in part because I'm kicking drugs and out of shape, but also because I'm scared shitless. I burst into the nurse's office, cradling my left hand in my right hand. I blurt out something about falling asleep and not being able to feel my hand. The nurse tries to calm me down. She presumes, not unreasonably, that this is just part of the *process*—anxiety and discomfort come with the territory in rehab. But it's not. This is different.

Within twenty-four hours I will be on hiatus from La Hacienda, sitting in the office of an orthopedic surgeon, who will run a hand along my biceps and down my forearm, carefully tracing the path of a nerve and explaining how the nerve has been freakishly compressed, like a drinking straw pinched against the side of a glass. When circulation is cut off in this manner, he explains, the nerve is damaged; sometimes it simply withers and dies.

"How long before the feeling returns?" I ask.

"You should have about eighty percent within a few months . . . maybe four to six."

"What about the other twenty percent?"

He shrugs. The man is all Texas, in movement and delivery. "Hard to say," he drawls.

There is a pause. Once more, nervously, I try to squeeze my

hand into a ball, but the fingers are unwilling. This is my left hand, the one that dances across the fretboard. The one that does all the hard creative work. The moneymaker, as we say in the music business.

"What about playing guitar?" I ask, not really wanting to hear the answer.

The doc draws in a long breath, slowly exhales. "Aw, I don't think you should count on that."

"Until when?"

He looks at me hard. Takes aim. Then he hits the bull's-eye. "Well . . . ever."

And there it is. The kill shot. I can't breathe, can't think straight. But somehow the message comes through loud and clear: this is the end of Megadeth . . . the end of my career . . . the end of music.

The end of life as I know it.

MUSTAINE

DADDY DEAREST

"No more of that shit in my house! You understand?"

FLIP THROUGH A STACK OF SCHOOL YEARBOOKS FROM MY CHILDHOOD OR ADOLESCENCE, AND MORE OFTEN THAN NOT YOU'LL FIND ONE OF THOSE GRAY SILHOUETTES, OR MAYBE EVEN A BIG QUESTION MARK—THE GREAT SCARLET LETTER OF YEARBOOKS!—WHERE MY PHOTO SHOULD BE. LIKE A LOT OF KIDS WHO BOUNCE AROUND FROM SCHOOL TO SCHOOL, TOWN TO TOWN, I WAS FREQUENTLY ABSENT AND THUS BECAME SOMETHING OF A PHANTOM, A SULLEN, RED-HAIRED MYSTERY TO CLASSMATES AND TEACHERS ALIKE.

THE JOURNEY BEGAN IN LA MESA, CALIFORNIA, IN THE SUMMER OF 1961. THAT'S WHERE I WAS BORN, ALTHOUGH IT'S POSSIBLE I WAS CONCEIVED IN TEXAS, WHERE MY PARENTS

My first recorded photograph with my father and sister Debbie.

had lived during the latter stages of their tumultuous marriage. There were two families, really: my sisters Michelle and Suzanne were eighteen and fifteen years old, respectively, by the time I came along (I often thought of them as aunts rather than sisters); my sister Debbie was three. I don't know exactly what happened in the years between the two sets of children. I do know that life unraveled in a great many ways, and in the end my mother was left to fend for herself, and my father became some sort of shadowy figure.

For all practical purposes, John Mustaine was out of my life by the time I was four years old, when my parents finally divorced. Dad, as I understand it, had once been a very smart and successful man, good with his hands and head, skills that helped him rise to the position of branch manager for Bank of America. From there he moved to National Cash Register, and when NCR transitioned from mechanical to electrical technology, Dad was left behind. As the scope of his work narrowed, his income naturally declined. Whether this failure contributed to his escalating problems with alcohol, or whether alcohol provoked his professional failures, I can't say. Certainly the man who ruled the Mustaine household in 1961 was not the man who married my mother. Much of what I know of Dad was passed down in the form of horror stories from my older sisters—stories of abuse and generally insane behavior perpetrated under the shroud of alcoholism. There are snapshots tucked away in the back of my mind, memories of sitting on Dad's lap, watching TV, feeling the razor stubble on his cheeks, smelling booze on his breath. I don't have memories of him *not* drinking—you know, playing ball in the backyard, teaching me how to ride a bike, or anything like that. But neither do I have a catalog of despicable images.

Oh, there is one—the time I was down the street, playing with a neighbor, and for some reason Dad came strolling up the driveway to take me home. He was angry, yelling, though I don't

David Scott Mustaine,
born September 13, 1961.

recall the exact words he used. Something about me being late. What I do remember is the sight of the channel locks in his hand. Channel locks are like pliers, only bigger, and for some reason I guess my father felt like he needed them to corral his four-year-old son. Or maybe he was working on something in the garage and forgot to put them down before setting off. Regardless of the motivation, the channel locks were soon taking a big bite out of my earlobe. I remember screaming and Dad seeming oblivious. He dragged me down the street, never releasing his grip as I stumbled and fell, then scrambled to my feet, trying to keep up, hoping my ear wouldn't just rip right out of its socket. (Do ears have sockets? I was a little kid—what did I know?)

Over the years I've generally defended my father against the allegations of abuse. But I have to admit—this particular incident does not serve as much of a defense. It doesn't exactly reflect the

My father, John Jefferson Mustaine.

actions of a sober, loving daddy, now, does it? But *sober* is the important word in that sentence. I know better than most that people under the influence are capable of unspeakably bad behavior. My father was an alcoholic; I choose to believe that this did not make him an evil man. A weak man, perhaps, and a man who did some bad things. But I have other memories as well. Memories of a benign man smoking a pipe, reading the newspaper, and calling me over to kiss him good night.

After the divorce, though, my father became a monster. Oh, not in the literal sense of the word, but in the sense that he was referred to by everyone in my family as someone to be feared and despised. He even became a weapon to be used against me, to keep me in line. If I misbehaved, my mother would yell, "Keep it up and I'm going to send you to live with your father!"

"Oh, no! Please . . . no! Don't send me to Dad's house!"

There were periodic reconciliations, but they never lasted long, and for the most part we were a family on the run, always trying to stay one step ahead of my father, who supposedly was devoting his entire life to two things: drinking and stalking his estranged wife and children. Again, I don't know if this was accurate, but it was the way things were portrayed to me when I was growing up. We'd settle into a rented house or apartment, and the first thing we'd do is run down to Pier 1 and get a roll of crummy contact paper to turn the shithole of a kitchen into something usable. Things would be quiet for a while. I'd join a Little League team, try to make some friends, and then all of a sudden Mom would tell us Dad had figured out where we were living. A moving van would show up in the middle of the night, we'd pack our meager belongings, and like fugitives we were on the run.

My mother was a maid, and we lived off her salary along with a combination of food stamps and Medicare and other forms of public assistance. And the generosity of friends and relatives. In some cases I could have done with a little less intervention. For example, it was during this period of transiency that we lived with one of my aunts, a devout Jehovah's Witness. Very quickly this became the center of our lives. And trust me—this was not a good thing, especially for a little boy. Suddenly we were spending all our time with the Witnesses: church on Wednesday night and Sunday morning, *Watchtower* magazine study groups, guest speakers on the weekends, home Bible study. Then I'd get to school, and while everyone stood with their hands over their hearts during the Pledge of Allegiance, I'd have to stand quietly with my hands at my sides. When the other kids were singing "Happy Birthday to You" and blowing out candles, I'd stand mute. It's hard enough to make friends as the new kid in school, but when you're the JW freak as well . . . forget it. I was a pariah, always getting picked on, always getting smacked around, which really hardened me.

I remember going to work one day with my mother, in a very wealthy neighborhood called Linda Isle in Newport Beach. There was a little sand pit near the boat dock, and a group of boys was tossing around a football, playing a game that is sometimes referred to as Kill the Guy with the Ball, although in the politically incorrect world of adolescent boys in the early 1970s, it was

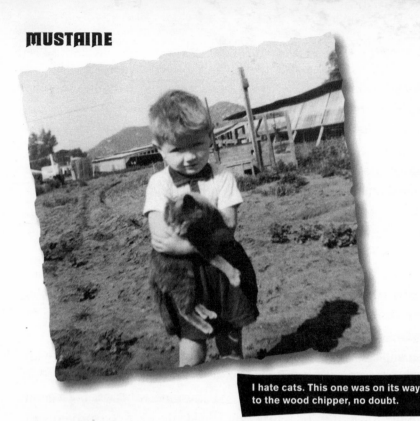

I hate cats. This one was on its way to the wood chipper, no doubt.

more commonly known as Smear the Queer. These guys were all bigger than me, and they took great joy in kicking the shit out of me, but I didn't care, and I had no fear. Why? Because by this time I'd grown accustomed to getting knocked around in school, and disciplined by aunts and uncles, and harassed by a variety of cousins. I blamed almost all of it on the Jehovah's Witnesses. I mean, the fucking insanity of having a brother-in-law or uncle spank me because I supposedly violated some obscure rule of the Witnesses. And this was all stuff that happened under the guise of religion—in the service of a supposedly loving God.

For a while, at least, I tried to fit in with the Witnesses, although from the very beginning it seemed like some giant, multilevel marketing scheme: you sell books and magazines, door-to-door, and the more you sell, the loftier your title. Total bullshit. I was eight, nine, ten years old, and I was worried about the world coming to an end! To this day I still have trauma caused by the Jehovah's Witnesses. I don't get all excited around Christmas, because I still have a hard time believing everything that goes along with the holiday (and I'm speaking as a man who now considers himself a Christian). I want to. I love my kids, I love my wife, and I want to celebrate with them. But deep down inside, there is doubt and skepticism; the Witnesses fucked it up for me.

WHAT DO YOU do when you're a lonely kid, a boy surrounded by women, with no father or even a father figure? You make shit up, create your own universe. I played with a lot of plastic models—miniature replicas of Jack Dempsey and Gene Tunney, whose rivalry was re-created nightly on the floor of my bedroom; tiny American soldiers stormed the beach at Normandy or invaded Iwo Jima. Sounds weird, right? Well, this particular world, the world in my head, was the safest place I could find. I don't mean to sound like a victim, because I've never felt that way. I think of myself as a survivor. But the truth is, every survivor endures some shit, and I was no exception.

Sports provided a glimmer of hope. Bob Wilkie, the chief of police in Stanton, California, was married to my sister Suzanne. Bob was a big, athletic guy (about six foot four, two hundred pounds), a former minor-league baseball player, and he was, for a time, something of a hero to me. He was also my first Little League baseball coach. Bob's stepson Mike (my nephew—how weird is that?) was the team's best pitcher; I was the starting catcher. I loved baseball from the very beginning. Loved putting on the hardware, directing the action from behind the plate, protecting my turf as if my life depended on it. Other kids would try to score and I would beat them down. I wouldn't do anything illegal, but I would put the fear of God into them if they tried to get past me. And I could hit—led the league in home runs that first season.

I don't mean to imply that I was destined for greatness in baseball, but I do think I could have been a jock if I wanted. Unfortunately, there was no stability in my life, and whatever extracurricular activities I chose to pursue, I did so largely without help. We would live with Suzanne for a while, until Dad would find us, and then we'd move out on our own, until the money ran out and we got evicted, and then we'd move in with Michelle or with my aunt Frieda. That was the cycle. One move after another, one home after another.

I wasn't lazy. Far from it, actually. I picked up a paper route to pay for some of my baseball gear and registration fees, and then I added a second route so I'd have some extra money for food and whatever else I might need. During that period we moved from Garden Grove down to Costa Mesa; both of my paper routes were in the Costa Mesa area, but my baseball team was in Garden Grove. So I'd routinely spend the afternoon on my bike delivering papers and then ride my bike up to Garden Grove—a distance of some ten miles—for baseball practice. Then I'd ride back home and fall asleep. The end of that insanity came near the end of the season, when our coach, having exhausted all pitching options during one particularly ugly game, ordered me to the mound.

"But I'm not a pitcher," I said.

"You are now."

I wasn't trying to be an arrogant prick or anything. It's just that I was exhausted and in no mood to play a new position; I didn't want to deal with the learning curve or the embarrassment and then have to pedal all the way back home, dejected and pissed off.

So I played, and I walked in several runs. And that, as it turned out, was one of my very last baseball games.

MUSIC WAS ALWAYS there, sometimes in the background, sometimes inching forward. Michelle had married a guy named Stan, who I thought was one of the coolest guys in the world. He was a cop, too (like Bob Wilkie), but he was a motorcycle cop, and he worked for the California Highway Patrol. Stan would get up in the morning and you'd hear the leather squeaking, the gestapo boots smacking against the floor, and he'd get on his Harley, fire it up, and the whole neighborhood would rattle. No one ever complained, of course. What could they do—call a cop? I liked Stan a lot, not just because of the Harley and the fact that he was clearly not someone you'd want to mess with, but also because

Even as a preteen, I was into staring people down, like here after a Little League victory with my team.

he was a genuinely decent man with a real fondness for music. Every time I went to Stan's house, it seemed that the stereo was roaring, filling the air with the sounds of the great crooners from the sixties: Frankie Valli, Gary Puckett, the Righteous Brothers, Engelbert Humperdinck. I loved listening to those guys, and if you think that seems odd for a future heavy metal warrior, well, think again. I don't doubt for a second that the sense of melody that would inform Megadeth took root back in Stan's house, among other places.

My sister Debbie, for example, had a terrific record collection, mostly hook-laden stuff by the pop stars of that era: Cat Stevens, Elton John, and of course the Beatles. That kind of music was always in the air, sinking into my skin, and when Mom gave me a cheap acoustic guitar as a present for graduating from elementary school, I couldn't wait to start playing. Debbie had some sheet music laying around, and before long I had taught myself some rudimentary chord progressions. Nothing great, of course, but respectable enough for the songs to be recognizable.

For a long time Debbie was my best friend, the person with whom I spent most of my time. She'd come home from school and we'd hang out together, watch TV, play music (Debbie on piano, me on guitar). We leaned on each other when things got hard; we also fought like siblings do, with Debbie usually getting the better of me in our disagreements.

As Debbie grew up and began dating, and eventually fell in love with a guy named Mike Balli, I was left behind. She was seventeen years old when they married. I knew even then it wouldn't last, and of course it didn't. Anyone who met Mike and saw him with Debbie knew it was a relationship doomed to fail. Whatever chemistry there was quickly evaporated, and they were left with an unbalanced union just waiting to die. Debbie was strong and dominant; she basically called the shots—a Big Momma kind of thing.

But Mike had his positive attributes, especially to a fourteen-year-old aspiring guitar player. For one thing, his mother was in some way related to Jack Lord, who at the time was the star of the hit television show *Hawaii Five-O*. In 1974, it didn't get a lot cooler than Steve McGarrett, and Mike didn't mind dropping the guy's name in casual conversation: "Dude, McGarrett's like . . . my second cousin or something!" Can't say I blame him. I would have done the same thing. Mainly, though, what I liked about Mike was the fact that he could play electric guitar, and he

My best friend growing up, my sister Deborah K. Mustaine.

didn't mind playing with me. Admittedly, his guitar was a complete piece of crap; it was called a Supra, and it was a ridiculous sunburst red, with three pickups, but it served its purpose. To my still uneducated ears, he seemed to be a fairly decent player.

Mike's little brother Mark was also a musician. He played bass in a band with a guy named John Voorhees (who later did a stint with a fairly successful band called Stryper). Mark and John heard me playing, asked if I might be interested in joining them.

"Sure," I said. "Just one problem."

"What's that?"

"I don't have a guitar."

No problem, Mark said. I could borrow his acoustic. I didn't really know what I was doing. I just knew I liked the feeling of having a guitar in my hands, making music, being part of . . . *something*. I was a smart kid but an indifferent student, even as far back as elementary school. I'd get in trouble for fooling around or failing to have my homework completed, and sometimes I'd have to stay after school. Frankly I found this embarrassing. But I knew in my heart that I was a natural learner, especially if it was a subject that captured my interest.

Like music.

I loved having that secret weapon, that bond—where you sit down with another musician, and you start talking, and everyone else at the table immediately takes notice, because you're speaking a language they don't even understand, can't hope to comprehend. It's like they think the conversation is going to be empty-headed, but it's not. It's just . . . different. And if you don't play music (as opposed to just listening to music), you really can't possibly know what I'm talking about.

So joining a band was about camaraderie as much as anything else, I suppose.

And sex, of course. Ultimately, when it comes to rock 'n' roll, it's always about sex.

ONE AFTERNOON WHEN I was about thirteen years old, we went over to Mark's house to rehearse. There were a bunch of people hanging out, including one of Mark's buddies, who lived across the street, and his girlfriend, whose name was Linda. When I walked into the house, Linda caught my eye. I wasn't exactly a player, even by junior high standards, but I noticed right away that Linda was giving me a hard look. She hung out while we jammed for a bit, and afterward, having seen that I was the new lead guitar player, she introduced herself to me. Within a matter of days, Linda had chucked her old boyfriend for me. Why? Not because of my looks or dynamic personality, but simply because I played guitar. And I recall thinking, as Linda sidled up to me and took my hand in hers, *Hmmmm . . . I kind of like this.*

The hormonal inspiration for picking up a guitar is a cliché; it's also fundamentally true, as pure and honest as any other muse. And it doesn't change, even as you go from gangly, pubescent teen to full-grown adult male. That was one of the things that surprised me most about the music business: you hear all this stuff about sex, drugs, and rock 'n' roll . . . and you laugh it off. Then you get to peek behind the curtain, and guess what? It's real! You go to Salt Lake City, the pristine capital of that most morally upright of states, and discover there's a reason the rock stars call it Salt *Lick* City. You discover the cliché is based on truth. It's absolutely real, and pretty soon you're trying to decide which of the two proverbial bulls you want to be: the one that charges down the hill, full speed, and fucks the first cow he meets, or the one who saunters down the hill slowly and fucks them all.

MARK'S HOUSE BECAME a place of inspiration and experimentation. One of the very first songs I learned to play was "Panic in Detroit" by David Bowie, followed by Mott the Hoople's "All the Young Dudes." There was a pot dealer who lived up the street, and he introduced us to a variety of great stuff (in more ways than one): Johnny Winter; Emerson, Lake and Palmer; Triumvirate; and, of course, Led Zeppelin. I mean, if you played guitar, you wanted to be Jimmy Page, right? And if you sang in a rock 'n' roll band, you wanted to be Robert Plant. Everyone was trying to learn "Stairway to Heaven," which I actually picked up pretty quickly. But you know what really got me hooked?

KISS.

Man, I really dug the early KISS stuff—not just musically but stylistically. I was not a Gene Simmons guy, either; I liked Ace Frehley, because he was a lead guitar player. I liked the whole rock star thing, and KISS seemed to have taken it to a new level. In the same way that Axl Rose made people hate rock stars, Gene Simmons and Paul Stanley made rock stars seem kind of decadent and megalomaniacal—which wasn't a bad thing at all, so far as I could tell. KISS was one of the first bands I saw live, and I couldn't help but notice that a disproportionate number of their fans looked like Dallas Cowboys cheerleaders: they all had blond hair and wore tube tops, and they seemed to be throwing themselves at the band. And if the band wasn't accessible, well, then the guy next to them in the audience would do.

My love for music, and especially my fascination with the lifestyle it promised, was viewed skeptically by some members of my extended family. My mother, of course, was forever conflicted: on the one hand, I know that she loved me and supported me, and wanted to see me happy and successful. On the other hand, there was no reconciling her son's drinking, drugging, and "devil music" with the tenets of the Jehovah's Witnesses; they were fundamentally incompatible. Similarly, my brother-in-law Bob Wilkie grew increasingly disenchanted with my changing interests. He liked me when I was a baseball player or an aspiring martial artist (I first took lessons at the YMCA in Stanton, which was located directly across the street from Bob's police station). Those were pursuits he could get behind. But playing in a band? Listening to heavy metal music?

Uh-uh.

One day when I was not quite fifteen years old, Bob came home and discovered me hanging out in his house, listening to Judas Priest's *Sad Wings of Destiny*. He walked in the front door, marched over to the turntable, and turned down the volume.

"What the hell is this?" he said, waving the album jacket in disgust.

"Judas Priest," I answered, somewhat sheepishly.

"Who does it belong to?"

I shrugged. "It's mine."

And with that Bob dropped the jacket, took two big steps in my direction, and punched me in the face.

"No more of that shit in my house! You understand?"

I stood there, stunned and dazed, holding a hand to my cheek, fighting back tears.

"Yes, sir."

What else could I do? I respected Bob too much to fight back. He would have kicked my ass anyway. I mean, the guy was a professional athlete—and a cop! Not only that, but Bob had come into our family—and into my life—as a good guy. He'd married Suzanne, adopted her son, and generally conducted himself in an old-fashioned, chivalrous manner. This seemed completely out of character.

But as I retreated to the kitchen to get some ice out of the freezer and applied it to my swollen jaw, I had to wonder: *Who the hell punches a fifteen-year-old?*

And . . .

What the fuck does he have against Judas Priest?

REEFER MADNESS

2

"He likes to pour A1 steak sauce on my pussy before giving me head."

I WAS THIRTEEN YEARS OLD THE FIRST TIME I GOT HIGH.

WE WERE LIVING IN GARDEN GROVE AT THE TIME, AND A FRIEND WHO LIVED DOWN THE STREET HAD INTRODUCED ME TO THE MAGIC OF MARIJUANA. THIS KID WAS ONE OF THOSE INGENIOUS LITTLE FUCKERS WHO, IF HE HAD MANAGED TO CHANNEL HIS ENERGY AND INTELLECT IN OTHER DIRECTIONS, MIGHT HAVE EARNED A PHD SOMEWHERE. AS IT HAPPENED, HE PROVED MAINLY TO BE GOOD AT FINDING WAYS TO INGEST POT.

WE WERE HANGING OUT AT HIS HOUSE ONE DAY AFTER SCHOOL, AND HE SUGGESTED WE SMOKE SOME WEED. BUT NOT IN ANY MANNER THAT I RECOGNIZED. RATHER THAN ROLLING A DOOB, THIS KID WENT TO HIS ROOM and returned with a homemade bong crafted out of a Pringles potato chip can!

"What do I do with this?" I asked as he proudly showed me the tube.

And then he demonstrated. A half hour later I was staggering back down the street, red eyed and giggling, absolutely loaded. And that was it. Game on.

I liked smoking pot, liked the way it made me feel, and so I started experimenting with it. From there I naturally branched out into alcohol and other drugs, and before long I was skipping school, killing entire days at my friend's house, sucking on the Pringles can. My grades quickly suffered, and I started to see how you could associate with the wrong people and make bad decisions, and pretty soon your life could be spiraling out of control. Not that I gave a shit. I'm just talking about awareness and the fact that as an adult, and a parent, I can look back now and see where it all sort of began. But you have to remember: there were no serious ramifications—none that mattered to me, anyway. Getting high on a regular basis did not make my life noticeably worse. In fact, it made life tolerable.

More than anything else (and this is true of most kids, I think), what I wanted was to feel as though I fit in somewhere. I wanted to *belong*. Music helped with that. So did smoking pot. Each time we moved to a new house, a new town, a new school, I endured an indoctrination period. I learned how to deal with this in a variety of ways—first through sports, then through music and partying, and eventually by breaking free of the Jehovah's Witnesses. There was no greater stamp of weirdness than to be associated with the Witnesses, and to escape that stigma I deliberately behaved in a manner that was inconsistent with the teachings of the church. My mom and my aunts and all the other Witnesses would warn me that I was destined to burn in hell if I didn't clean up my act, but frankly I didn't care. I just wanted to get away from them. I wanted some semblance of *normalcy*, whatever that might mean.

There were times when I felt like the sad hero of some fairy tale. You know the kind—where the kids are left in the care of an evil stepmother or stepfather, or some other surrogate caregiver who really couldn't give a flying fuck about the kids' welfare. And the dreary circumstances of my life seemed less appealing than retreating to some make-believe world in which all I had to do was smoke weed, play music, hang out with like-minded slackers, and maybe try to get laid once in a while. Music, in particular, was my avenue of escape—everything else just went along with it.

THERE WAS, HOWEVER, one significant problem associated with cultivating a healthy appetite for drugs and alcohol.

Cash flow.

By the time I was fifteen we'd moved into an apartment at a place called Hermosa Village (which was actually located not in Hermosa or Hermosa Beach, but in nearby Huntington Beach), across the street from Golden West College, where I would eventually take classes. When we moved in there, I lost some friendships and the easy access to pot that came with them, and so I had to figure out how to keep the grass growing, so to speak. At the time, pot was going for roughly ten bucks an ounce. So, with no consideration whatsoever given to consequences or moral conundrums, I borrowed ten bucks from my sister, bought an ounce of pot, and went to work. I rolled forty joints and quickly turned around and sold them for fifty cents apiece. In a matter of just a few hours, I had doubled my money. Now, I was far from an economics wizard, but I knew a good thing when I saw it. From that moment on, I was in business: a low-rent pot dealer who made enough cash to stay high and to put food in his belly when the fridge was empty, which was more often than you might imagine. Before long, the going price for a joint went up to seventy-five cents. Then a dollar. Then Mexican weed gave way to the more potent and expensive Colombian, which in turn gave way to rainbow and to Thai. The culture embraced pot smoking with increasing fervor, which was good for my wallet and maybe not so great for my head. I didn't really care. I was home. All I needed was some dope and music, and some buddies to hang out with.

I remember seeing *Reefer Madness* at the old Stanton Picture Palace, a theater in my brother-in-law's jurisdiction. There were virtually no rules there in the 1970s; you could drink and smoke as much dope as you wanted. And when the cops came, the owner would get on the public address system and say, "Ladies and gentlemen, so as not to violate fire codes, please extinguish all smoking materials now." And then the fans would come on and clear the fog, and the cops would leave and everyone would light up all over again. What a great place! I saw *Fritz the Cat* there, too, and *Gimme Shelter.* I'd have my little two-dollar pipe and my bag of pot, and I'd sit there for hours on end, hiding out, watching the movies. That was the culture. That was my life.

Mom naturally approved of none of this, and I can't say that I blame her. On more than one occasion I'd be getting ready to leave, to go hang with my friends or play some music, and I'd have to alert my mother to the possibility of a delivery.

"Uh, Mom?"

"Yes?"

"There's a good chance this dude will come by around three o'clock. He's going to pick up a package. It's in my room. Just give it to him. And tell him I need twenty-five bucks."

Mom would look at me like I was insane. "What exactly is in this package, David?"

"Doesn't matter, Mom. Just give it to him. Really, don't worry. It's cool."

Remarkably enough, she went along with it. At least for a while. It's hard not to love your kids, I guess, even when they're making your life miserable.

Eventually Mom had had enough. Unable to reconcile my behavior with her own religious beliefs (and no doubt dreading the day when the cops would break down the door and arrest all of us for drug trafficking), Mom moved out of the apartment. I was not invited to join her. I was fifteen years old and, for all intents and purposes, totally on my own. An emancipated minor.

Fortunately, the two guys who ran the apartment complex wound up being terrific customers of mine. So if I was a little short on cash when it came time to pay the rent, all I had to do was broker a deal. A few joints here and there usually settled the issue and left everyone happy and high. By this time I was no longer just dabbling in the field; I was moving a considerable amount of dope. And I had no problem with it whatsoever. Here's the truth of the matter: when you're a hungry fifteen-year-old with no viable means of income and no parental support or supervision, you don't have many options. You aren't old enough to get a real job, so you have to be more . . . *creative*. Desperation fueled my entrepreneurial spirit—that and the knowledge that if I didn't sell dope, about the only other way to make money was to sell myself. Peddle my ass. I knew enough kids who'd gone that route, or at least had heard about them, seen them working the streets, and there was no fucking way I was going to let that happen.

Under the right circumstances, though, I didn't mind trading sex for drugs, or drugs for sex, or whatever. There was, for example, a girl named Willow who worked at a music shop at Westminster Mall. We got to know each other through my frequent visits to the store, during which I'd wander around for hours, thumbing through the stacks of vinyl, trying to figure out what I wanted to listen to next, whether there was some way to advance my knowledge. I was a pothead and a dope dealer, but I really did love music, and I wanted to be a great guitar player—I just had no idea how to make it happen. Eventually I struck up a friendship with Willow, who was maybe a year or two older than me, and the friendship evolved into something else. In exchange for free dope, Willow would give me free records. We'd smoke the dope and listen to the records while having sex at my apartment. Not a terrible arrangement, all things considered. It was Willow, after all, who gave me my first AC/DC album, a gift that kept on giving for years to come, long after we'd stopped having sex or even seeing each other casually.

I never labored under the illusion that I was anything more than a diversion for Willow, someone who shared her taste in music and didn't mind trading dope for sex. But even at that age I had some meager standards, which bubbled to the surface one afternoon during a postcoital round of pillow talk.

"You know, my boyfriend likes it when I shave my pubic hair into a heart," Willow said.

"Yeah, I noticed. Cool."

"You know what else he likes?"

"What?"

She leaned over and put her arms around me, then whispered into my ear. "He likes to pour A1 steak sauce on my pussy before giving me head."

"Whoa . . ."

And that was that. Not even the prospect of an endless supply of records was enough to wipe from my brain the indelible image of Willow and her boyfriend and a big sloppy bottle of A1. We never had sex again.

WHEN BUSINESS SLOWED and my stomach rumbled, I had precious few options. I couldn't really move back in with my mother—our relationship was simply too fractured, and her ties to the Jehovah's Witnesses precluded accepting my increasingly decadent way of life. Salvation, then, lay to the north. Specifically, in a little town near Pocatello, Idaho. My sister Michelle had moved up there with Stan, who in addition to being a motorcycle cop was also a skilled carpenter. As tourism and an attendant real estate boom hit the region, work for guys like Stan became plentiful; he ditched the badge and uniform and went off to make some serious money. Tired of trying to support myself, and weary of the life I was leading at home, I called Michelle and asked if I could come up and live with her for a while. She graciously accepted, although strict parameters were placed on the arrangement.

For one thing, I had to get my ass back in school. I also agreed to get a part-time job. Michelle helped me land a gig bussing tables at a restaurant where she worked, a place called the Ox Bow Inn. My nephew Stevie (Michelle's son) worked there as a busboy as well, so it was kind of a family affair. Stevie, though, turned out to be a real pain in the ass. He wanted to start a band but lacked the money to buy proper equipment. So he kept borrowing gear from other bands playing at the Ox Bow. There were a lot of people who weren't best pleased.

That, however, was nothing compared to the grief Stevie caused me at school. Before I even arrived, he had spread the word about the imminent arrival of his uncle Dave, "the kung fu master from California." Well, of course, I wasn't a kung fu master; in fact, I hadn't yet studied kung fu at all. I'd been taking martial arts classes* for about three years and had progressed to the point where I could handle myself in a fight, if necessary. But it wasn't like I was a black belt or anything, and I certainly didn't brag about it. The study of martial arts has been an important part of my life—spiritually and physically—for nearly four decades now, but I was nothing more than a novice at the time, taking classes to enhance my self-esteem and foster some sense of discipline in an otherwise chaotic life.

Stevie saw it differently, and so did everyone else. By the time I got up there, half the school was ready to fight me just for the sheer fucking sport of it. On the first day of school some dude walked by me at my locker and drove his elbow into my stomach. I was still trying to catch my breath when he looked at me and said, with a nasty, gap-toothed smile, "You and me, boy? We're gonna fight after school today."

"Who the fuck are you?"

He didn't answer, just walked away, laughing, with a posse of rednecks.

Turned out his name was Wilbur. He was—I shit you not—the son of a pig farmer, which actually gave him a relatively prominent place in this particular backwoods social stratum. I had no way out of this. I had to take the bus home, and by the time I got on board, everyone knew there was going to be a showdown between the kung fu master and the pig farmer. Now, getting to and from school in rural Idaho involved numerous transfers and lots of bus time. My rendezvous with Wilbur occurred at one of the transfer points, while waiting for a second bus that would take me back to the mobile home where Stan and Michelle lived. Within

---

* Specifically in Shorin-ryu karate. I competed in my first tournament around this time and discovered how challenging the sport can be. I won my first match after my opponent was disqualified for hitting me in the face and groin. Unfortunately, I was unable to continue fighting and had to withdraw.

seconds of getting off the bus, Wilbur and I found ourselves at the center of a big, heaving circle of bloodthirsty teenagers.

Damn it, I did not want this to happen.

Wilbur put up his hands, like some bare-knuckle fighter, and smiled confidently.

"Come on, motherfucker," he yelled. "Hit me! Flip me or something."

For some reason I heard that—*"Hit me! Flip me . . ."*—and the thought occurred to me that it sounded like the title of a punk song. A calm washed over me. The whole thing just seemed so ridiculous, me standing there in the middle of a bunch of strange, screaming kids, getting ready to fight this big Idaho pig farmer's son. I thought I'd left California to get away from dangerous situations. How the hell did this happen?

"Come on, man! You gonna give me a karate chop or what?! Kung fu faggot!"

Stalemate. Wilbur didn't want to hit me first because he was bigger; I refused to hit him because I had been taught by my sensei that I was to strike only in self-defense. And so it went, the two of us dancing awkwardly, until the bus arrived. We boarded, uneventfully, and the bus pulled away.

Crisis averted.

Or so I thought, until we reached Wilbur's stop. As he exited the bus, he cocked his arm and drilled me in the back of the head with an elbow. I knew instantly I was fucked—and not because I was now compelled to engage Wilbur in battle, but rather because I'd worked up a sizable wad of chewing tobacco, a big chunk of which was now sliding down my throat. If you've ever accidentally swallowed chew, you know what came next. Within seconds I was incapacitated; by the time I got home I was vomiting from my shoes.

In response, I did what anyone in my situation would have done: I put a hex on the guy.

Well, maybe not anyone, but anyone with a sister who was heavily into witchcraft and black magic. Indeed, for me, this was the beginning of a very long and disturbing flirtation with the occult, the effects of which haunted me for years. At the time, though, it seemed just a handy tool to have at my disposal. Having been baptized Lutheran and harassed into stupefaction by the JWs, I was by my teenage years an empty vessel when it came to religion. Contrary to popular belief, while I did read *The Satanic Bible* I never became an actual Satanist—the whole concept seemed kind of silly, to be perfectly candid—but I certainly did dabble in the dark arts, and I don't doubt for a second that it fucked with my head to an almost immeasurable degree.

I believed in the occult, and some people will say, "How can you believe in the occult and practice black magic and not be satanic?" Well, there's a line there. Talk to anyone who has been involved in the occult and they will tell you that there are a lot of different factions for different types of magic. And as with anything else, there are good and bad aspects to the occult.

I only know that both witchcraft and the Jehovah's Witnesses caused me a good deal of pain for a great many years. They're different, of course. The pain from getting into witchcraft was residual. The pain of the religiosity of the Jehovah's Witnesses, that was causal. It's like when people say, "Hey, you're on drugs, so your relationships are shitty," and you respond with, "No, my relationships are shitty, and that's why I'm on drugs." Either way, you're fucked-up.

But that afternoon, as I tried to calm my raging stomach? Witchcraft seemed like a perfectly reasonable coping mechanism.

Since Michelle was reluctant to offer, I stole some of her books; after just a few days of study, I went to work, crafting a doll out of bread dough, using poppy seeds to spell out W-I-L-B-U-R and tying a noose made out of string around the doll's neck. Then I recited an incantation from the book of spells. Finally, at the very end, I picked up the doll and snapped off one of its legs.

Did it work?

I can't say for sure, but I do know that a short time later Wilbur was involved in a car accident; his leg was broken. Given the nature of life in that part of the world—the way people drank heavily and drove without regard to consequence—and given that Wilbur was an imbecilic jerk, I suppose some sort of crippling episode was inevitable.

Then again . . .

Kind of creepy, huh?

AFTER MY HIATUS in Idaho, I returned to Orange County and loosely resumed the pursuit of a rock 'n' roll lifestyle. Since I liked cars and knew a little bit about how they worked, I got a part-time job working at a garage; this helped tide me over until I could cultivate enough clients to resurrect my business selling pot. I took classes at night in the hope of getting a high school diploma and found companionship in the arms of a girl named Moira, who became my first serious love interest.

Musically, I was a sponge, listening to anything I could get my hands on, trying to learn my favorite licks and mimic my favorite guitar players. During the day I hung out at the beach with my best buddy, Mike Jordan, and some other pasty-skinned friends of Northern European descent, drinking and trying not to fry. At night we wandered from neighborhood to neighborhood, from kegger to kegger, sometimes fighting, but usually just drinking, smoking pot, and laughing at the amateurish bands that passed for "entertainment."

Even the worst of them, though, managed to tap into something primal and to achieve a minor level of celebrity, with all the attendant perks. I remember hearing about a guy named Pat Knowles, the one guitar player in our neighborhood universally viewed as a badass musician. Then I met him for the first time. What a disappointment! The guy was a skinny little vanilla-pudding, Peter Pan–looking motherfucker. Just a really soft kid. But Jesus . . . could he play! And then there was John Tull, who was almost the antithesis of Pat Knowles. John was a big lumberjack kind of guy, with thick arms and a cinder block of a skull. You know how they say the typical adult male has a forehead equal to the width of four fingers? Well, John was definitely a five. Maybe even a six. He had a black Les Paul with three pickups, and he was playing songs like no one I'd ever seen. Not locally, anyway. Good songs, too—songs I listened to on the radio and on my eight track, and as I watched him play, I couldn't help but be impressed.

Man . . . this guy is good.

That was only half of it. When the band went on break and John put down his guitar, the chicks were all over him. And bear in mind, Mr. Five-Finger Forehead was not exactly the most handsome guy in the room. But it didn't matter—it was the guitar and the magic of the music that made John attractive to the opposite sex. I wanted to be like him, and to be like Pat Knowles.

Only *better* than them.

IT BEGAN AT the age of seventeen, with a kid named Dave Harmon, a drummer from Huntington Beach whose home life seemed to be the exact opposite of mine. Dave came from a stable family, with a mother and father who supported everything he wanted to do, including becoming a musician. They understood

In a Michael Schenker (of UFO at the time) inspired pose, in concert at a house party with Panic.

that I was basically on my own, and so they took pity on me, opened their home to me, and treated me with kindness and understanding. For me, it was like winning the lottery. I was living on my own, drinking generic beer, eating ramen noodles and macaroni and cheese like they were going out of style. Then I meet this kid with cool parents and a fridge full of food.

Dave and I started talking about playing together and maybe putting together a real band, one that would kick the shit out of anything we'd seen at the neighborhood parties. To play guitar, Dave recruited a friend of his named Rick Solis, who had a beautiful Gibson Flying V. Like me, Rick studied martial arts, so we hit it off right away. Rick was also the first aspiring rocker I'd met who actually looked the part—he was like a cross between Vinnie Vincent and Paul Stanley. This was no accident. Rick was one of those guys with an innate understanding of image—he favored sleeveless shirts, long hair, and a weird assemblage of rock star jewelry. He also had an enormous nose and dark skin, which gave him a really exotic Mediterranean appearance, and was one of the most hirsute guys I'd ever met. He took the good with the bad—the bearskin rug on his chest (hey, in the seventies this was considered the height of virility) and the monobrow that stretched from one side of his head to the other.

Rick was the first guy I met who seemed committed to playing well and to becoming a rock star. We taught each other a bunch of songs, from "Fire" by Jimi Hendrix to most of the Judas Priest catalog to almost anything else that sounded interesting. Like me, Rick was still developing his taste for music. Before long he was behaving in a manner that was profoundly weird and unacceptable, which led not only to his expulsion from the band but, I can only presume, to a premature demise (Rick often drove while fucked-up, and died in a motorcycle accident just a few years later).

With Rick gone, Dave and I went about the business of building a new band. First to join was a guitar player named Tom Quecke, a friend of mine from night school. Tom came from a family with three brothers. The oldest worked for the government in national security; a terrific, great upstanding guy. The middle brother I didn't hear much about—he was the black sheep of the family. And then there was Tom, who was like a black sheep gone good. Or trying, anyway. Truth be told, he was kind of a mediocre guitar player, but that's all we really needed, because he only played rhythm; I handled lead.

Next on board was Bob Evans, a bass player who reminded me of that character Junior from the hillbilly TV show *Hee Haw*. He was heavyset, with short hair and bangs, and he wore overalls all the time. Bobby looked . . . well, kind of like a simpleton. But he was actually a pretty sharp kid. As was his father, who was an accomplished sound engineer who had built some incredible sound cabinets for his home. These things weren't just bass cabinets; they were like bass enclosures from Royal Albert Hall or something.

We'd go to play with this dude, and I'd have my little cabinets, and Bobby would be firing up these enormous cabinets, stacked eight feet high, and would hit that first bass note—*BWOWWW-WWW!*—and sterilize the neighborhood. Bobby had money and a car, so naturally we were happy to have him in the band.

At that point all we needed was a singer—I hadn't yet considered the possibility that I might handle the microphone myself—and we found one in Pat Voelkes. Pat was lean and muscular, with long straight hair—he looked like a singer. He was also a couple years older than the rest of us, a little bit more mature, a little smarter about the practical side of putting together a band. We built a rehearsal studio in Pat's garage and got together as often as possible to practice. But we all had lives on the side. Mine revolved around the trafficking of illicit substances. By this time I'd gravitated from selling pot to selling anything I could get my hands on: hash, LSD, Quaaludes, cocaine. When it came to making money, I was indiscriminate.

I don't say that with pride. It's just the way it was. I needed cash, and this was the easiest, most efficient way to raise it. Moreover, you have to consider the cultural and political climate of the times. Chemically speaking, the late 1970s was a pretty liberal time. I didn't see anything particularly dangerous or immoral about ingesting or distributing drugs. It seemed absolutely normal to me. Given my background and family history, this isn't exactly a surprise.

We called the band Panic. I don't even remember why—probably just because it sounded kind of cool, wild and anarchic. Our first performance was in Dana Point, at a party hosted by my cousin John. It was something of a makeshift affair. Dave Harmon was unable to play that night, so we recruited a substitute drummer named Mike Leftwich. We played pretty well, and the crowd loved us. The set list was a random collection of songs I'd heard at various keg parties—Def Leppard, the Scorpions, Judas Priest—along with some more obscure stuff that I liked, such as Budgie and Sammy Hagar (as a solo artist). Everyone had a blast, and by the end of the night the apartment had taken on the atmosphere of an orgy, with drunken girls removing their clothes and having sex with guys in the band.

I couldn't have been happier.

The next day, though, brought horrific news. The band members had all gone their separate ways after the party. Mike had left with a friend named Joe, a big-hearted, unassuming kid who had doubled as our sound guy for the concert. On the drive home, on Pacific Coast Highway, just south of Huntington Beach Pier, Mike and Joe had been involved in a terrible accident. I got the news from Tom Quecke, delivered through the haze of an early-morning hangover.

"Joe fell asleep at the wheel," he said, his voice catching. "They're both gone."

AT SEVENTEEN YOU don't instantly make the cause-and-effect connection between drinking and death, but I was beginning to understand that the lifestyle I was leading—and at times loving—had its consequences. For one thing, when I drank, I tended to get really violent. Pot had a soothing, almost soporific effect. Alcohol, though, provoked anger. I was probably sixteen the first time I drank to the point of blacking out. It wouldn't be the last. Invariably, my mood turned dark on these occasions. My intent was never to hurt anyone. It wasn't like I popped open the first beer with the goal of finding a fight by the end of the evening. My motivation was much simpler: to feel good and find somebody who wanted to commiserate naked with me. Typically, though, the plans went awry. Let's put it this way: I did not get in trouble every time I drank, but every time I got in trouble, I'd been drinking. That's for sure. Smoking pot was an entirely different experience. I'd get up in the morning, wake and bake, watch MTV, sing along with the Buggles, play some guitar, take a nap, and get on with the day. No harm, no foul.

All of it was of an ever-expanding piece: the music, the lifestyle, the drinking, the drugs, the sex. For the longest time I was incapable of acknowledging even the slightest possibility that I might have a problem with substance abuse. I looked in the mirror and saw a prototypical rock star. A party animal. It wasn't until many years later that I took another look and saw something else:

Oh, my God. I'm not Keith Richards. I'm Otis from Mayberry! A fucking drunk!

But that took time. Pot was for the most part a socially acceptable drug in the seventies; to a lesser extent, so was cocaine, although I shunned it initially because it was linked in my view to the disco movement and then to house music and techno. Cocaine was for the Village People and Donna Summer crowds, or the pussies you'd see at a Flock of Seagulls concert. For metal fans, especially for metal musicians, there was booze and drugs. The hard stuff.

A FEW DAYS after the accident, Dave Harmon and I went over to Mike's house and tried to speak with his family. We awkwardly offered our condolences, and they graciously accepted, but it was a painful encounter. I suppose on some level they blamed us for what happened to Mike, if for no other reason than because of his association with the band. Someone had to be at fault, right? Isn't that the way tragedy works?

We tried to resuscitate the band, even played a bunch of shows in Dana Point, Huntington Beach, and the surrounding areas over the next couple months. But the spirit was lacking; there was too much baggage, too many reminders of what had happened. Too much guilt, maybe. I can only speak for myself, and for me, it just didn't feel right. The kinship that drives a band during the formative years was lacking. We didn't like each other enough, and we didn't want it badly enough.

Drug use around Panic was common. I was doing drugs with the band members, fronting people stuff, getting high on my own supply . . . spiraling down the path of drugs and alcoholism. Even the greatest of all fringe benefits—random, indiscriminate sex—began to lose its luster. I told Moira one day that I'd had a dream about engaging in a threesome with her and one of her best friends (this was true, incidentally); that afternoon, when I came home from rehearsal, Moira and Patty were standing on the front porch, naked and smiling, awaiting my arrival. One might reasonably assert that such a greeting would boost the spirits of any red-blooded American male. And it did . . . for a while. But something was missing. I just didn't know what it was.

I'd gotten into rock 'n' roll for the lifestyle, not because I aspired to great musicianship. I didn't sit around waiting for people to come up and say, "Gosh, Dave, you arpeggiate so beautifully!" No, it wasn't that at all. I was a rock 'n' roll rebel. I had my guitar strung across my back, I had a knife in my belt, and I had a sneer on my face. And that was it. That was enough.

Or so I thought.

AROUND THE SAME time, I briefly reconnected with my father. It was June of 1978; I was seventeen years old, and for some reason I got the urge to track him down. Mom and Dad had been divorced for so long, and he'd been such a shadowy figure in my life, that I just had to see for myself whether everything I'd heard was true. So distant were the memories that they couldn't be trusted, any more than I could trust the lurid stories of abuse spewed by my sisters and my mother.

It didn't take long to track him down, and when I called him up and suggested we get together, he seemed genuinely moved.

"I'd like that, yeah. When?"

"How about this weekend?"

We met at his apartment, a dark, sparsely furnished little place with bad wallpaper and rented furniture. It was Father's Day, but that was almost beside the point. I didn't feel like his son, and I don't know that he felt like my father. We were just two people—strangers really—trying to connect. Whatever emotion I expected—anger, joy, pride—was overwhelmed by the sadness of his pathetic little life. My father did not look like the bogeyman of my nightmares; nor did he look like the successful banker he'd once been. He just looked . . . old. At one point I opened up the refrigerator looking for something to drink and was stunned by its emptiness. There, in the door, was a little jar of mayonnaise, crusty at the rim. On the center shelf was a loaf of bread, open and spilling out of its bag. A few random bottles of beer were scattered about the fridge.

That was it.

I didn't know what to say, so I just shut the door and took a seat at the kitchen table. I don't remember exactly how long the visit lasted. I do recall apologizing for being such a terrible son, an acknowledgment that brought tears to his eyes and a dismissive wave of the hand. When I left, we hugged and agreed to make an effort to get together more often.

That didn't happen. The next time I saw my father, about one week later, he was in a hospital bed, on life support. His job at the time was hardly glamorous—servicing cash registers for NCR.

Apparently, as I understand it (although there is some dispute regarding the events leading up to his death), Dad was in a bar when he slipped off a stool and hit his head. I'd like to think that he was working on a cash register at the time, that his death was in some minor way noble. But the likelihood of that is small. It's like the guy who gets caught in the whorehouse and says, "Uh . . . I was just looking." My father was an alcoholic, and he suffered a cerebral hemorrhage in a bar. Hard to imagine he was sober when it happened. The tragedy is that he might have been saved, but by the time the doctors tracked down anyone who could give them permission to crack his skull and relieve the pressure, he'd already lapsed into a coma. Imagine that. You have an ex-wife and four children all living in the area. You have several brothers and sisters. Grandchildren. But on the day that you suffer a terrible accident, there's no one to call, no one who cares.

When I got the call from my sister Suzanne, I kind of freaked out.

"Dad's in the hospital," she said. "You'd better get down here right away."

"What happened?"

"Just hurry."

The first thing I did—the very first fucking thing—was grab a pint bottle of Old Grand-Dad whiskey. I tucked it into my shirt pocket, then ran outside, hopped on my moped, and drove off down Goldenwest Street toward the Pacific Coast Highway. Funny thing is, I hated whiskey; it wasn't even my bottle, just some shit left behind after a party, no doubt. But I saw it and knew I wanted to hurt someone, and I figured whiskey would help get the job done.

The trip to the hospital in Costa Mesa was one I could have made in my sleep, even though I'd never been there before. I knew my way around the whole region because I'd been like a flea, jumping from dog to dog through Orange County, Riverside County,

Los Angeles, and San Diego. I raced down the highway, drinking with one hand, opening the throttle with the other. When I got to the hospital room, my father was in the fetal position, wires snaking from his body to various monitors and life-support equipment. My sisters were already there, lined up at the foot of the bed like the Three Wise Monkeys. Nobody said a word, until finally Suzanne drew close, smelled the liquor on my breath, saw my bloodshot eyes and the near-empty bottle of Old Grand-Dad poking out of my shirt pocket.

"You know what?" she said, her voice dripping with disdain.

"What?"

"You're going to end up just like him."

She put the emphasis on the last word—"*him*"—in such a way that I wasn't sure which one of us—me or my father—was the true object of her contempt. I knew only that I was furious. I was angry that my father was dying just as I was getting to know him. I was angry that my sister saw in me the same character flaws that had led my father to such a miserable end. Most of all, though, I was angry at myself. I feared in my heart that she might be right. Maybe I would end up just like my father, curled up in a hospital bed, my brain drowning in its own juices, surrounded by blank-faced people who didn't seem to give a shit whether I lived or died.

3

LARS AND ME,
OR WHAT AM I GETTING MYSELF INTO?

"You got the job."

PANIC DIDN'T SO MUCH BREAK UP AS DISSOLVE, THE RESULT OF A LACK OF COMMITMENT AND CHEMISTRY.* ONE OF OUR LAST SHOWS, IN LATE 1981, WAS ALSO ONE OF THE MORE MEMORABLE. IT WAS A BENEFIT CONCERT FOR A BIKER WHO HAD PASSED AWAY. NOW, COMPILING A SET LIST FOR A GROUP OF BIKERS—AND I'M TALKING ABOUT SERIOUS BIKERS, NOT THE GUYS WHO TRADE THEIR BEEMERS FOR HARLEYS ON THE WEEKEND—CAN BE A CHALLENGE. MY OWN TASTES WERE KIND OF ECLECTIC. I REALLY LIKED A LOT OF STUFF BY INDIVIDUAL BANDS I'D DISCOVERED JUST BY KEEPING MY EARS OPEN.

* The spiritual kind, I mean—chemicals we had in abundance; chemistry we lacked.

The holy trinity of Metallica to some: me, James, and Cliff at the Old Waldorf in San Francisco. Photograph by William Hale.

For example, there was a little-known band called Gamma, which was Ronny Montrose's follow-up to his solo project. I loved Montrose, loved how they sounded and what they stood for. They were just a really solid rock band. Most of the bands you saw at backyard parties in this era were all playing the same stuff: Robin Trower, Rush, Ted Nugent, Pat Travers, Led Zeppelin, KISS. Some of it I liked more than others, but I digested all of it and figured out what it was people wanted to hear. In that way I could formulate a reasonably satisfying set list. But figuring out what kids from the suburbs want to hear is a little easier than meeting the expectations of a gang of drunken bikers. So one of the songs we learned specifically for this show was "Bad Motor Scooter" by Sammy Hagar. If nothing else, at least we'd done our homework.

The show took place out in the boondocks, at a big campground in a nature preserve. And I have to say, it was exciting—probably the most intense night Panic had known, or ever would know, as it turned out. These were hard-core bikers. Gang members. Now, I had seen *Gimme Shelter*, the 1970 documentary about the Rolling Stones' infamous and tragic performance at Altamont, during which security provided by the Hells Angels resulted in murder and mayhem. So I had some idea what to expect. Was I scared?

Hell, no!

I thought I had *arrived*.

But the night was both more and less than I had anticipated. There were two distinct odors filling the air throughout the evening: pot . . . and chili. That's right—chili. Vats of it, the result of a chili cook-off; these, unbeknownst to me, were fairly common at this sort of event. There were thirteen kegs of beer at the center of the compound—I specifically remember the number because of its symbolism (good luck, bad luck, as the case may be). We didn't do a sound check or anything like that. We just hung out, smoking dope, eating chili, drinking beer with these guys, until one of them yelled, "Start playing!" And that's what we did.

We roped off an area at the front of the compound and set up our gear. This was a time when cordless gear was still relatively rare (and often prohibitively expensive). But I rigged a cordless setup using a Radio Shack stereo, an amp, and a device known as a Nady wireless system. I was one of the first guys I knew who had a wireless setup, and I could tell it freaked out the bikers who watched us play that night. You could almost see them thinking, *How the fuck is he playing that thing without any wires?*

Anyway, we ripped through our set, playing fast and flawlessly. Tons of energy, no mistakes (none that were noticeable, anyway). We finished with a scorching version of "Bad Motor Scooter," thanked the crowd for their support, and began to pack up.

That's when things got ugly. The guy in charge approached the "stage."

"The fuck are you doing?"

At first I said nothing, which was clearly the smartest approach. I thought about getting right in his face. I mean, I was a drug dealer, right? I understood the rules of marketing and fair trade. They had paid us to play. We played. How dare they not honor our contract?

Well, they were bikers, of course. They did what they wanted to do. And what they wanted, at that moment, was more music. Fortunately, we had a diplomat in our midst: Pat Voelkes, who, as I've mentioned, was the oldest member of the band and easily the most mature when it came to dealing with other people. Pat negotiated with them for a few minutes, then returned with a new contract. Here were the terms: we'd play another set; they wouldn't pay us another dime. They did, however, agree to give us a bag of hallucinogenic mushrooms.

Deal!

So we did one more set, and everybody ate the magic mushrooms

Metallica sound check at a show in San Francisco, March 1983.
Photograph by Brian Lew.

and tripped out spectacularly, resulting in one of worst experiences of our professional lives. We all said things we didn't mean, divulged secrets that should have been left unspoken. By the time we got home, the brotherhood had been destroyed. And getting home was no small task. Our primary means of transportation, Tom's Volkswagen Rabbit, had blown a clutch on the way out. At first, we tried to push the thing home, and what a sight that must have been: a bunch of scrawny, anemic teenagers leaning into a couple thousand pounds of unwilling steel. It was hopeless, so we ended up sleeping overnight in the back of a flatbed truck that we had used to transport our equipment. With us that night were two buddies who had been helping with my drug trade—basically just keeping an eye on my house while I was traveling with the band or working at the garage. These guys were Dumb and Dumber but likeable enough under most circumstances. Unfortunately, their minimal brain power was diminished even further by the mushrooms, and at some point they thought it would be a good idea to steal a keg from the bikers.

It all went bad very quickly, of course. The keg got away from them and started rolling down a hill, clanging and clattering, banging against rocks, and waking up everyone at the campground. It finally came to rest in a stream.

Oh, shit . . .

Suddenly our little adventure had turned into *Friday the 13th*.

The perpetrators (Dumb and Dumber) remained at large, trying to communicate with us through bird calls and whistles, while the rest of us were corralled by the bikers and held prisoner in the back of the flatbed. Eventually, a settlement was reached (we played another set), the keg was retrieved, and everyone lived through the night. By the time we got back home, though, something had changed. It was like that scene in *Almost Famous*, where the band has survived a terrifying bout of turbulence while flying from a concert at the end of a tour, and everyone is sick and exhausted, and you just know the end is near.

That's the way I felt. I had nothing left to give to Panic. And Panic had nothing for me.

A FEW WEEKS later I was leafing through an alternative newspaper called the *Recycler* when I came across a classified advertisement by an as-yet-unnamed band that was in search of a guitar player. This was nothing out of the ordinary—the *Recycler* was filled with these sorts of announcements on a weekly basis; they were required reading for just about every aspiring musician in Southern California. Few of them sparked my interest, largely because I had no desire to be a hired gun in someone else's band. I knew I was a pretty good guitar player; I also was beginning to come to the realization that I liked to be in charge. I was not good at taking direction.

This particular ad caught my attention, though, since it was the first to reference not one or two but three of my favorite bands. The first was Iron Maiden. Nothing really special about that—you couldn't play metal and *not* appreciate Iron Maiden. The second was Motörhead. Nothing unique there, either. The third, however, was a band called Budgie. Just seeing the name in print made my heart race. I'd been introduced to Budgie, a groundbreaking band from Wales—in fact, they are regarded in some quarters as the first heavy metal band—one night a few years earlier, while hitchhiking on PCH. The driver worked for a radio station in Los Angeles.* He was a decent enough guy. Shared some Quaaludes, kept the music blaring, and at one point, after finding out I played guitar, he smiled and said, "Dude, you gotta listen to these guys." Then he inserted a Budgie tape in the cassette deck.

I was instantly blown away. The speed and power of the music, without abandoning melody—it was like nothing I'd ever heard.

Now here I was, reading the *Recycler*, wondering what to do with the next phase of my life, and it was like I'd been sent a message.

Budgie!

That day I called the number in the ad.

"Hey, man, I'm looking for Lars."

"You got him." The guy had a strange accent that I couldn't quite place. He also sounded very young.

"I'm calling about your ad? For a guitar player?"

"Okay . . ."

---

* He claimed to have at his house a replica of the obelisk made famous on the cover of Led Zeppelin's *Presence*. Looking back now, I totally get it: major-market DJ participates in graft to put an album in circulation. At the time, though, as a kid, it just seemed like the coolest thing in the world.

"Well, I know Motörhead and Iron Maiden," I said. "And I love Budgie."

There was a pause.

"Fuck, man! You know fucking Budgie?!"

That was all it took. You see, Lars Ulrich, the kid (and, yeah, he was just a kid, as I would soon discover) on the other end of the line, was an avid collector of music from the New Wave of British Heavy Metal (NWOBHM). And when I dropped the name of a band that was at the forefront of that movement, I was in. The thing is, I didn't even realize until later that Budgie held such a prominent place in that world; I just liked their music. And Lars respected that, which just goes to show you that deep down inside, a very long time ago, we really were kindred spirits.

We met a few days later at Lars's condo in Newport Beach. Actually, it was his parents' house, which I didn't realize until I arrived. The drive was like a trip down memory lane, as Lars lived in a neighborhood not far from where my mother had worked as a maid when I was growing up. At one point, after exiting the Pacific Coast Highway, I came to a stoplight and realized that if I made a right turn, I'd be driving into Linda Isle, where my mom had cleaned toilets for the rich folks. If I took a left, I'd be at Lars's place in just a couple minutes. After making the turn, I remembered that once, many years earlier, I'd put on a little bow tie and white shirt to help out while my mom worked for a caterer at a private party in this very same neighborhood.

You can imagine what I was thinking when I pulled into the driveway in my old Mazda RX-7, with the rusted-out muffler rattling so hard I thought the windows might crack:

"Silver spoon motherfucker . . ."

Lars's father, Torbin Ulrich, was a former professional tennis player of some renown. His mom was a housewife; I never knew too much about her. Lars was born in Denmark. Not surprisingly, he'd begun playing tennis at a very young age and was something

Backstage with Lars Ulrich and my longtime friend John Strednansky. Photograph by William Hale.

of a prodigy himself. Supposedly, he'd come to the States with the idea of furthering his tennis career, but that soon took a backseat to his real passion: music, specifically playing the drums. I didn't know any of this when we first met. All I knew when he came to the door that morning was that he was very young (I was twenty years old; Lars was not quite eighteen) and obviously had come from a different world than the one I had known.

I had no great expectations regarding this initial encounter. In a lot of ways, I was still very innocent. I had some pot and figured if nothing else, I'd hang out with this kid, get high, and listen to his plans for conquering the music world. We shook hands and went right upstairs to his bedroom, presumably to get down to business (whatever that might mean). The first thing I noticed when I walked into his room was that he had an assortment of interesting shit on the walls: pictures of bands, magazine covers. One that stood out right away was a big poster of Philthy Animal, the drummer from Motörhead, hammering away at this incredible drum kit, the skins of which were adorned with what appeared to be gaping sharks' mouths.

Very cool, I thought.

A little more disconcerting was the gigantic stack of Danish porn on the nightstand. I was no prude. By this time I'd lived out my fair share of *Penthouse* fantasies. But this shit was strange. Not the kind of stuff you'd see in mainstream American skin magazines, but hard-core European strangeness: girls getting fucked by baseball bats and milk bottles, things of that nature.

"Dude, this is a little weird, huh?"

Lars shrugged. Part of it, I think, was that he looked so young. He could have passed for thirteen or fourteen, and it just seemed odd to be hanging out with him, leafing through Danish porn and talking about starting a band. And smoking dope, of course, which is what we did next. Lars had a bamboo bong sitting right out in the open (his parents rather obviously ruled with something less than an iron fist), and naturally the conversation gravitated to drugs. We traded war stories for a bit, and Lars told me about his favorite method of smoking hash. He'd dig a hole in the ground, bury the hash while it was burning, then dig a little tunnel and inhale the smoke through a screen on the other side. I tried to picture that: this little kid facedown in the dirt, sucking hash smoke into his lungs. I couldn't imagine doing that myself, and I'm not sure what advantage this method provided over more traditional modes of delivery . . . but I had to admit it was inventive.

So we talked for a while, got high, and eventually I asked Lars if he had any samples from the band he was trying to form. There were three people in the lineup already, he said: a singer named James Hetfield (James had not yet begun focusing on playing guitar for the band), a bass player named Ron McGovney, and Lars, the drummer. They needed a guitar player—a really kick-ass player—to complete the lineup. Really, though, the band was still in its embryonic stages. It had no name, no history of performing. What it did have, apparently (although I didn't know it at the time), was an agreement between Lars and a producer named Brian Slagel, whose new label, Metal Blade, was about to release a heavy metal compilation called *Metal Massacre*. A spot on the album had been reserved for Lars's venture; all he had to do was come up with a song, a band, and a recording.

"Listen to this," Lars said. He inserted a cassette into his stereo and played a rough demo of a song called "Hit the Lights," written by James and one of his buddies from a previous band. The guitar work was by a guy named Lloyd Grant, who had played with Lars and James briefly, before I came along. The song wasn't bad; the playing was uniformly sloppy, the sound quality even worse, and the singer had little pitch control or charisma. But there was energy. And style. When it ended, Lars smiled.

"What do you think?"

"You need more guitar solos, that's for sure."

Lars nodded. He didn't seem offended. I think he wanted to hear my honest opinion. Lars had been looking for a guitar player who matched his taste in music, and maybe I fit the bill. Crude as it was, the tape reminded me of the NWOBHM stuff I'd been hearing. I understood the way those guys played guitar from a riff point of view. It wasn't so much about strumming chords or arpeggiating—picking from one side of the guitar to the other—it was more like picking the same string over and over, to the point where it almost became monotonous. In that way, the riff had to carry the weight of the whole song. If that sounds simple, well, it isn't. It's incredibly challenging, because the guitarist is reliant on such a small measure of music. The effect, when executed properly, is almost hypnotic.

I came away from that meeting with minimal expectations. Lars was painfully laid-back. Moreover, as I said, he was just so young—it was hard to imagine that he had any kind of grand plan for assembling what would eventually become the biggest heavy metal band in the world. Like a lot of kids with vaguely defined rock 'n' roll dreams, he was just sort of stumbling along. I'd been there myself.

The afternoon ended with a handshake and a promise to keep in touch, and then I drove back to Huntington Beach, bleary eyed and stoned. I didn't know if I'd ever hear from Lars again. But he called just a few days later, wanting to know whether I'd be able to meet him and the other guys in Norwalk, where Ron McGovney lived.

"For what? An audition?"

"Yeah, kind of like that," Lars said.

I said sure, again figuring I had nothing to lose. It was either play this one out to its logical conclusion—see if these guys had any potential at all—or return to Panic, which was clearly a dead end.

Classic Mustaine/Hetfield pose. We were destined for greatness–just not together. Photograph by Brian Lew.

McGovney was a question mark to me. I knew nothing about him. Nor did I know much about James, who, as it turned out, was living with Ron. The two of them had been pals since middle school and were now sharing a duplex owned by Ron's parents. In fact, they owned several units in the neighborhood, and Ron was given free reign to live in one and turn the garage space into a studio. It was hardly a lavish life—the entire neighborhood had a cheap cookie-cutter feel to it—but compared to the way I'd been living (selling dope to put food on the table), Ron appeared to have life by the balls. As did Lars.

Ron did not make a great first impression. I was a bit of a hard-ass, a wanna-be street kid, and I was suspicious (and probably a bit envious) of anyone who seemed to have been handed an easier path in life. At the time Ron was working—or at least dabbling—as a rock 'n' roll photographer, with a particular interest in heavy metal. He was always pulling out photos of other bands, most prominently Mötley Crüe. For some reason Ron was a huge fan of the Crüe, and I guess he figured it would impress people to show them pictures of Vince Neil spray-painting his hair or putting his clothes on. I didn't understand it, and I still don't. Any more than I understood the way Ron was dressed that first day, in his knee-high go-go boots; Austin Powers–style, skintight stretch jeans; studded belt; and carefully pressed Motörhead T-shirt.

Yuppie metal. That was the look.

I remember being fairly quiet that day. It was almost like I was a gunfighter, and I took the matter with an appropriate degree of seriousness. Mind you, I had never been on an audition before. Whenever I'd played in a band, it had been my band. There was no "trying out" for someone else's band. Fuck that! I was a leader, not a follower. Playing backseat to someone else really didn't sit well with me and indeed had put me in a bit of a foul mood. Simply by agreeing to drive up to Norwalk and endure the process of being evaluated and interviewed, I'd compromised my own integrity and standards. That's the way I looked at it, anyway. What can I tell you? I was arrogant. And I was angry. But I had to swallow my pride. I was tired of dealing drugs and playing with a dysfunctional band. Maybe this other thing was worth a shot.

There was a weird vibe almost from the moment I arrived at Ron's place. In addition to Lars, Ron, and James, there were a few other people hanging out, including Ron's girl-friend and a guy named Dave Marrs, a friend of Ron's who would later work briefly as a roadie for Metallica. I'm not sure what they expected from me. I'd been pretty honest with Lars about how I filled the day. I told him I played music and sold

I tend to flip people off a lot. Here's proof. Me having fun backstage. Photograph by William Hale.

pot on the side; in reality, of course, I sold pot and played music on the side. Regardless, he didn't seem to care. And neither did anyone else.

Lars introduced me to everyone as I unloaded gear from my car and brought it into the garage. While I set up, everyone else went into another room, which I thought was kind of weird. There didn't seem to be any excitement about what we were doing. And as far as I could tell, I was the only one competing for the job.

I plugged in my amp and calmly went about the business of warming up. Then I warmed up some more. I kept playing, faster and louder, figuring eventually somebody would walk in and start jamming with me; at the very least, I thought they'd come in and listen, ask me a few questions. But they never did. They just left me there to play on my own. Finally, after maybe a half hour or so, I put down my guitar and opened the door into the house. The entire group was sitting there together, drinking and getting high, watching television. I noticed, by the way, that James and Lars were drinking peppermint schnapps, which was almost comical. I didn't know anyone who drank schnapps—it was an old ladies' drink.

"Hey—we gonna do this thing or what?" I asked.

Lars kind of smiled at me and waved a hand. "No, man . . . you got the job."

Huh?

I looked around the room. Was it really that easy? I didn't know whether to feel like I'd been offended or complimented. My response vacillated between relief and confusion. Did they not care? Were they so impressed by my warm-up that they just had to have me in the band? (I knew I was pretty good, but I didn't know I was *that* good.) The way I see it, looking back on it years later, maybe they didn't want to conduct a real audition—with all of us playing together—because it would have given me the opportunity to gauge their level of skill and musicianship. That strikes me as a bit ironic now, given the sometimes acrimonious nature of our relationship over the years, and the fact that I have often been portrayed as someone who was lucky to be in the right place at the right time, filling a temporary hole in the Metallica lineup.

But I didn't know any of this at the time. Both physically and in the way he dressed, Lars was as foreign looking as he had been

the day we met, but I attributed that largely to his European upbringing. Ron was doing his thing, and James . . . well, James was
rail thin, with black spandex tights tucked into boots and a chee-
tah-print shirt. Displayed prominently on his wrist was a wide
leather bracelet with a clear patch in the middle of it—almost like
the kind of thing a quarterback wears on game day, with the plays
written on it. James, you could just tell, was trying really hard to
look like a rock star. He had long hair shaped into a windswept
coif, so that he resembled Rudy Sarzo, the bass player for Ozzy
Osbourne.

I tried not to laugh.

Oh, my God. What am I getting myself into?

4

METALLICA—
FAST, LOUD, OUT OF CONTROL

"You keep talking like that, I'm going to punch you in the mouth."

IN THE BEGINNING IT WAS AS MUCH ABOUT STYLE AS SUBSTANCE.

I REMEMBER GOING OUT SHOPPING ONE DAY WITH LARS AND MARVELING AS HE SPENT THE BETTER PART OF THE AFTERNOON TRYING TO EDUCATE ME ON THE FINER POINTS OF PURCHASING HIGH-TOP SNEAKERS. IT WAS, APPARENTLY, SOMETHING OF A SCIENCE, AND LARS AND I DISAGREED ON THE PROPER FORMULA. CHECK OUT THE EARLY PHOTOS OF METALLICA AND YOU'LL SEE ME WEARING SHINY WHITE LEATHER CONVERSE ALL-STARS WITH RED STARS ON THE SIDE. THIS WAS MY CHOICE, NOT LARS'S. FOR SOME REASON, HE WAS OF THE OPINION THAT ROCK STARS WORE TRADITIONAL CHUCK TAYLORS.

The Young Metal Attack is right; I am just a kid here still in Metallica. Photograph by William Hale.

"Fuck that!" I said. "That's like the kids on *Fat Albert*. I'm not wearing that shit."

I could be wrong, but I remember this as my first disagreement with Lars. It may sound like a petty detail, but I think it points to the inevitability of the dissolution of Metallica as it was in its infancy. Too many cooks in the kitchen. I was a band leader. So was Lars. Inevitably, the failure to agree on a common goal or to accept specific roles rose within the framework of the group. I've seen it time and again. Egos clash, combustible personalities ignite. The odds of surviving these obstacles—to say nothing of the financial, artistic, and managerial challenges—are astronomically bad.

And yet, in retrospect, I understand what Lars was doing because I've done it myself: he was trying to form an image as well as a musical entity. His heart, I think, was probably in the right place. To me, it was his taste that was misguided. One day he pulled out a photo of Diamond Head, a British heavy metal band that he admired to the point of obsession—he'd even trailed them, Deadhead style, on a European tour the previous year.

"Look at this," he said. "These guys look like rock stars."

I just stared, slack jawed. There was a lot to like about Diamond Head, but fashion was not high on the list. I looked at that picture, saw all the black spandex, the white boots, the long, flowing dress shirts unbuttoned to the waist with the bottom tied into a knot, exposing the singer's hairy navel, and I wanted to gag.

"Lars, I can't even believe a dude would dress that way. He looks like a chick."

See, there were lines of distinction that couldn't be blurred. You had to decide what type of music you were going to play, and your appearance had to properly reflect that music. In that sense,

Diamond Head was not my cup of black coffee. A lot of bands were like that. Consider the importance of hair. Everyone had long hair in those days, with the exception of the punk bands. In hard rock and metal, hair was long, and within that framework a decision had to be made:

Up or down.

You were either like Page and Plant (hair down, and thus cool) or you were like KISS, Mötley Crüe, and so many other imitators (hair up, and thus not so cool). My hair went down. Always did, always will.

Next came the name. Every band needs a great moniker, right? We discussed and discarded several, including Leather Charm, which had been the name of a short-lived band in which James and Ron had both played. This was one of those names that just seemed incredibly wrongheaded to me. Leather Charm? What are you after with that one? Who's your audience? It sounded kind of questionable in terms of projecting your notion of a good time, if you know what I mean.

It was Lars who suggested "Metallica," and, it was an undeniably great name. The logo came from James. The first time I saw the Metallica logo, and everyone was raving about how cool it was, I remember thinking, *Wow, it really is.*

Whether Metallica had any reasonable chance for success, I couldn't say. I do know that the first time I saw Lars play the drums, I was shocked at his mediocrity. Still, you had to admire his determination. The kid loved music (and good music, at that), and he wanted to be a rock star. That he would eventually become the Machiavellian character he is today . . . well, I didn't see that one coming.

We obviously didn't have a lot of material when we first started rehearsing together. Set lists in the beginning consisted primarily of cover songs, as well as songs written by James and

his former bandmate Hugh Tanner. Most new material we had was written by me.

In early 1982 Metallica went into a studio for the first time. We hadn't been together for very long, but somehow we ended up at a little place in Orange County, recording "Hit the Lights." When it came time for the guitar solo, I nailed it, and everybody started freaking out about how great it was. For some reason, though, when the first version of that demo came out on *Metal Massacre* several months later, it also included some of Lloyd Grant's guitar work. That struck me as somewhat odd and not really in the spirit of brotherhood that fuels a band, but I didn't get all worked up over it. Things were happening rather quickly, and I was excited to be part of it.

Our first live show was on March 14, 1982, at Radio City in Anaheim, California. It was a raw, unpolished, but wildly energetic performance in front of about two hundred metalheads, many of them friends of ours. Still, a respectable audience for an unknown band playing its first gig. To give you an idea of where we were musically, nearly half of the nine-song set list consisted of Diamond Head covers. We also did "Hit the Lights." The only song that could reasonably be considered a Metallica original, at that time—a song written exclusively by one of the members of the band—was "Jump in the Fire."

That was mine.

I point this out simply as a way of illustrating that my role in Metallica was actually quite prominent. I was the lead guitar player and one of the primary songwriters. A band member's role doesn't get much more vital than that. Not that I was particularly concerned with territoriality at the time. We were just

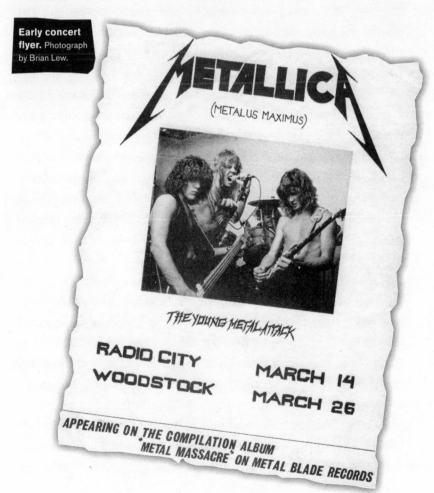

Early concert flyer. Photograph by Brian Lew.

METALLICA

(METALUS MAXIMUS)

THE YOUNG METAL ATTACK

RADIO CITY
WOODSTOCK

MARCH 14
MARCH 26

APPEARING ON THE COMPILATION ALBUM
"METAL MASSACRE" ON METAL BLADE RECORDS

having fun, playing music, partying like crazy, trying to get better with each performance. We were all in it together, at least for a while.

We each had our strengths and weaknesses, and it's interesting to look back now and see what Metallica looked like in those early days. Intent on playing the role of front man and singer, James did not pick up a guitar that night in Anaheim, nor for some time afterward. But there was a bit of a problem: James was not a naturally gregarious fellow, particularly onstage. At one of our earliest shows, I can remember him standing at the microphone, freezing, afraid to say a word. I don't mean during a song—James had no problem singing or performing, and later, when he began playing guitar, he proved to be a sturdy guitarist as well. But the stage banter? That was hard for him. At one point, sensing his anxiety, I walked over to the microphone and started talking. That was the beginning of my persona as an unusually provocative and loquacious guitar player. A shit stirrer, in other words. Tradition, of course, dictates that guitar players perform wordlessly. They can jump up and down, rip off their clothes, maybe even set their instruments on fire. They are not supposed to speak. That role is assigned to the singer. Everyone knows that's the way it's supposed to work.

I didn't care. I was doing what came naturally.

Two weeks later we got a huge break, playing a pair of shows in one night at the Whisky in Hollywood, opening for Saxon. Credit must be given to Ron for this one, since it was his connections with Mötley Crüe that helped open the door. Ron had taken a three-song demo tape to the club, hoping for an audience with the club's manager. While there, he ran into the guys from Mötley Crüe and told them of his plan, and they offered to help out. If that sounds gracious, well, it really wasn't. Mötley Crüe had originally been booked to open for Saxon, but

It is obvious talking while not being the front man is humorous to me while in Metallica. Photograph by William Hale.

at some point they, or their management, had decided that they were now too big to be an opening act; they wanted to headline. And since we were ready, willing, and able, with a solid demo as a calling card, the timing couldn't have been better.

Again, during both shows, we played mostly covers. This time, though, we did two of my compositions, "Jump in the Fire" and "Metal Militia." Although we were tighter and made fewer mistakes than in Anaheim, we certainly weren't perfect. I recall taking the mike from James again and generally flailing all over the stage while playing guitar. In the days that followed, we generated considerable buzz, although the mainstream rock press was not initially impressed. Indeed, our first review was a stinging jab directed at almost everything about Metallica.

With one notable exception.

"Saxon could also use a fast, hot guitar player of the Eddie Van Halen ilk. Opening quartet Metallica had one, but little else. The local group needs considerable development to overcome a pervasive awkwardness."

Ouch!

I don't recall taking any pleasure in being singled out as the one bright spot in an otherwise forgettable show. (I'm sure I stood up in defense of my bandmates.) We experienced growing pains no different from those endured by all great bands. The truth is, we were doing something radical. We were fast and loud and dangerous, on the cutting edge of heavy metal. Practically speaking, thrash began with early Metallica, in both form and attitude.

The next few months brought a kaleidoscopic blur of rehearsing, writing, performing, and partying. Everything happened so fast. There was a four-track demo (commonly referred to as *The Power Demo* in Metallica lore) that we recorded in Ron McGovney's garage. That tape included two of my songs, "Jump in the Fire" and "The Mechanix," along with "Hit the Lights" and "Motorbreath," which was credited to James (although I believe in its nascent stage it belonged at least in part to James's former Leather Charm bandmate Hugh Tanner).

I'm not sure how we managed to accomplish as much as we did, given the lifestyle we were leading—all that fucking and fighting, drugging and drinking and vomiting. But we did. Our repertoire expanded, our performances improved. Very quickly we realized that in order to achieve the heaviness we wanted, we needed another guitar player. Since James still wasn't interested in anything other than singing, we recruited a guy named Brad Parker. The first day of rehearsal he showed up wearing a striped shirt with high French cut sleeves—the kind you might see on a Russian sailor. He wore eyeliner and a white feathered earring. I took one look at this guy and started laughing.

Dude, if you last a day in this band, I'll be shocked, I thought.

He actually lasted a few days—maybe weeks—but not long enough to matter. He played one show with us, at a place called the Music Factory in Costa Mesa. Before we took the stage, he turned to me and said, "Listen, while we're out there, call me Damien, okay?"

"What?"

"Damien . . . Damien Phillips," he said.

"Who the fuck is Damien Phillips?"

He smiled.

"I am. It's my stage name."

That was the first and only time Brad Parker and/or Damien Phillips played with Metallica. Our next gig was one month later, shortly before Memorial Day 1982, with James playing rhythm guitar and singing lead. By this time we had dispensed with the poseurs and the endless search for another guitar player and simply decided to encourage James to handle the job himself; he turned out, of course, to be a formidable player.

Throughout the summer our schedule intensified, and so did our reputation. We played at least one gig a week at various venues around Southern California: the Troubadour and Whisky in Hollywood, the Woodstock in Anaheim, any number of smaller parties and concerts at places you've never heard of. The first version of *Metal Massacre* was released in June, and within a month we found ourselves in a studio, working with a record company executive by the name of Kenny Kane. This guy owned a punk label and apparently had gotten the impression that Metallica would somehow appeal to the label's demographic, so he offered us a chance to record an EP. When he heard the tapes, well, I guess he wasn't thrilled, since (obviously) Metallica was not a punk band. He withdrew the offer and we kept the tapes. The resulting demo, titled *No Life Till Leather*, consisted of seven songs: "Hit the Lights," "Mechanix," "Phantom Lord," "Jump in the Fire," "Motorbreath," "Seek and Destroy," and "Metal Militia."

I was the primary writer on four of those songs: "Mechanix," "Phantom Lord," "Jump in the Fire," and "Metal Militia." Without meaning to sound bitter, it's important to note that this demo, which provided the spark for the underground phenomenon that Metallica became, stands as a rather indisputable piece of evidence in the war between those who think my contributions to the band were significant (Megadeth fans, mainly) and those who don't (Metallica fans). When Metallica released its first album, in 1983, all four of those songs were included (although "Mechanix" had been reworked and given a new title, "The Four Horsemen," I still received a writing credit).

No Life Till Leather became our calling card, and we used it to build an audience from L.A. to San Francisco. We had no formal contract, no means of distributing songs, but that was far from an insurmountable obstacle. Tapes were copied and passed around, and pretty soon we were playing in front of fans who knew the words to our songs, which I have to tell you is about as thrilling a thing as a young rock star can experience. We were getting better and we knew it.

We also were completely out of control. I will never deny that I was a handful in those days. I was aggressive, driven, and unpredictable, and I drank way too much. But so did everyone else in the band. We practically lived in our cars, driving up and down the coast, drinking before and after rehearsals and gigs. It wasn't unusual for one or more members of the band to pass out during those trips and wake up to discover that his face or body had been painted. We shared homes, money, equipment, drugs, alcohol, girls. It was a life of utter decadence (and at times one hell of a lot of fun). For all of us.

The difference, and I suppose it is an important distinction, is that we were different types of drunks. I was often an angry, hostile drunk; Lars and James were happy drunks. Harmless, for the most part, although their antics were juvenile.

As word of *No Life Till Leather* spread, so too did our reputation. We found ourselves spending increasing amounts of time on the road, driving up and down the coast between L.A. and San Francisco. Invariably, those trips became exercises in humiliation. On every trip, it seemed like someone's shoes would be tossed out the back of our truck, just so Lars or James could watch them get pissed off. If they had treated me that way, I would have left.

Admittedly, the person I was onstage—pissed off, trying to play my guitar so fast that it would nearly burn my fingers—was not far from who I was off the stage. When I drank, I would often get combative. I didn't always go looking for a fight, but I certainly never walked away from one. Even when it involved my friends and bandmates.

Prior to the formation of Metallica, I'd bought a couple dogs to dissuade people from breaking into my house (which had happened on occasion, in part because of my "business" interests). These were formidable pups—Staffordshire terriers (which are similar to pit bulls) cross-bred with Rhodesian ridgebacks—and they quite naturally scared the shit out of most people. But they were also very affectionate and loyal, and I cared for them immensely. When I traveled to Ron's house for rehearsal, or to a gig, I'd usually leave them behind to protect the house. Sometimes, though, one of the dogs would keep me company. One day in the summer of 1982, I drove to rehearsal, and when I let the dog out of the car she began running around. Dogs do that when they've been cooped up for a while. At some point the female jumped up on the front quarter panel of Ron's car, a beautiful Pontiac GTO, prompting James to give the dog a hard kick across its chest. The dog (she was still just a puppy) let out a yelp and scampered away.

And I went nuts.

"What are you doing?"

"She's scratching the car, man," James said, as if that was an acceptable excuse for kicking a dog.

"Fuck you!"

The actual fight didn't happen right there. They call it a hang fire, like when there's an unexpected delay between the trigger of a gun being pulled and the actual discharge of the weapon. You know it's coming, and there's no stopping it. It's just a matter of time. James and I alternately cursed at each other and refused to speak, until eventually we were both in Ron's house, preparing to rehearse, and tensions boiled over. There was another round of accusations and insults, more cursing, more threats.

"You keep talking like that, I'm going to punch you in the mouth," I said.

"Fuck off!"

In the middle of this exchange, Ron walked out of the bathroom and into the living room. He and James went way back, and despite the fact that James often treated him like shit, Ron instinctively defended his friend.

"You hit him, you'll have to hit me first."

"Shut up and sit the fuck down," I said.

And then James jumped to Ron's defense. "You touch him, you're going to have to hit me first."

Jesus, I thought, *what is this, some kind of fucking game show?*

I realized I would have to make a decision.

"Okay, you win," I said, and with that I threw a right cross that landed flush against James's face, turning his mouth into a pile of bloody Chiclets. To my surprise, Ron immediately jumped on my back. Reflexively, I gave him a hip toss; he flew across the room and landed on an entertainment center, sending shards of particleboard all over the place and destroying the old Pong video game hooked up to the TV. The fight might have gone on longer if not for the presence of my friend and martial arts training partner Rick Solis, who quickly intervened. I was enraged, ready to kill both Ron and James, when Rick came up from behind and grabbed my elbow, pinching the ulnar nerve and rendering me incapacitated.* We stood there together for a moment, saying nothing, when suddenly James began screaming at me.

"You're out of the band! Get the fuck out of here!"

* This is similar to the injury I would suffer to my left arm many years later, except it was a temporary thing. When the nerve is compressed, it sends a shock wave to the victim, who usually is rendered immediately helpless.

Ron was yelling, too. Lars, meanwhile, was standing in a corner, just sort of twirling his hair, and trying unsuccessfully to mediate a settlement. "Come on, man . . . I don't want it to end this way."

"Fuck you! I quit!"

"Good! Fuck you, too!"

WHILE OUR DISAGREEMENTS had never reached this level of intensity, it should be noted that by this time Metallica was already a band struggling with personality conflicts. Each of us was guilty of pointing the finger of blame at one time or another. My job was safe, as far as I could tell, although obviously I'd failed to assess the situation properly.

The dismissal lasted roughly twenty-four hours. I returned for rehearsal the next day, apologized to everyone, and was welcomed back into the fold. Everything was fine. Except it wasn't. Some things can't be undone, and this was one of them. In many ways, it was the beginning of the end. Ron and I grew increasingly annoyed with each other. I thought he was smug and spoiled and not particularly talented; he viewed me as unpredictable and dangerous—not inaccurate, I must confess. When a break-in at Ron's place was traced back to acquaintances of mine (not friends, mind you, and I certainly had no idea what they had done), Ron became angry and accusatory. My response, and I don't say this with any pride, was to walk into the rehearsal room one day when Ron wasn't around and pour a can of beer into the pickups of his Washburn bass, effectively destroying a very expensive piece of equipment.

I knew this would infuriate Ron, but I didn't care. My rationale went something like this:

I don't like you, I don't like that you pinned this break-in on me, I don't like that you're a mama's boy, I don't like that you seem to have everything going on, everything handed to you, and you don't appreciate it. It doesn't seem like you're one of us.

By this point, in the late fall of 1982, Metallica had begun performing regularly in San Francisco, where the metal scene was significantly less artificial than it had been in Los Angeles. Hair and makeup mattered less than the music. When it came to playing music, Metallica was like nothing anyone had seen or heard before. But there was always room for improvement. And that's where Cliff Burton came in.

Unloading speakers before a show with Ron.
Photograph by Brian Lew.

Cliff was the star bass player for a Bay Area band called Trauma. That term alone—"star bass player"—should tell you something, because bass players are typically at the bottom of the rock 'n' roll food chain. Guitar players and singers are at the top, drummers in the middle, bass players at the bottom. I was once quoted as saying, "Playing the bass is one step up from playing the kazoo," which predictably pissed off a lot of bass players, but it's essentially true. Of course, there are exceptions

Backstage with Metallica. Our first photograph with Cliff Burton in 1983. Photograph by Brian Lew.

to every rule, and Cliff was definitely not a glorified kazoo player. He was brilliant. The first time I saw him play, I knew he was something special, and so did Lars and James, which is why they began surreptitiously courting Cliff while Ron McGovney was still in the band.*

Cliff was worthy of pursuit, and I think we all (with the exception of Ron) saw him as the "missing piece." We had arrived

* As it turned out, the same sort of thing happened with Kirk Hammett, who later took my spot on guitar.

in San Francisco as the band of the moment, an underground sensation that quickly surpassed everyone, even the popular local thrash kings Exodus. We were locked and loaded, with an exhausting stage show featuring a dangerous, loudmouthed motherfucker on guitar and a variation on heavy metal that was at once heavier, faster, and more melodic. We were the real deal. As was Cliff. Trauma was nothing special, but everyone knew the band was worth watching if only to witness Cliff's wizardry with a wah-wah pedal. It's not often that a bass player stands out as the star of a band, but Cliff, with a wild mane of hair and an athletic, muscular style of playing, pulled it off. He was an innovator.

He also was reluctant to join Metallica or any other band not based in the Bay Area. But Lars kept pursuing Cliff. Eventually, when Ron departed, just a few days after the violation of his Washburn bass,* the door was open for Cliff to join the band. But concessions would have to be made. Cliff was impressed by what he'd seen of our work and more than willing to trade Trauma for Metallica. Under one condition.

We'd have to move to San Francisco.

If there was any hand-wringing over this decision, I don't recall it. We all knew Cliff was talented enough to present what would ordinarily be considered an outrageous bargaining chip: *Relocate the whole band? For a bass player!* He was that good. And we were that driven; we were willing to do anything to be successful. I think we all recognized that by adding Cliff, we could become the greatest band in the world.

---

* Whether he was fired or quit remains a point of contention, depending on whom you ask. Certainly Ron would have been fired if he hadn't left; either way, it was not an amicable parting.

THE TRANSITION TOOK a few months, during which we altered living and professional arrangements in a half-assed attempt to save some money and prepare for the move to San Francisco. Shortly before Christmas 1982, James got the boot from Ron McGovney (no surprise, since Ron was understandably reluctant to continue supporting James after splitting with Metallica). I'd already moved back into my mother's house because . . . well, because I was broke. So I invited James to come and live with me and my mother, creating a variation on the *Three's Company* theme with predictably disastrous results. Suddenly you had two heavy metal warriors living with my mom, the quiet little housekeeper. To say she was bummed by the whole arrangement would be an understatement, and not merely because of her religious affiliation. The lifestyle we were leading—the drinking, fighting, carousing—was enough to give any parent cause for concern. But to have it happening under her own roof? It couldn't have been easy. Especially as she came to realize that it wasn't merely a phase. I was pretty good at playing guitar, and I was serious about making a living at it. But that wasn't

Playing with Cliff Burton at the Metallica mansion (Mark Whitaker's house).
Photograph by Brian Lew.

the only reason I played. It wasn't only about strutting and getting laid and trying to become famous. When I held a guitar in my hands, I felt good about myself. When I played music, I felt a sense of comfort and accomplishment that I'd never known as a child. When I replicated the songs that I loved, I felt an attachment to them and to the musicians who had composed them. And when I started writing songs of my own, I felt like an artist, able to express myself for the very first time. Maybe my mother sensed all of this, and that's why she put up with all the craziness. Or maybe that's just what mothers do.

Regardless, out of respect for my mom (and fear of getting caught), I stopped dealing drugs and tried to earn some cash in a more reputable manner. Lars had gotten an overnight job delivering newspapers for the *Los Angeles Times*, and he asked me if I wanted a job, too. I did it for a little while, but I hated the hours and the drudgery of the work. Sometimes, just to make it more interesting, Lars and I would deliver papers together. We'd drive around in his mom's AMC Pacer, careening through neighborhoods, sometimes sideswiping parked cars or mailboxes. There were few images funnier than Lars driving the Pacer, which was basically a fishbowl on wheels. To see him weaving down the street in one of the ugliest cars in history, chucking newspapers out the window, with no regard for where they landed, you couldn't help but laugh. It was like a video game: *Evil Danish Paperboy!*

All you needed was Orson Welles or James Earl Jones providing the narration: "Metallica is coming to get you!"

By February of 1983 we had relocated to the Bay Area, specifically to the El Cerrito home of Exodus manager Mark Whitakker, who would soon become Metallica's road manager and facilitator. Mark's place, affectionately known as the Metallica Mansion, became ground zero for all things related to the band. Lars and James moved right in and took the two available bedrooms. I settled for a shitty little box of a room—with no shower, sink, or refrigerator—at the home of Mark's grandmother, roughly an hour away. I lived out of a Styrofoam cooler, into which I would pack everything I needed for the day . . . or for two days . . . maybe even three. One of the guys, usually Cliff Burton, would pick me up in the morning and drive me to rehearsal. Cliff and I got pretty close in those first couple months, simply because we spent so much time together. We'd drive back and forth, smoking some of Cliff's horrible homegrown pot, talking about music and listening to music. And not just metal or even vintage hard rock, but stuff you'd never associate with Metallica. I can recall several instances in which we were driving along, sharing a joint, and singing out loud to Lynyrd Skynyrd.

When rehearsal would end, and the other guys would start talking about doing something else with the rest of the day, I'd suggest we keep playing. Not necessarily because I loved rehearsal, but because I couldn't stand the idea of going back to that little house by myself. Sometimes I would just refuse to leave; I'd sleep on the couch for days on end. It was a strange and surreal hand-to-mouth existence. I'd been there before, of course; I'd grown up poor, panhandled for beer money, knew how it felt to wear the same pair of dirty jeans for days on end and to live off boxes of Kraft macaroni and cheese. I think it was harder for Lars and James. And for that reason, along with the fact that I considered us to be brothers-in-arms, I often found myself standing up for them.

There was, for example, the time we were all at a party, and in walked the guys from a band known as Armored Saint. As sometimes happens in these situations, harmless verbal jousting gave way to nasty, personal insults, paving the way for a physical confrontation. They targeted Lars, probably because he was the smallest. I don't remember exactly how it began; I do remember jumping off my chair and telling them to leave my friend alone. They laughed at me, much as they had been laughing at Lars, which was not a good idea. Lars may not have been a fighter, but I was. I had training and expertise. More important, I didn't give a shit.

As the guys from Armored Saint dog-piled on top of Lars, I ran across the room and applied a side kick to the first person in my path. His name was Phil Sandoval, and he was the band's lead guitarist. The first thing I heard was a loud *crack!* Like the sound of a branch snapping in half. And then the sound of someone wailing as Phil fell to the floor and grabbed his lower leg.

I'd broken his ankle.

Needless to say, that was the end of the fight. I tell this story not to brag, but simply as a way of pointing out how I felt about Lars, James, and Cliff. I would have done anything for them. They were my friends.*

Although he looked the part of a gunslinger, James wasn't big on confrontation either. One night I went to the Mabuhay Gardens, a nightclub in North Beach colloquially known as the "Old Mabuhay," with James and his girlfriend. While we were waiting outside for the club to open, a girl came running out of a nearby alleyway, flailing her arms and screaming at the top of her lungs.

"He broke my nose! He broke my nose!"

* Interestingly enough, Phil is my friend, too, to this day, and for the longest time I felt terrible about what I did to him.

"What can I do to make it up to you?" I eventually asked him.

"Well, it's not really necessary, but if it'll make you feel better . . ."

"It will."

"I can always use a new guitar."

So, a couple years ago, I bought Phil a nice guitar, and we're all cool now. That chapter is closed and I wish him nothing but the best in his life and career.

I had no idea who she was or what had happened. And I didn't care. Instantly I felt the rush of adrenaline you get before a fight. I looked at James, didn't say a word. I just smiled, and I could tell what he was probably thinking.

Oh, what's this crazy fucker gonna do now?

Finally, I touched him on the shoulder and said, "Let's go, dude!"

So we ventured into the alley, hardly able to see a thing. I was quiet, but behind me, James was grunting, snorting, yelping half-baked threats.

"Gonna kill you, motherfucker!"

I almost laughed. James wasn't so much threatening anyone as he was whistling past the graveyard. You know, like you did when you were a kid, trying to convince yourself that you weren't afraid of anything when in reality you were about to shit your pants.

At the end of the alleyway was a parked van. As we drew near, with James still yelling, the driver's-side door opened, and out stepped this big son of a bitch.

"Which one of you assholes wants to kill me?" he said, the look on his face signaling either inebriation or a complete lack of fear. Maybe both.

Before I could respond, James took a quick step backward.

Thanks a lot, brother . . .

There wasn't time for an explanation. The big guy lunged at me, and as he moved forward, I opened my hand, thumb pointing down, and grabbed the back of his neck. Then I swept his foot out from underneath him, threw him on the ground, and started rabbit-punching his head until he was unconscious.

A few minutes later the cops arrived and took the guy away in handcuffs. James and I went back to hanging out in front of the club, acting like nothing had happened, but inside I was pretty shaken up. When I woke the next morning my hand was swollen and sore, like I'd punched a wall. When James asked me if I was okay, I just nodded. We never talked explicitly about the way that incident unfolded. There was no point.

DUMPED BY ALCOHOLICA

"You're a bad motherfucker!"

SAN FRANCISCO, WITH ITS THRIVING CLUB SCENE AND VIGOROUS METAL FANS, PROVED TO BE A WARM AND WELCOMING PLACE FOR METALLICA. WE PLAYED OUR FIRST SHOW WITH CLIFF ON MARCH 5, AT THE STONE. ON MARCH 19 WE PLAYED FOR A SECOND TIME, AT THE SAME CLUB. IN BETWEEN, WE RECORDED ANOTHER DEMO AND WATCHED OUR POPULARITY SOAR. IT SEEMED AS THOUGH WE HAD TAKEN OVER THE CITY IN A MATTER OF JUST A FEW SHORT WEEKS. NOT THAT ANYONE SEEMED TO MIND THE INVASION; IT WAS ACTUALLY A NICE ENVIRONMENT UP THERE, WITH A LOT OF BANDS PURSUING SIMILAR GOALS, PLAYING AND LOVING THE SAME TYPE OF MUSIC, WHAT WOULD COME TO BE KNOWN AS THRASH METAL. THE JEALOUSY AND POSTURING THAT TYPIFIED THE L.A. CLUB

Playing a fierce solo on Lars's belly while carefully avoiding the wang bar.
Photograph by William Hale.

scene was mostly absent in the Bay Area, and we bonded quickly and easily with other musicians, most notably (and ironically, as it would turn out), those in the band Exodus. At one point I even became blood brothers with some of the guys in their band. Like, real blood brothers—cutting our hands and swapping fluid in a manner that, in retrospect, given the lifestyles we led, can only be termed reckless.*

ANYWAY, METALLICA SEEMED to be moving at warp speed. One morning in April 1983, I rolled out of bed, bleary eyed, hungover, and smelling like bad cottage cheese, and saw a U-Haul was in the driveway. Everything had happened so fast that I didn't even know (or, frankly, care about) most of the details. If anyone wonders why I became such a control freak later in my career, well, the evolution has its roots right here. I was perfectly content to go along for the ride.

The *No Life Till Leather* demo had drifted east and wound

---

* I spent a fair amount of time hanging out with their lead singer, a guy named Paul Baloff. We had a lot in common, having both grown up under challenging circumstances that involved fending for ourselves at a ridiculously young age. Paul's life had been even harder than mine, and (like me) he had issues with drugs and alcohol. But what an incredible spirit! Boundless energy, prodigious talent, great sense of humor.

In the end, though, I think Paul was basically a street urchin who never really adapted to the regular world. He was kicked out of Exodus a few years later, and in 2002 he passed away from complications related to a stroke. A memorial was held in his honor and donations were solicited on behalf of the Save the Wolves Foundation. This made sense, given that in his latter years Paul was periodically homeless and supposedly living mostly in the wild, with a gray wolf as his loyal companion. I don't know if this is true or merely apocryphal, but it certainly adds to the legend of Paul Baloff. And it seems somehow appropriate. Rest in peace, brother.

up in the hands of a guy named Jon Zazula. "Jonny Z" owned a popular record shop in New Jersey called Rock and Roll Heaven that was well known for finding and promoting underground artists. He also was an aspiring record producer; after hearing the demo, and seeing the reaction to it among customers, Jonny Z offered Metallica an opportunity to play a few shows in and around New York and to help the band secure a recording contract. Most of the discussions regarding this arrangement went on without my knowledge or involvement. Days later, when we arrived in New Jersey and I discovered that my name wasn't on any of the contracts and got a little nervous, Lars suggested that I was overreacting.

So I let it go.

I suppose I could blame Lars or James or even Mark Whitakker for cutting me out of the loop, which they did, but I also have to take responsibility for failing to keep my eye on the ball. I was too busy fucking and getting fucked-up. These guys were my friends, and despite our periodic disagreements, I trusted them.

My mistake.

Just one of many, as it turned out.

A woman I'll call Jennifer was my bed partner the night before we left San Francisco. She was, at the time, the semiserious girlfriend of Kirk Hammett, the guitar player from Exodus (like I said, we shared a lot of things with the guys in Exodus). Jennifer was a cute girl who liked guitar players, and I certainly didn't mind hanging out with her. As I walked out of the bedroom, Lars and James were waiting.

"Sorry," I said. "Give me a few minutes to shower. I can't go all the way to New York like this."

They nodded. Everything seemed perfectly fine. But it wasn't. I had no idea that my time in the band was nearing an end.

There has been much dispute regarding the timeline of

Metallica posing on the side of Mark's house. Photograph by Brian Lew.

events during this period of Metallica, but here is what I believe happened. At some point in the preceding weeks, or maybe even months, a flirtation had begun; Lars and James—Lars, mainly—had discussed with Kirk Hammett the possibility of Kirk joining Metallica. Since there was neither room nor need for a second lead guitar player, his role was clear: he would replace me.

Regardless, I never saw it coming.

WE PACKED A twenty-four-foot U-Haul and attached James's pickup truck to the back. At any given time, three of us rode up front, in the cab of the U-Haul. The other two passengers, including Mark Whitakker, who was now officially Metallica's road manager, slept in the cargo bay, where the temperature alternately soared and plummeted and the vibrations rattling off the sheet-metal walls made it feel like the inside of a trash can. We stopped for beer less than a mile after pulling out of the driveway and remained in a drunken stupor for most of the trip.

For the first few hundred miles, we fed off the adrenaline of embarking on a new venture. I remember crossing a bridge out of California into Nevada and feeling a rush of excitement and accomplishment, as if for the very first time I was doing something important with my life. I was in love with the idea that I had been presented with a gift: the opportunity to play music for a living. And it was almost like that Willie Nelson song, "On the Road Again," which so perfectly captures the appeal of the circus life, of playing music and performing in front of crowds. He totally nailed that aspect of the troubadour's existence.

Everything gets old, though, doesn't it? After a while, as the miles clicked away, we all grew irritable and weary. Whenever it was my turn to get in the back I'd feel a wave of anxiety; I'd imagine someone falling asleep at the wheel and the U-Haul tumbling off a bridge, and I'd see myself drowning in the back, the last moment of my life devoted to gulping stale air out of one of Lars's tom-toms. The sunshine and warmth of California gave way to the gray clouds and snow of Utah and Wyoming, and I took a turn at the wheel. I was a surfer kid who had grown up driving in little cars on crowded but pristine highways, so this was new territory for me, in more ways than one. I'd never driven a commercial vehicle, and only a couple times (on ski trips) had I driven in the snow. So I was totally unprepared when we hit a patch of black ice and began sliding sideways across the interstate.

For a moment everything slowed down, just like they say it does in an accident. The only way I can describe the sensation is to equate it to surfing. Like when you're riding a wave and you walk down the nose of the board, and the fin pops out of the water, leaving you rudderless. It's a feeling of helplessness and inexplicable exhilaration. And it's exactly what I felt as the U-Haul truck careened across the highway, completely out of control, eventually spinning to a halt with half of its body on the shoulder and the other half facing oncoming traffic. We all jumped out of the truck, laughed nervously, the way you do when you can't believe you're still alive, and prepared to go on with the trip. Suddenly, though, an eighteen wheeler went roaring by, swerving at the last second. And then came a Jeep Wrangler, right at us. We froze for a moment and then began diving for cover, just as the Jeep spun out and slammed into the front of the U-Haul. I grabbed Mark Whitakker at the last second, pulling him out of the path of the oncoming vehicle and perhaps saving his life in the process.

Fortunately, no one was hurt. The Jeep was hauled away and we drove the truck to another U-Haul center, where we were given a replacement vehicle. But the mood had changed. There was less laughter, more hostility. It could have happened to any one of us. We were all stoned or drunk, and we all lacked the expertise to drive the truck through snow-covered mountain passes. Unfortunately, I was behind the wheel at the time, and so the weight of the incident—the *blame*—fell on my shoulders. For the rest of the journey I felt like an outcast.*

* Many years later both James and Lars would identify the trip as a breaking point; the two even acknowledged that while I was out of earshot, tucked away in the cargo bay of the U-Haul, they were up front listening to tapes of other bands, secretly "auditioning" guitarists who might take my place.

Ron Quintana, James, and me.
Photograph by William Hale.

One night while I was sleeping in the back of the truck, we hit a bump and some shards of rust were shaken loose from the ceiling. I could feel them falling onto my face, and when I looked up to see what was happening, rust fell into my eyes. The pain was excruciating. That, combined with the fact that I was growing delirious from a diet of alcohol and potato chips, provoked a bit of a panic attack.

"Guys, we have to stop," I said. "I need to get to a hospital, right away."

They would have none of it.

"You'll be fine, man," Lars said. "Go back to sleep."

We fought for miles. At one point, when we pulled over for gas, I even called my mother and told her it looked like things weren't working out; I asked if she would send me the money to come back home.

That sounds crazy, I know, but it's how I felt at the time. I'll take responsibility for my part in all of this. I wasn't always the easiest guy to get along with. But I know that if the roles had been reversed—if it had been Lars or James who wanted to see a doctor, for any reason, I would have steered the U-Haul to the nearest hospital. Immediately. Booze obviously played a big role in all of this. But I wasn't the only one who drank. That's why they called us "Alcoholica." A name that endured, incidentally, long after I had departed.

AFTER A WEEK on the road, we arrived in Old Bridge, New Jersey, at the home of Jon Zazula. I have no idea how Jonny Z sold himself or what he had told Lars prior to our leaving San Francisco. If what we expected was some hot-shit promoter or rising record company executive, what we got was something else entirely. Jonny Z and his wife lived in a little two-story home in an unappealing suburban neighborhood. Aside from a rusted-out car and other white-trash detritus, the yard was free of any sort of landscaping.

In reality, Jonny Z had little in the way of a résumé. But he had balls, and obviously he was smart enough to see something in Metallica that was worth pursuing. Still, what a letdown. Jonny Z had promised a hero's welcome.

"Wait till you get to my house," he had said. "We'll have a full bar and a big steak dinner to celebrate."

It may sound like a small thing, but the thought of that steak had kept us going for much of the previous week. I imagined Jonny Z out on the patio of his mansion, next to the in-ground pool, grilling away on a giant Weber. There would be top-shelf liquor and silk sheets in the guest suite. When we got to Jonny Z's house, I figured, there would be no doubt that Metallica had arrived.

What we got instead was a single hunk of low-grade sirloin cut into strips and split among the entire gang, and a handful of walnut-sized roasted potatoes—washed down with seven-ounce bottles of Michelob. I remember being embarrassed by the entire affair and almost feeling sympathy for Jonny Z. Just when I thought the evening couldn't get any worse, Jonny Z stood up from the table and excused himself.

"Sorry, boys, I have to leave now."

I looked at the clock on the dining room wall. Six P.M.

You've got to be kidding! We just drove across the country, I'm almost blind from getting rust fragments dumped in my eye, we're all starving and sick and exhausted . . . and you've got someplace better to be?

I wondered if perhaps Jonny Z had another meeting, maybe with a more important client. Another band, perhaps. That wouldn't have been such a terrible thing—at least it would have given the impression that the guy actually had some juice in the industry. Maybe we were in good hands after all.

No such luck. The truth was far more disconcerting.

Jonny Z said he had a curfew. He was due at a halfway house.

"I got busted," he explained with a shrug.

"No shit?"

"No shit."

For all I know, it was nothing more than Jonny Z's idea of a joke; more likely, he thought it would somehow impress us. Either way, that initial meeting left much to be desired. I couldn't believe that this guy was now responsible for the success or failure of Metallica.

THE FIRST FEW days in New Jersey passed in a blur. We partied relentlessly, grabbed free food whenever it was offered, and generally pursued decadence with a fervor we hadn't known even in San Francisco. The partying was ferocious and at times dangerous. I remember one night being at one of those little upstairs/downstairs houses that looked like the house where *Amityville Horror* took place. We were listening to music when all of a sudden the evening took a twist and alcohol and cocaine gave way to crystal meth. Even back then, when I thought I was virtually indestructible, this was one of the few drugs that actually scared me; it was evil shit. I had tried it a couple times while partying in San Fransico, but found it completely unappealing. Some people really liked crystal meth. It was considered a poor man's cocaine, with roughly the same pulse-pounding effect at a fraction of the cost. But what nasty side effects. To me, crystal meth was like a line in the sand that you did not cross. Coming from a guy

Lars and James doing an imaginary Captain Morgan rum commercial, yet soon to become very real treasure chests. Photograph by William Hale.

who has been addicted to both cocaine and heroin, that might sound strange. But it's the truth. When it came to provoking aberrant behavior and placing the user's life at risk, crystal meth was in a league of its own. People talk about a lot of different drugs, and it's true that each carries its own particular metaphorical warning label. But methamphetamine's should be the most graphic. The shit that goes into it, and the people cooking it? You're talking about twelve-year-old kids mixing it up in their bathtubs. Or worse.

Anyone with half a brain should know better. And yet, crystal meth was everywhere. James met some girl almost as soon as we got to the East Coast. I could tell right away that she was a meth junkie. She had the bad complexion—ruddy, pockmarked skin, boils and other lesions—that comes with habitual meth use. It isn't so much the drug itself that causes the eruptions; it's the toxic shit that fills out the recipe.

"Ladies and Gents ... Cliff Burton!" I was proud of playing with him. Photograph by William Hale.

Frankly, I did not understand the appeal. I preferred organic partying—I tried not to put anything into my body that hadn't been distilled or harvested. What can I say—we all have our standards.

DESPITE HIS OBVIOUS lack of clout in the music business, Zazula had done his homework where Metallica was concerned. Say what you want about the guy—he saw an opportunity and seized it. Shortly after we arrived in New Jersey, we did a promotional gig at his store, which was housed in a big indoor flea market in nearby East Brunswick. I can't say that the idea of performing at a flea market made us feel like rock stars—it seemed like a comedown after what we'd experienced in San Francisco. But my opinion quickly changed when we got to the store. There were hundreds of kids lined up, buying our demo tapes and waiting for an opportunity to meet the guys in the newest, heaviest, hottest heavy metal band in the world: Metallica.

I have no idea how much money changed hands that day, and I certainly never saw any of it. It really didn't matter. I know only that we stayed for hours, signing T-shirts, tapes, posters, albums . . . whatever. By the time we left, I realized there had been a huge paradigm shift. Standing in that flea market, surrounded by adoring fans, I felt like a rock star.

It was all incredibly exciting and disorienting and vaguely unsettling. We'd been starving for days, and all of a sudden people were throwing food at us. I remember looking at myself in a mirror when I woke up one morning and noticing that my stomach was grotesquely distended. Of course, that could have had something to do with the fact that I was drunk or stoned virtually every waking moment. The party never stopped. Booze, cocaine, pot, meth—it was everywhere, and it was mine for the asking. Along with groupies, the quality and volume of which seemed to be improving by the day. We'd do an appearance or

One of the last times that I ever played in San Francisco with Metallica. Photograph by William Hale.

a gig, or just show up at a party, and everyone wanted to hang with us.

"You're a bad motherfucker!" they'd shout.

I'd nod approvingly. I *was* a bad motherfucker. And proud of it.

For the first week or so we stayed in the basement of Jonny Z's house. He tolerated the nonstop debauchery for a while, probably because he'd invested so much in our success. This way, at least, he could keep an eye on us. Soon, though, we became too much to handle. The proverbial last straw was the uncorking, and subsequent guzzling, of a very old and very special bottle of champagne that had been stored in the Zazulas' liquor cabinet since the day they were married. After that, Jonny Z kicked us out. Well, he didn't put it that way. Instead, he suggested that all parties might be happier if we just moved into a living space above our rehearsal hall, a place called the Music Building in Jamaica, Queens. I call it a "living space," but it wasn't an apartment or anything like that. It was just a big empty room, with no stove, no refrigerator, no shower. Just a single sink and a toaster oven. The five of us—Mark Whitakker was there, as well—lived out of a cooler, into which we stuffed beer and packets of bologna. That was the diet. We'd wake up in the middle of the day, eat, drink a little bit to take the edge off the hangover, hang out, and then go back to sleep. Sometime after sundown we'd wake again, like a pack of fucking vampires, and start playing. We'd rehearse for a few hours, then drink until we passed out. The next day we'd do it all over again.

Lather, rinse, repeat.

This was the rhythm of our lives.

During this period we struck up a friendship with the guys in the band Anthrax. The Music Building was their home as well, although only during the daylight hours, when they were rehearsing. I'm friends with a few of those guys to this day, including guitarist Scott Ian.

No doubt shredding, James is singing behind me.
Photograph by William Hale.

Anthrax was a very different band than they are today—less polished, less refined, with a vastly different lineup—but they were still interesting, and I remember watching them play a few times and thinking that things would work out for them. The camaraderie we'd known in the Bay Area was largely absent in New York, but we saw a glimpse of it with Anthrax. One day I walked into the studio and started talking with Danny Lilker, a bass player and a founding member of the band (along with Scott). I can still see the look on his face—a mixture of amusement and pity—as we talked. I can only imagine how I must have looked . . . and smelled.

"Dude, you want to come over to my house and grab a shower?"

He didn't have to ask twice. On the way, we stopped at a pizza place and Danny bought me a couple slices. It's a small thing, perhaps, but it was a gesture of kindness that struck me as completely genuine, and I've never forgotten it.

Meanwhile, back at the Music Building, clandestine shit continued. I was completely oblivious to Metallica's master plan, if there was such a thing. Certainly I had no idea that my tenure in the band was about to come to an end, and that indeed plans for my dismissal were already in the works. It is a testament to my naïveté—or perhaps to my alcohol-induced complacency—that even as strange things happened, I failed to take any action. One day we were driving around, drinking and smoking some weed, just keeping the party rolling (or so I thought), when we suddenly stopped at some guy's house to check out musical equipment. This dude had a bunch of shitty, low-grade amplifiers, Fender Bassmans, and I couldn't figure out why we had any interest in them. I had plenty of gear already—really high-quality stuff.

"What are we doing here?" I asked Lars.

He just shrugged. "You can never have enough gear."

James and Lars ended up borrowing a pile of shit from this guy. The first time we played a show in New York, suddenly my amps were on James's side of the stage, and the lousy amps were on my side of the stage. They offered some bullshit explanation for it, and I swallowed it without a fight. But in my heart, I knew something was wrong. The pendulum was swinging back and forth, and it was only a matter of time before it cut into my skin.

I played just two shows with Metallica in New York, on consecutive nights. The first was April 8, 1983, at the Paramount Theater in Staten Island. The second was April 9, at L'Amour in Brooklyn. On both nights we shared a triple bill with Vandenburg and the Rods. In my recollection, both shows went well. Steve Harris from Iron Maiden was in attendance, and he told me afterward how much he enjoyed the way I played guitar; considering the source, this was no small compliment.

Afterward, as was our custom, we all went out drinking. This was our way of celebrating. It was also our way of consoling ourselves. We drank when we were happy, we drank when we were sad. We drank to fight boredom. We drank for inspiration and consolation.

We drank. A lot.

By now it had become a pattern. The more we drank, the more our personalities diverged. I mentioned this before, but Lars and James would get weird, and by weird, I mean silly—childish. The more they drank, the goofier they became. With me it was a different story. The more I drank, the more I sought an outlet for my rage and frustration. I wanted to get out and do some cruising and bruising. So this night was nothing out of the ordinary. I've thought about it many times, tried to recall a specific incident that might have provoked what followed, but I keep coming up empty. The night ended as it usually did, with the five of us passed out on the floor of the Music Building, drunk and sexually satiated, too numb to give a shit about the price we would pay the next morning.

I find it interesting that the execution was delayed for more than twenty-four hours. I don't know why, but for some reason they waited until Monday to give me the news. We hung around all day Sunday, recovering from our hangovers, patting ourselves on the back for bringing New York to its knees on consecutive nights. Then we rehearsed a little bit, drank some more, and passed out again. When I awoke on Monday morning (April 11), they were standing above me, all four of them, grim resignation etched on their faces. My bags were behind them, packed and ready to go.

James and Cliff were inherently meek and nonconfrontational, so their role was mainly supportive. It was Lars and Mark who took the lead.

"What's going on?" I asked.

"You're out of the band," Lars said, without a trace of emotion. "Get your stuff; you're leaving right now."

I didn't know what to say. All previous foreshadowing notwithstanding, I was shocked. Everything I had worked for, everything we had accomplished—together—was crashing down in front of me, and I couldn't do anything about it. I felt like I was back in grade school, when I had no control and every day was a vertiginous nightmare.

"W-what, no warning?" I stammered. "No second chance?"

They looked at each other, slowly began shaking their heads.

"No," Lars said. "It's over."

Fighting seemed pointless. Anyway, I wasn't willing to surrender whatever dignity remained with me by groveling for my job. If they felt that strongly about it—and obviously they did—there was no sense in trying to change their point of view.

"Okay," I said. "When does my plane leave?"

There was a long pause as they exchanged glances. Lars handed me an envelope.

"Here's your bus ticket," he said. "You leave in an hour."

There have been more than a few bad days in my life, but this one remains right up there with the worst of them, right alongside the day my father died. In fact, this hurt more.

"Okay," I said. "But don't use any of my stuff."

I was referring not to my amps or other equipment (all of which took weeks to make its way across the country), but to something more precious. Something more personal.

My songs.

Of course, we have different recollections of the whole thing. James had been named the designated driver, probably because he was my closest friend in the band. We threw my stuff into the back of the truck and drove out of Queens in silence, bound for the Port Authority bus terminal. We barely made eye contact as we drove through the city. James has cultivated an image of toughness and machismo over the years, but I've known him a long time. I know who he is deep inside. When he dropped me off at the bus terminal, there were tears in his eyes. We were both hurting.

"Take care of yourself," he said.

"Yeah."

We embraced one last time, and then I pulled away and walked into the terminal. I didn't look back. It wasn't until I took a seat in the waiting area that I realized something important: I was dead fucking broke. Not a dollar to my name. I was looking at a four-day bus trip from New York to California with no food, no water, nothing. I had only a bag of dirty laundry and my guitar. Why they couldn't have given me a few bucks—survival money—for the trip, I don't know. Maybe it hadn't occurred to them. Regardless, I spent the next four days in a hobo's hell, panhandling for change, accepting whatever handouts my seatmates offered—a doughnut here, a bag of chips there. More than one person took pity on me. It's interesting how nice people can be when they don't even know you, when they have no reason whatsoever to help you or to trust you, when you are in the throes of a hangover and about to be suffering from withdrawal because you can't even afford to buy a drink, and you reek of sweat and alcohol. But those people are out there, and when you run into them it can restore your faith in humanity.

Not that I was particularly concerned with looking on the bright side of life at the time . . . or for quite a long period thereafter. At one point I was sitting in the back of the bus, my stomach rumbling, my head throbbing. On the floor I spotted a pamphlet. I picked it up and began reading, just to pass the time, really. It turned out to be a handbill authored by California senator Alan Cranston. The discussion focused primarily on the dangers of nuclear proliferation. For some reason, one line in particular stood out:

"The arsenal of megadeath can't be rid no matter what the peace treaties come to."

I let that swim around in my aching head for a few minutes—*"the arsenal of megadeath . . . the arsenal of megadeath"*—and then, for some reason I can't quite explain, I began to write. Using a borrowed pencil and a cupcake wrapper, I wrote the first lyrics of my post-Metallica life. The song was called "Megadeth" (I dropped the second "a"), and though it would never find its way onto an album, it did serve as the basis for the song "Set the World Afire."

It hadn't occurred to me then that Megadeth—as used by Senator Cranston, *megadeath* referred to the loss of one million lives as a result of nuclear holocaust—might be a perfectly awesome name for a thrash metal band. But then again, I hadn't looked that far ahead.

I just wanted to go home.

BUILDING THE PERFECT BEAST: MEGADETH

"Dude, if you want to be a great musician, you have to try heroin. You'll see. It's like being back in the womb."

BY THE TIME I GOT BACK TO CALIFORNIA, I WAS BASICALLY SHATTERED. I'D LOST MY BEST FRIENDS, MY BAND, MY LIVELIHOOD. PRACTICALLY SPEAKING, I'D LOST MY IDENTITY, WHICH HAD BECOME THOROUGHLY INDISTINGUISHABLE FROM THAT OF METALLICA. I WAS THE FACE OF THE BAND, AND NOW I HAD NO BAND. I HAD NOTHING. WITH NOWHERE ELSE TO TURN, I CRAWLED BACK TO MY MOTHER, WHO BY THIS TIME WAS IN POOR HEALTH (SHE WOULD DIE OF CONGESTIVE HEART FAILURE SEVEN YEARS LATER). THE HUMILIATION I FELT UPON RETURNING TO THAT HOUSE, TO THE VERY SAME ROOM WHERE

This was an unusual sight to me. On a dare from David Ellefson, I became Megadeth's singer one New Year's Eve. I have no idea what is happening to my mouth, but here is how the "snarl" started. Photograph by Harald O.

James and I had briefly lived together, was almost unbearable. Every morning brought a stark reminder of failure.

For a while, I must admit, there was only self-pity and depression. Mom kept me fed, gave me a place to sleep, and at night I turned to the comfort of old friends and acquaintances. But this, too, was uncomfortable, because the circle had once included the guys from Metallica. Now they were gone, and I was back, and it all seemed a little hard to explain. I was hanging out with my friend Heidi one night, just drowning my sorrows in alcohol, when the conversation turned to Metallica.

"It's just as well that I quit," I said. "Those guys were really starting to get on my nerves."

Heidi had known me for years. There was no bullshitting her. She shook her head and laughed.

"Come on, Dave. You know you didn't quit. They fired you."

I was stunned. "Who told you that?"

"Lars," Heidi said. "He called me last week."

Even then Lars was an agile spinmeister—when it came to his reputation, or the reputation of his band, he left nothing to chance. And so he had meticulously reached out to the people we had in common, to make sure they got his version of the story. Fair enough, I guess, since I was equally guilty of trying to twist the story in my favor.

Regardless, the realization that Lars had been criticizing me from afar, while Metallica moved forward with its career, served as a powerful motivating factor. In that moment, sitting across from Heidi, caught in a lie and seeing pity in her eyes, I was ashamed. But I was also righteously pissed off.

"Okay, you're right," I said. "They did kick me out. But I was going to quit anyway. I want to start my own band."

That was half-true. I don't know that I would have quit Metallica, but I do believe we were destined to fracture. And in giving voice to a new dream—*"I want to start my own band"*—at least I was doing . . . something.

Over the next few months, the dream would become an obsession, thanks in no small part to a seemingly never-ending stream of fawning publicity surrounding the emergence of a new type of heavy metal, one typified by the sound of a garage band from New York by way of California:

Metallica.

Imagine my shock when Metallica's debut album, *Kill 'Em All*, was released in the summer of 1983, and four of my songs were included: "The Four Horsemen" (formerly "Mechanix"), "Jump in the Fire," "Phantom Lord," and "Metal Militia." The same four songs that had been included on the *No Life Till Leather* demo. The writing credits were altered, I assume, to reflect changes made in the songs during the recording process. James or Lars (or both) took a share of the credit for all four songs. On each, my name was placed last, so that songwriting credit for "Jump in the Fire," for example, reads as follows: Hetfield/Ulrich/Mustaine.

I listened to these songs with a blend of wonder and indignation. To suggest that the modifications made to these songs somehow reflect a collegial atmosphere or a more balanced division of labor is, as far as I'm concerned, inaccurate. The day after I was dismissed from Metallica, Kirk Hammett was in New York, taking my place at the Music Building, auditioning for my role in the band, and mimicking the blistering lead guitar solos I had created, solos that stand today as the genesis of thrash metal.

Did they think I wouldn't notice?

Did they think I was that easily pushed around?

Probably not. More likely, they just figured I'd never amount to anything and thus would not present any sort of a challenge to them.

But they were way the fuck wrong.

BUILDING THE PERFECT beast—in this case the perfect band—takes time. I didn't want to rush into it and take the first few people I met, without regard to personality or commitment. Given what I knew about the music business and what I would later learn, I don't think it's possible to avoid conflicts and clashes within the structure of a band. Over the long haul, there are bound to be problems, as there are in any family. At the very least, though, I wanted to find a group of musicians who were talented and ambitious. I was out for blood. I wanted to kick Metallica's ass, and I couldn't do that with amateurs. The mission was too important for dilettantes.

To gain a measure of self-esteem and independence, I dived back into the workaday world, a place I hadn't visited in a very long time. Rather than returning to the soul-sucking (and frankly dangerous) life of a drug dealer, I went to work as a telemarketer: phone sales. This would be my last "real" job, and it's now been in

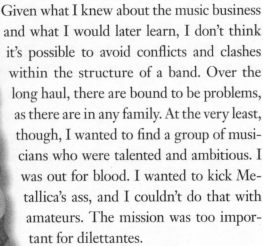

At the first Megadeth show in 1983 at Ruthie's Inn in Berkeley, California. I had bullet belts and dummy hand grenades on for this show. I wanted to make a statement.
Photograph by Harald O.

the rearview mirror for more than a quarter century. It was an awful job, about as boring and depressing as you might imagine, and made tolerable only by the "colorful" people with whom I worked. My supervisor was a woman named Marjorie. Marjorie, bless her heart, understood instinctively that the people in her charge were there primarily because they had no other options. Not one of us aspired to telemarketing greatness. We just needed a paycheck. Marjorie was a demanding but fair boss. She walked around the office in a generally perturbed state almost all of the time, but you got the sense that she was actually a decent person. She was just . . . cranky. But funny, too, in a militant feminist (think Janeane Garofalo) sort of way.

Half the time I showed up high or got high on my "smoke break." Marjorie knew it, sort of expected it, didn't really care one way or the other. I mean, how lucid do you have to be to dial a phone and have someone hang up on you? Marjorie was fascinated by the culture of pot that permeated her office, and on one of my last shifts she even pulled me aside and said, "Can you get me some weed, man?"

Indeed I could. And did. A bunch of us got baked together, and then I went off to be a guitar player again. Full-time.

Although I was far from a telemarketing whiz, I did make enough money to get back on my feet and into my own apartment, on Vernon Avenue in Hollywood. The first two guys in my new band—which briefly carried the name Fallen Angels—were named Robbie McKinney and Matt Kisselstein. Robbie, who had helped me get the telemarketing gig, played guitar. Matt, another telemarketer, played bass. They were both nice kids with some talent, but I could tell our venture wasn't going to last. We lacked the chemistry, the energy, the spark—or whatever you want to call it—that gives a band life in its infancy. But that's okay. It was through my friendship with Robbie that I met a young woman named Diana

Aragon, with whom I would fall in love and carry on a relation-ship that lasted more than seven years.* My goal at the time was to assemble a band, at any cost necessary, and then upgrade the parts as needed until I had the leanest, meanest fighting machine possible. It's taken a while, but I think I've finally done that. And this band, like the first incarnation of Megadeth, was a necessary step in that journey.

I WOKE ONE morning, hungover as usual, to the rhythmic pounding of a bass guitar. Not to the recorded sound of a bass coming out of a stereo or boom box, but an actual bass, coming from the apartment beneath mine. When you're a musician—ac-tually, even if you're not a musician—you know the difference; you can feel it in your bones, especially when you've been out late the night before and your head is throbbing and all you want to do is sleep it off.

Bwomp . . . Bwomp . . . Bwomp . . . Bwomp . . .

I rolled out of bed, pounded the floor with my foot, and screamed, "Shut up!"

Bwomp . . . Bwomp . . . Bwomp . . . Bwomp . . .

On and on it went, one of the simplest and most famous bass lines in the history of rock music: the opening of Van Halen's "Runnin' with the Devil."

Bwomp . . . Bwomp . . . Bwomp . . . Bwomp . . .

I pounded the floor again. Still no response. I staggered into the kitchen and threw open a window.

---

* Not monogamous, of course; I remained an alcoholic with a wandering eye for some time to come.

"Hey! Shut the fuck up!"

Bwomp . . . Bwomp . . . Bwomp . . . Bwomp . . .

Enough was enough. I picked up a potted plant from the windowsill and heaved it downward. It exploded on the air-conditioning unit of the offending apartment. And that did it. The music—such as it was—stopped.

I shambled back into the bedroom, pulled up the covers, and prepared to sleep for a few more hours, only to be interrupted by a knock at the door.

Oh, man . . . these guys are really asking for trouble.

I marched back into the living room and threw open the front door. There, before me, were two of the least imposing kids you'd ever want to meet. Both wore bell-bottom jeans and canvas high-tops, with cheap leather jackets that looked like the kind you'd pick up on QVC for $29.95—you know, the ones with the belt around the middle, so you can attach the optional tackle box or Trout Unlimited patch. The younger-looking of the two had long brown hair. The other kid was going prematurely bald, with only a tuft of hair on the crown of his head, and had a protruding Adam's apple that reminded me of Beaky Buzzard, the sad-faced cartoon vulture of Looney Tunes fame.

Before I could yell at them, the one with the long hair smiled.

"Hey, dude. You know where we can get some cigarettes?"

I slammed the door, barely getting out the words, "There's a store on the corner," before it closed in their faces.

Not more than two minutes passed before there was another knock at the door. Now I was really getting pissed. I sauntered back into the living room and answered the door again, this time fully prepared to hit one of them in the face.

"Hey," the younger one said, still smiling. "Uhhhhhh . . . are you old enough to buy beer?"

They were simultaneously endearing and irritating. And what the hell? A little hair of the dog didn't sound half-bad at that point.

"Okay," I said, smiling. "Now you're talking."

We went down to the corner and got a case of Heineken, and over the next few hours began cultivating a friendship that would evolve into a partnership. The one with the long hair was named David Ellefson, the son of a farmer from Jackson, Minnesota. David had come to Los Angeles ostensibly to study music at a place called the Musicians Institute, which was located just a block away from my apartment building. The Musicians Institute might have been held in high esteem in some circles, but to me it was worthy of scorn—the kind of place where you went to learn how to play Toto covers at wedding receptions and graduation parties. For David, though, it might as well have been Juilliard. Or so he told his parents. While his brother, Elliott, stayed home in Minnesota to help run the family farm, David went off to California to pursue his dream of becoming a musician. They gave him their blessing, along with a credit card, and turned him loose. It couldn't have been easy for them, but I suppose they were reassured by the knowledge that at least their son had enrolled in a respectable academic program at a fine institution of higher learning.

Except he hadn't. David never took a course at the Musicians Institute. Instead, after driving the family van all the way to Hollywood, he and a few of his high school buddies (including Greg Handevidt, the one with the hefty Adam's apple) went about the lonely business of trying to make it in the music business. At the time that I met them, they were barely eighteen years old and utterly clueless. But likeable as hell.

We sat around for hours that first day, tossing back Heinekens, talking about playing, sharing some of our musical likes and dislikes. David and Greg had been in a band called the Killers back in Minnesota (for some reason, I guess there was a small but thriving metal scene in the Upper Midwest), which was influenced, of course, by Iron Maiden, so I knew some of the stuff they'd been playing. I copied a few of the licks, showed them what

I could do. I could tell they were impressed. I was a little older and, despite my recent setbacks, more experienced in the music business. It might be a stretch to say that I was like a big brother to these guys, but I definitely became the leader of our odd little melting pot of a band: Mustaine and the Minnesota boys.

Not long afterward I asked both David and Greg to join my new band. They both happily accepted the invitation. David and I were good friends right from the beginning, and the fact that he was a really good bass player made the transition even easier. Greg was a little more problematic. A nice guy, and not a bad guitar player, but he was such an awkward and unusual-looking character. Not in a bad way—he was just a guy desperately in need of a rock 'n' roll makeover. Half the battle would have been trying to cultivate hair. That might not sound like a big thing, but it was to me. I had a very precise image of what my band would look like—what any real heavy metal band *should* look like—and it did not include bald heads and leather. Yeah, I know, fans of Judas Priest might cry foul, but the fact remains that skinheads and leather signify something I wasn't crazy about embracing. To each his own, you know? I wanted a more traditional look to go along with our decidedly unconventional, hard-assed sound. We were going to be the fastest, loudest, most dangerous band in history, and we had to look the part.

Greg didn't look the part.

Greg developed a friendship with a guy from the telemarketing firm and drifted off into obscurity.

So Greg was out. He remained a part of our circle of friends for some time to come, before eventually returning to Minnesota and joining another band. Much later, after giving up the dream, as almost everyone does eventually, he became some sort of mortician. Or so I heard.

And then it was just the two of us, me and Junior. "Junior"— that's what I called David Ellefson. I had decided shortly after inviting him into the band that we couldn't have two guys named Dave. Too confusing.

"What's your middle name?" I asked.

"Warren."

"Oh, man. That's not going to work. How about we shorten it? We can call you 'War.' You know, play off your Scandinavian heritage. All that Viking shit."

I thought it sounded pretty cool. David disagreed.

"All right then. But I'm not calling you Dave. From now on, you're Junior."

And that's what I called him for the better part of twenty years.

In the beginning I was skeptical about my own singing ability, so we brought in a vocalist named Lawrence "Lor" Kane. Lor wasn't in the band long, but give credit where credit is due: it was Lor who suggested Megadeth as the band's name. It happened when we were driving around one night, talking about finding exactly the right moniker. Lor knew I had already written a song entitled "Megadeth" and thought it would work equally well as a band name.

And he was right. So, thanks for that, Lor.

We kept a revolving door for drummers as well. The first was Dijon Carruthers, whose father was a journeyman actor named Ben Carruthers, whose credits included, most notably, *The Dirty Dozen*. Dijon was tall and lanky, with a smooth complexion and a very relaxed demeanor. It was hard to tell much of anything about him, aside from the obvious fact that he was a fantastic drummer, since he was such a weird and mysterious guy. Dijon described himself as being of Spanish descent, but he really didn't look Spanish. He'd write lyrics occasionally that were truly twisted and sadistic, not at all what you'd expect from a guy whose favorite musician was the Italian violinist Paganini. Once, at rehearsal, he showed up wearing a Pilgrim's hat and what appeared to be a wig; no explanation was offered. Then again, none was expected.

Anyway, one night while we were having dinner at Dijon's house, in walked this guy with a bass slung over his shoulder. Just opened the front door, strolled through the house like he owned the place, offered nothing more than a nod of the head and a cursory "Hey, man."

I looked at Dijon. He seemed uncomfortable.

"Who the fuck is that?" I asked.

"Oh . . . that's my brother."

This came as something of a surprise, given that the dude who had just passed through was a black man, and Dijon was suppos-edly Spanish. And therein was the heart of the mystery with Dijon Carruthers. His brother was Kane

One of the first live shots of me and my best friend for nearly two decades, David "Junior" Ellefson. Photograph by Harald O.

Carruthers, the bass player for a band known as the Untouch-ables. Dijon, it turned out, was of mixed racial heritage.

This revelation proved to be a formidable obstacle in my re-lationship with Dijon. I don't know whether he was embarrassed about his lineage or whether he harbored some suspicion that I was racist. Regardless, damage had been done. I couldn't possibly have cared less whether Dijon was black or white, but I did care that he hadn't told me about something that was, to me, so fundamentally important. This was about who he was and how he presented himself, and if he couldn't trust me or Junior with this information, then how could we possibly trust him?

Next came a drummer named Lee Rausch, another strange cat who played pretty well but who had some serious personality quirks. Lee's nickname was Jughead, so you can probably imagine what he looked like, and he had some pretty far out religious beliefs. Now, because of my background, that totally changed the way I looked at this guy. I knew we'd never be able to play together for a long period of time. Even though I wasn't a Christian, I found this shit weird.

I wasn't exactly militant in my stance on religion, however; thus the band's brief flirtation with Kerry King. Kerry, of course, was a founding member of Slayer, a thrash metal band that, like Megadeth, came of age in the early 1980s in Los Angeles. Although it had already garnered a substantial underground following by the time I was trying to put together a band, Slayer had not yet received the backing of a major label. I figured Kerry, a talented guitarist, might be open to the possibility of joining us, at least in the short term, while we tried to find a second guitar player. Slayer has often been mislabeled as a satanic band, and Kerry has frequently (and, again, inaccurately) been branded a Satanist. These days he's more likely to refer to himself as an atheist, although our divergent views on the subjects of religion and music provoked a feud (for lack of a better term) that only recently cooled.

Back in the day, though, I had no problem with Kerry. He was a very young, clean-cut, and ambitious guitar player, the son of a sheriff, who didn't drink alcohol or take drugs. Yet he was in a band called Slayer. Go figure. While he was in Slayer and I was putting together Megadeth, Kerry and I hung out together quite a bit, and we actually became pretty close friends. I shared with him a bunch of stuff on the guitar, including the infamous Devil's tritone, a complicated musical interval spanning three tones. The Devil's tritone requires some dexterity, but it's cool primarily because of the folklore attached to it. For a period of time in the Middle Ages, the Devil's tritone was banned by the Catholic Church; supposedly, musicians who disregarded this edict were severely punished and sometimes even beheaded. Whether there is truth to these tales, I do not know, but their existence was enough to inspire legions of heavy metal guitar players to incorporate the tritone into their songs. Kerry had never heard of it; but once introduced to the Devil's tritone, he became a big fan, and just about every Slayer song now includes that chord progression.

Kerry actually joined Megadeth for a few gigs in San Francisco in the spring of 1984. We were still searching for a new guitar player but didn't want to miss out on the opportunity to play live, so I asked Kerry to sit in with us. Some part of me was hoping he might agree to leave Slayer and join Megadeth on a permanent basis. But that didn't happen. Far from it, actually.

We prepared for those shows at a rehearsal studio in L.A. run by a guy named Curly Joe. This place was party central. We went back there one night after rehearsal and the studio was jumping with folks who were basically out of their minds on drugs. Remember, this was the early 1980s, when cocaine was not only socially acceptable but seriously strong shit. I'd become a formidable partier by this time, so there wasn't a lot that I considered shocking. But the scene at the studio was truly disturbing. We walked in and the revelry was at once obscene and terrifying—kind of like something out of the movie *Less than Zero* (set in the eighties, not coincidentally), where you open the door and some guy wearing a pig mask has his face stuck between another dude's legs.

"Holy shit!"

We were out of there fast, running down the stairs because we didn't want to wait for the elevator. At the bottom of the stairs,

**Me, Chris Poland, and David.
Obviously I am soloing.**
Photograph by Harald O.

spray-painted on the wall, was a gigantic swastika, along with the words *Curly Joe is a hippie Jew.*

Fucked-up and running for our lives (or so we thought), we crashed into each other on the way out the door, causing Lee Rausch to stumble and break his foot. Our first show in San Francisco was just a week away, and Lee naturally wanted to cancel, but I talked him out of it.

"When it's time to do the show, we'll cut off the cast," I suggested. "Then you can get it recast the next day."

The show must go on, right?

But when Lee had the cast removed, his foot was black, just fucked-up beyond recognition.

"Oh, man, that's nasty," I said. "You sure you can play?"

Lee nodded, took the stage, and did a commendable job. More than that, actually. I mean, talk about playing in pain. Lee had to be one of the toughest guys I've ever known. That incident took its toll on him, though. Or maybe something else did. Regardless, when we got back to Los Angeles, Lee announced that he was going off to find himself, to search for some deeper meaning in life. The last time I saw Lee he was getting into his truck, singing out loud, and acting like the happiest guy in the world.

I never spoke with him again.

SO, ONCE AGAIN, Megadeth needed a drummer. We found him in the person of Gar Samuelson. David Ellefson and I were working together at a place called Mars Studio at the time, and it was there that we "interviewed" Gar. If you can call it that. Gar was an incredibly sweet kid with big, sleepy eyes and full lips—he reminded me of the actor Don Knotts, especially the caricature Don Knotts (like in *The Incredible Mr. Limpet*, for example). There were differences, of course—Gar had long hair and a slow, almost guttural way of talking. I would soon learn that he was also a heroin addict, and that fact, more than any other, colored his day-to-day existence. But for all his problems, Gar was a genuinely likeable person who had a gift for making people light up.

On the day of his audition and interview, Gar arrived at Mars Studio completely strung out on dope. In order for him even to be capable of taking the meeting, Gar had to go out and score some heroin in advance. Timing, however, is everything in the life of the junkie (as I would later discover). Presumably, Gar had planned to get high earlier in the day and thus achieve a state of relative lucidity by the time he was scheduled to meet his potential bandmates (and employers). But because he hadn't scored right away, and had probably ingested a little too much, the process had evolved in a slightly different fashion. Gar had quickly gone from "Aahhhh," to "Whoops," to "Oh, shit . . . I'm falling asleep."

When I walked into the room to meet Gar, he was sitting in a chair, head hanging, eyes fluttering, a cigarette dangling between his fingers. The cigarette was down to the filter; I could see that it already had burned his skin. Gar didn't even notice.

"Wow, this is going to be fun," I said to Ellefson. "The guy's like a sadist or something. What's next, a cattle prod?"

I walked around the room a bit, looked at Gar, tried to size him up . . . tried to imagine him in Megadeth. The first thing I noticed (after the cigarette, of course) was the footwear. Capezios! The guy was wearing fucking Capezios. I had a flashback to my days in Metallica, when we played at a roller-skating rink with a band called Ratt, and one of their temporary guys had been wearing Capezios. Something about that just struck me as wrong. If you're a guitar player and you dress up like a chick, you aren't a metal guy, you're a metal cross-dresser. You don't belong in Metallica, you don't belong in Megadeth. If you're going to be metal, you have to have the lifestyle, and that lifestyle does not include sitting in front of a mirror and putting on eyeliner and lipstick—and Capezios! It's like saying you have to wear eyeliner to be a fisherman. It just doesn't happen. It shouldn't happen, anyway.

Whatever trepidation I might have had about Gar, though, melted away after he woke up and started playing. Within just a few seconds I knew he was the right guy to take over for Lee Rausch. Gar created these amazing jazz-influenced drum fills that immediately and instinctively challenged my guitar playing. Technically he was a marvel—using both hands to create a crossover technique that was at once flashy and effective. Gar's style, informed by years of jazz training, became a big part of the first couple Megadeth records. For a while, in the early days, when people would ask me to describe the type of music we played, I'd say, "We're a jazz-oriented punk band with some classical influences." I'd say it to mess with people's heads, but it really was close to the truth.

GAR CAME TO Megadeth's attention through Jay Jones, a cocaine dealer who became our manager. Jay was an extraordinarily odd character with a skull that was grossly disproportionate to his body (think Fred Flintstone) and a voice like Ratso Rizzo. All twisted vowels and nasal twang. Every sentence, it seemed, began with *"Hey, dooood."*

I don't mean to imply that Jay was incompetent or that we failed to do any due diligence before turning our career over to him. We did some research. Not a lot. Jay was not entirely without street cred. He'd been involved with a few reputable punk bands, including the Circle Jerks, as well as some artists who were on the cutting edge of what would come to be known as hip-hop. Jay had some interesting ideas; he was more than just a drug dealer and a junkie.

But he was both of those things.

We were frequently together, traveling from the studio out to where Jay would go to score heroin. He'd get cheap Mexican heroin that had been cut with shoe polish or something. It had a purple tint to it, so that when you'd snort it and then run your hand across your nose, you'd get a shit-colored snot line on your hand. Jay's hands were always streaked with these lines, and he didn't even seem to care or notice. Why, you might ask, did we allow an acknowledged cocaine dealer and drug addict to be our manager? Simple: he had the sales pitch, baby. He had the patter.

Also, he had easy access to cocaine and heroin, which meant Megadeth had easy access to cocaine and heroin, a fact that took on great importance as the band evolved.

Jay, incidentally, is deceased now, and the way he expired was just as outrageous as the way he lived. His father had been in the military and had been involved in some sort of explosive accident that had left him permanently disabled. Jay and his brother had never left the family home, and indeed shared a bedroom into middle age. With bunk beds, no less. They had two big, sloppy, mange-infested dogs that shared the room with them. And a barrel of kibble in the corner. So you can imagine how this room smelled when Junior and I would pay a visit. We'd go over to get Jay, and he'd be in his room, and he'd tell us to wait a second, and we'd have to wait outside the house, which was like a kennel, or worse, in his bedroom, which smelled like the service entrance of a veterinary clinic; you'd gag just walking through the door.

Some years later, long after he and Megadeth had parted company, Jay Jones was stabbed to death with a butter knife during—rumor has it—a fight over a bologna sandwich. That's not funny, of course. But, if you knew Jay, neither is it particularly surprising.

Thanks to Jay, though, Megadeth had its drummer. In the months after he signed on, we found out quite a bit about Gar Samuelson—some of it good, some of it not so good. On the positive side, he was, as advertised, an absolute virtuoso on drums. On the negative side, his drug addiction was even more pronounced than I had suspected. Gar and Jay made for a formidably fucked-up tandem, and with the two of them now so deeply ingrained in the band, it was only a question of time before cocaine and heroin surpassed alcohol as the drugs of choice in Megadeth.

I remember being at Gar's house one day, hanging out, when the conversation turned to recreational drug use and a philosophical debate over the merits of particular substances. Chemically speaking, I was far from a virgin. I could best be described as a functional alcoholic who also liked to smoke weed, snort the occasional line of coke, and experiment with other drugs. There was little I hadn't tried. But heroin?

Never.

"I don't understand why you guys like to do that shit," I said.

Gar laughed. "You mean smack?"

"Yeah. What's the big deal?"

He nodded, smiled knowingly. "Dude, if you want to be a great musician, you have to try heroin. You'll see. It's like being back in the womb."

Back in the womb . . .

That sounded pretty cool. And, shit . . . I wanted to be great. Next thing you know I was bent over a table, pulling a line of heroin into my nostril. It was a small amount, so there was no great rush, just a warm sensation, followed by a short nap.

When I woke up, Gar and his brother were hunched over the kitchen stove, bleary eyed and silent, and smoking crack. I remember seeing them and thinking, *Wow, this is really stupid.*

"Don't knock it till you've tried it," Gar said, giggling like a child.

Full disclosure: I had smoked cocaine once before, back when I was playing in Panic. There was one night when we were scheduled to play a gig, and I wasn't feeling well. One of the guys in our little entourage (not a band member, I should point out) liked to freebase, and he suggested I give it a try. Better than Tylenol, he said. One hit and my headache would be gone. But that was freebase, not crack; I didn't know there was much of a difference until I joined Gar and his brother at the stove.

I took a single hit and immediately felt as though the whole world had been pulled out from under my feet. The room began to spin furiously, and suddenly I found myself lurching awkwardly toward the bathroom. I threw open the door, fell to my knees, and vomited into the toilet. I stayed there on the floor for a few minutes, retching, sweating, trying to regain my equilibrium.

Never again. I swear to God . . . never again.

And then it passed. The nausea and dizziness were gone, replaced by the most amazing euphoria I'd ever experienced, and at that very moment . . . I got it. I understood exactly why Gar and his brother had their faces over the stove. I understood heroin and why you might want to mix it with crack. It all made sense to me now. These guys were jazz guys, and in the jazz world . . . well, anything goes. Not every jazz musician is a drug addict, obviously, but in my experience there is no corner of the music universe where hard-core drug use is more commonly found— and accepted. That includes heavy metal. As I said, in metal we liked to drink; in jazz, smack was everywhere. And now I had been indoctrinated.

I don't recall any regret about this transition, at least not in the beginning. Quite the contrary. This was in some ways just another notch on the holster. Rock stars did drugs, and I was a rock star. Now I'd smoked crack and snorted heroin—on the same day, no less!—which in my estimation put me one step closer to being Jimi Hendrix or Keith Richards. Forget for a moment that Hendrix was dead and Keith looked worse than dead. The thing about being a drug addict is that it is not all piss and puke. Sometimes it's actually a lot of fun, in a very twisted, *Trainspotting* sort of way. Until it gets out of hand, which it invariably does, and then it takes your fucking heart and soul, and everything else you have to give.

The descent was slow, in the beginning, mainly because Gar and Jay (like the rest of us) were always broke and so there was never enough smack or crack to go around, never an opportunity to really go nuts with it. It wasn't unusual to arrive at rehearsal and see Gar kind of moping around sadly, hands stuffed in his pockets. Then you'd realize that his cymbals were missing. Or his drumsticks. Or even his whole drum kit.

"Gar, man, where the hell is your gear?" I'd say.

He'd just shrug in that innocent way that made you want to hug him and take care of him, rather than slap him for being so stupid.

"Sorry, Da-vey," he'd drawl. "Had to pawn it so I could get well."

"Well" was a euphemism. It was the word we used to describe getting over being dope sick. If you had heroin, you would be well; if you knew where to find heroin, and had the money to purchase it, you could get well. We had a guy—a dealer, or a "conduit"—called the Rug Doctor. For the longest time, I didn't even understand the nickname, didn't particularly care, as long as he could deliver, or made house calls, or however you want to put it. Later, I found out the name stemmed from his ability to get people well, to get them "up off the rug," which is where you were when you were sick and going through withdrawal. When you're a heroin addict, that's pretty much every day. You spend each waking moment chasing, snorting, smoking, shooting. Anything to get rid of the withdrawal symptoms.

THERE HAD BEEN times in my life when I'd been relatively sober, but I was kind of like that old Western joke:

What do you get when you sober up a drunken horse thief?

A horse thief.

I was a frustrated guitar player who had a real hard-luck story growing up, and to deal with my pain and anger and loneliness, I medicated myself. But I didn't really find any solutions until I started to do heroin. For me, heroin was the magic bullet. It changed the way I looked at the world. It killed all the pain, even more so than alcohol. Drinking stoked my anger. When I did smack, I mellowed. Growing up I never would have anticipated that I'd be a junkie. Especially a heroin addict. I was a Jehovah's Witness, and I can still see the issue of the *Watchtower* with its painfully earnest antidrug message and the picture of a junkie on the cover, a filthy, fetid old guy drawing his injection up out of a rusty bottle cap.

But that's not how heroin addicts get loaded, unless they're locked up in a Turkish prison or something. Heroin was a much more accessible and mainstream drug than I had been led to believe. Far more insidious, too. You do a little heroin and the brain gets confused. It says, "Hmmm, looks like we don't need to excrete any dopamine today. Already enough in the system!" So the brain instructs the pituitary gland to take a vacation. As long as you keep feeding the body (and thus the brain) more opiates, the masquerade continues. But here's the problem: if the body's natural mechanism for producing dopamine (and endorphins) shuts down for a day, and then starts up again, you're going to feel a little icky. If it stops for three days, you're dope sick.

I was willing to pay the price, to take whatever risks were involved. Frankly, it all felt like part of the package. I was a rock 'n' roll rebel in a hot band. I had a beautiful girlfriend and a widening musical reputation, bolstered by the fact that most people who followed heavy metal knew of my role in Metallica.

One of those people was Chris Poland, a guitarist who had previously played in an L.A. jazz fusion band with Gar Samuelson. The two of them, in fact, had been high school buddies back in Buffalo (hence the name of their band: the New Yorkers), and they'd come out to California in search of fame and fortune and God only knows what else. Chris, like Gar, was a friend of Jay Jones.

"Dooood, you gotta check this guy out," Jay said. "He played with Gar, and he's fuckin' awesome."

On that point, Jay was correct. Unlike Gar, who was preternaturally laid-back and almost anemic in appearance, Chris was solidly built and ambitious. He introduced himself to me after a Megadeth show one night and basically asked for a spot in the band. Upon meeting Chris I was actually somewhat surprised that he appeared to be so robust, given his relationship with Jay and Gar. I just sort of expected another sickly jazz junkie. But in both demeanor and appearance, Chris was strong, in part due to the fact that Chris had a girlfriend named Lana whose parents owned a fleet of mobile burrito stands ("maggot wagons," we called them) that delivered to construction sites around town. So Chris rarely had any trouble finding his next meal (or "getting well"), unless he got in trouble with the girlfriend or she got in trouble with Dad, all of which would eventually happen. The junkie's life is rarely a straight line.

I listened to Chris for about ten minutes before making up my mind. The guy was an impressively dexterous guitar player—better than I was at the time, for sure—and, like Gar, he was informed by a jazz background that added nuance to his playing. Equally important was the fact that he and Gar already had developed a certain chemistry from having played in another band together and from having been friends for so many years. That was important to me, especially after the ugliness of my breakup with Metallica. I longed for that closeness. I've always said that when you are in a band with someone, playing music together, you can't get any closer . . . unless you have sex with each other. Now, the truth is, most guys in bands do have sex with each other, in an in-

Our first backdrop for Megadeth.
Photograph by Harald O.

direct sort of way—pulling trains on girls, tag-teaming, sharing girlfriends, because, you know, when you're in a band nothing is "mine" and everything is "ours."

But I digress.

The point is, Chris was a nearly perfect fit. So we offered him the job on the spot.

Then we all went out and got loaded to celebrate.

7

MISSION:
TO BREAK ALL THE RULES OF GOD AND MAN

"And by the way, when you see your guitar player, tell him I said thanks for biting my pussy."

JAY JONES TOOK CARE OF US, IN A MANNER OF SPEAKING. HE'D SHOW UP AT MARS STUDIO NEARLY EVERY DAY, AROUND NOON, JUST AS ELLEFSON AND I WERE STIRRING FROM OUR SLUMBER. TO HELP CLEAR THE COBWEBS, JAY WOULD TAKE US TO A PLACE CALLED NORM'S, A REALLY GROTESQUE NEIGHBORHOOD LUNCHEONETTE WHERE $5.99 GOT YOU A HUNK OF DRY MEAT, POTATOES (MASHED, BAKED, OR FRENCH FRIED), A SIDE OF WILTED ICEBERG LETTUCE, AND A BOWL OF JELL-O FOR DESSERT. OH YEAH—AND A BOTTOMLESS GLASS OF ICED TEA OR LEMONADE. THE FOOD WAS HORRIBLE, BUT WE DIDN'T COMPLAIN. THERE WAS PLENTY

A good role model and a bad role model.
Photograph by Ross Halfin.

of it and we weren't paying. It's amazing how little you need to survive when you are young and chasing goals both noble (artistic success) and ignoble (the daily heroin or cocaine score).

We had learned how to eat for literally pennies a day. Jay didn't mind paying, even though he had little money himself, because Megadeth was his ticket to a better life. I think he also genuinely liked our company—we were a rolling party at the time, and Jay was our facilitator. After lunch we'd go to a nearby pub, where Jay would complete the day's transaction, dispense a balloon of heroin, and we'd all get well, just in time to start rehearsing. Each of us had his preferred method of getting high. I started out snorting heroin, then (as with cocaine) advanced to smoking, which provides for a faster, more intense intoxication. Gar and Chris Poland were far more experienced; both were intravenous drug users by the time we met them. Addiction, though, is addiction, and I don't mean to minimize or distort my own capacity for self-destruction, but I could see right from the beginning that shooting smack was a whole different game, and frankly a little too scary for my tastes. I shot heroin only a couple times. Didn't like the way it felt, didn't like needles, didn't like the whole culture surrounding it (which often involved sharing needles). It just seemed dangerous and unhealthy and, well, gross.

That we were able to make music—sometimes great music—while living this way remains something of a marvel. But we did. We were young, ambitious, talented, and indestructible. Or so we told ourselves. Prior to Chris joining the band we had recorded a three-song demo ("Loved to Death," "The Skull Beneath the Skin," and "The Mechanix") that swiftly began making its way through the underground network of tape trade and distribution, much as *No Life Till Leather* had done for Metallica. We played up and down the Pacific Coast, mostly in L.A. and San Francisco, putting on ferocious stage shows that were sometimes brilliant, sometimes sloppy, but never boring. By this point Metallica's first

BACK TO MARAUD!

LIVE FOR METAL - DIE FOR....

MEGADETH

THEIR CONVENTICLE GATHERS AT/ON

BERKELEY KEYSTONE **15**

PALO ALTO KEYSTONE **16**

THE STONE S.F. **18**

A. P. R.

THE MEGADETH FAN CLUB
438 Joshua Way
Sunnyvale, California 94086

FAST... LOUD... AND RUDE!

IN-STORE APPEARANCE AT THE RECORD VAULT!
APRIL 18   NO WIMPS!

TICKETS ON SALE AT BASS OUTLETS
FOR SHOW INFO. —
(415) 391- 8292/8289

Flyer for an early Megadeth show.

record had become a hit and the band was gathering momentum. I tried not to pay attention, but it was hard (and would only become harder). In interviews, Lars Ulrich would occasionally denigrate my contribution to Metallica, alternately describing me as a temporary guitar player or a mere footnote. More than once he actually criticized my guitar playing. Well, that was more than I could handle. If you want to say I was a drunk, fine. I was a drunk. If you want to say I was a handful, okay. I was a handful. I should have cleaned up my act. But don't lie about my playing ability; don't suggest that I wasn't a major contributor to everything the band accomplished in its embryonic stage. Without my songs and my solos—without my energy—I don't know that Metallica ever would have become the band that it was. A bold statement, perhaps, but there you have it. And I was righteously pissed that Lars couldn't at least do me the courtesy of being respectful.

I responded in the most cutting and juvenile manner possible. Over the next couple years, as Megadeth carved out its own niche, battling Metallica for thrash metal supremacy, journalists and disc jockeys often requested interviews. Invariably, I'd calmly deflect any discussion of Lars, sometimes by speaking in Danish.

"Godmorgen," I'd say with a smile.

The chip I'd been carrying on my shoulder since childhood only grew heavier as Megadeth cultivated a reputation. Our live shows, combined with the demo, naturally provoked interest from record companies. My goal was to land a deal with a major label right out of the starting gate, but it became apparent in fairly short order that we didn't have the juice to make that happen. Rather, we couldn't make it happen on our terms.

During a trip to New York we carried on a brief flirtation with a major record label. The company's A&R director at the time was a charismatic gay man, very much out of the closet. I can say with a degree of certainty that while he may have known his business, he was also an intensely strange and aggressive character. I saw it for myself one night at the Limelight, a popular club in New York. The record company executive had taken us there as part of our recruiting trip, and it definitely had the desired effect. One of the first people I saw when I walked in was the guitar player for the Cars, which was an A-list band at the time. "Let the Good Times Roll" was among the first songs I had learned when I played in a band back in high school, so I couldn't help but smile as I passed him, thinking, Man, I've made it now—I'm hanging out with the guy from the Cars!

As often happened at clubs in New York in the 1980s, we ended up in the bathroom snorting lines of cocaine. And in walked the record company executive. I'd been out with him before, so I knew of his prodigious capacity for partying, but this particular incident took me by surprise. He walked up to us, took a couple pills out of his pocket (ecstasy, I presume), stuck them in our mouths, and then tried to seal the deal with a big kiss.

Junior, the midwestern boy far from home, stood there with a blank look on his face. The record company executive, meanwhile, laughed like a madman. I managed only a weak "What the fuck?!"

I don't know if this was the guy's idea of a joke or just his way of showing his guests a good time. Maybe, I thought, this was the first in what he expected would be a long line of favors traded. But I wasn't going there. If getting a major-label record deal meant I'd have to introduce my dick to some guy's ass . . . well, then Megadeth would be going the independent route.

We met first with representatives of Enigma Records, a small label with a reasonably strong list of artists in its portfolio. When that didn't pan out, we turned to Combat Records, an independent label out of Long Beach that was in some small way part of the Sony empire. Representing Combat in that meeting was Cliff Cultreri, the vice president.

Cliff was accessible. New York–born and –bred, he was thick around the middle, spoke with the nasal twang of Adam Sandler, and appeared more interested in being our buddy than in playing the role of record company executive. As I recall, in that meeting, Junior and I were somewhat cocky. We'd been romanced by labels large and small, and more were knocking at the door. It seemed unlikely that we were going to come out of this whole thing without a contract. Indeed, not more than five minutes after we left the offices of Combat Records, Cliff Cultreri came running out into the street, screaming, "Wait! Wait!" By the time he caught up with us, his face was flushed and covered with sweat, his breathing labored. For a moment I thought he might have a heart attack.

"I . . . called . . . New York," Cliff gasped. I presumed he was referring to the parent company, but he didn't elaborate. Probably because he was too tired. Or too excited. Maybe both. "They want . . . to . . . sign you."

So we signed with Combat Records, and before long the showbiz pigs were sniffing around, trying to take advantage of us, teaching me why I needed to count my fingers whenever I shook somebody's hand and why I needed to keep my back against the wall. The education would take time. I wasn't terribly interested in the business end of things in those days. I wanted to make music, get high, and get laid. Not necessarily in that order. Megadeth facilitated the achievement of those admittedly hedonistic goals, and we had little concern for damage done to friends or family or reputation.

After moving out of the studio, I was essentially homeless, although Ellefson let me stay at his place for a while. I was smoking cocaine and heroin. We were junkies, we were bad boys, we were alcoholics. We smoked pot, got in fights, and fucked chicks. And we were utterly remorseless. As Chris Poland once said, "I guess our mission statement was to break all the rules of God and man, and we pretty much did."

Actually, there was another mission statement, one that more accurately, if not more articulately, expressed our creative aspirations. Although it mutated with some regularity, the sentiment was consistent: to make Megadeth the "fastest, utmost-heaviest, most ultra-furious heavy metal band in history."

Or some such nonsense. It sounded good at the time, and if the verbiage left something to be desired, at least the spirit was admirable. We would be heavier than heavy metal, faster than the fastest of speed or thrash metal bands. We would redefine the genre. On our own terms.

Despite the rampant promiscuity that was so much a part of our lives, we were all hanging with specific girls at this time. These were relationships of convenience and nothing more. Diana remained my true love, but since Diana lived with her parents and I needed a place to stay, I moved in for a time with a girl named Sharon.

Anyway, one night we were driving around in Ellefson's van, working our way through some China white (synthetic heroin), when Chris Poland and I began to get into it a little bit. Chris was a volatile personality—probably not the best match for someone like me—and we had already had heated arguments by this time. These were due in part to the combustible nature of our relationship, but also to the fact that heroin has a tendency to make you . . . shall we say . . . grumpy. Not usually when you're high, of course—smack users are generally pretty laid-back, so long as they're well stocked. But when you're not well, it's a very different story. You get intensely irritable—Poland used to call it "the heroin bitch"—and in that state, it doesn't take much to set you off.

I forget exactly how the fight began. I just remember Poland bickering incessantly with Sharon and Ellefson's girlfriend, Robin, and then me, the volume increasing, the insults and threats getting uglier. The screaming continued as Ellefson hit the brakes and pulled over. Poland was in my face and wouldn't let it go, so I yanked him out of the van and started rabbit-punching his head, trying with all of my might to knock him unconscious. But he wouldn't go down. The guy was so completely fucked-up that he refused to quit, so essentially it became a technical knockout. Only the intervention of Scott Menzies, one of Chris's closest friends (and a future Megadeth road manager), prevented me from perhaps killing Chris that night. Scott jumped on my back and pulled me off; as he and Ellefson tried to calm me down, Sharon climbed into the driver's seat of the van and hit the accelerator. The van jumped off the curb and rocketed toward a Bob's Big Boy across the street. Fortunately, Scott was working in hero mode that night. Just as Sharon hit the gas, he dived headfirst into the van, fought her for control of the wheel, and rammed the gearshift into park.

The van let out a horrible groan and crawled to a stop. I still believe that if Menzies's death-defying leap had been a second or two late, Sharon would have taken out half the customers at Bob's Big Boy. She was capable of such madness, and if not for the fact that I needed a warm bed and food, I'm sure I wouldn't have lasted as long as I did with her. But this was the end of the line. It took the better part of an hour to pick up the pieces of this mess. We tracked down Chris, who had wandered off, then drove to Sharon's house. By the time we got there, she had passed out in the back of the van, so we deposited her on the front lawn of her apartment building. Then we tossed a few empty vodka bottles at her feet, to heighten the disgust of any neighbors who might happen by.

When I came back later that night, feeling not the slightest bit guilty and simply needing a place to sleep, Chris was on the sofa in Sharon's living room. I didn't care, didn't think anything of it. We landed where we landed in those days. I woke the next morning with a brutal hangover and immediately reached for a Quaalude to dull the pain. After getting a glimpse of Poland, I decided to split the pill in half.

"Hey, buddy," I said, wincing at his bruised and swollen face. "I think you're going to need this."

He took the pill, thanked me, and off we went to rehearsal, with no hard feelings. Sharon, however, was a different story.

When I returned to the apartment that evening, my shit was piled up in the hallway outside the door. Nearly everything I owned—records, stereo, clothes, even a little cookie tin containing a quarter-pound of pot—had been removed from the apartment. The only thing missing, oddly enough, was my pet scorpion (a gift from one of my customers). Except to the extent that I no longer had a place to stay, I didn't care much about the dissolution of my relationship with Sharon, and I certainly didn't blame her for kicking me out; I hadn't exactly treated her well. But I was pissed that she'd left everything in the hallway, where it could have been stolen, and I wanted my scorpion back.

I tried knocking on the door for a while; no one answered, so I convinced a neighbor to let me in and then tried to gain access to Sharon's apartment from the outside, climbing from balcony to balcony, three stories above the ground. Eventually I reached her apartment, and what I saw inside scared the shit out of me. There was Sharon half-dressed, with a 250-pound gray-haired woman I had never seen before and who looked like a man.

"What do you want?!" the woman growled.

"Uhhhhhh . . . I want my scorpion back."

Sharon then came to the window and began screaming at me.

"Yeah? Well too fuckin' bad. You're not getting your scorpion back." She paused, smiled. "And by the way, when you see your guitar player, tell him I said thanks for biting my pussy."

I had no response for that one. All I could do was stand there slack-jawed, thinking, *Whoa . . . Poland. You fucked my girlfriend. Touché to you, bro.*

THE FIRST MEGADETH record was called *Killing Is My Business . . . and Business Is Good!* From concept to finished product, it was an adventure, during which I learned more about the music business than I ever imagined. And most of it was not particularly encouraging. Oh, the run-up was fine—crafting the riffs in rehearsal, writing the songs themselves, learning to have confidence in my own ability not only to play guitar but to sing. The latter was the bigger hurdle. Right up until we went into the studio, I was still considering the possibility of hiring a full-time vocalist. Prior to making our demo, we had a guy we liked. His name was Billy Bonds, but he showed up for rehearsal one night wearing makeup and eyeliner, and that was the end of that. I didn't care if the guy could sing like Robert Plant—there was no way some glam-band wannabe would be the face of Megadeth.

Second show ever, Ruthie's Inn Berkeley, 1984.
Photograph by Brian Lew.

"Fuck it," Ellefson said. "Why don't you just try singing?"

It took time to learn proper technique. I didn't know how to breathe efficiently or how to pace myself so that I wouldn't wreck my vocal cords. Consequently, I developed a unique singing voice. Not everyone is a fan, of course. But there's no questioning the originality. When you hear a Megadeth song, you know it. My voice is every bit as recognizable as James Hetfield's or Axl Rose's. Giving up the security of (relative) anonymity that a guitar player enjoys was equally challenging. Say what you want about lead singers: they're arrogant, egotistical, immature, petulant, hypersensitive. They also have huge balls. Without that particular attribute, you can't get out onstage and sing. It's just not possible.

After receiving the contracts from Combat Records and finding the language almost indecipherable (I've since grown far more savvy about these things), I had to find an attorney. Jay Jones suggested a lawyer with whom he had done some business in the past, and we figured, well, if Jay says he's good, then he's probably good. As it turned out, this was not a decision that worked in my favor. I remember looking at the contract and wondering why it seemed to be so one-sided, with everything favoring the record company. I noticed incentives for the attorney, but I wasn't discriminating enough to question any of it. I just wanted to make music and have a good time. That's all any of us wanted.

By this point we were full-blown junkies. On more than one occasion David Ellefson and I would visit the attorney, and I would fall sound asleep the minute he began speaking in legalese. Junior would stay awake and try to pay attention, but he didn't know what the fuck the attorney was doing, and I'm sure he'd be the first to admit it. By the time the ink had dried on all the contracts, we wound up with one of the most pathetic deals in the history of rock 'n' roll. Even by the sorry standard of independent labels, we got fucked over.

Our entire budget was eight thousand dollars, a figure so insultingly low that it was almost laughable. And yet, we were undeterred. The album would be recorded at a studio called Indigo Ranch in Malibu. The studio was originally built by and for the Moody Blues in the 1970s (thus the name *Indigo*), so there was a legacy of professionalism and success attached to it, which was important to us. Every artist gets a charge out of walking into a studio or concert venue and standing in the same spot where great musicians have performed in the past. You like to think that the history seeps into your marrow, becoming a muse of sorts. If that sounds a little mystical, well, it's true nonetheless, and despite the perversely minuscule budget, I was excited about getting into the studio and putting our mark on the world.

Unfortunately, things began to go wrong almost from the day we arrived. Gar and Chris showed up with Jay Jones, armed with about a hundred pounds of frozen hamburger meat and a huge cache of cocaine and heroin. Basically, we spent about four grand on drugs and four grand to make the record, which is just one of the many reasons why *Killing Is My Business* did not come out the way I had hoped it would. Simply put, we ran out of money.

Incredibly enough, we also ran out of dope within a week. Without dope, we were incapacitated. Without dope, there could be no record. So I called a friend and begged for assistance in finding some cocaine. We ended up driving all the way from Malibu to Manhattan Beach to get the coke, and it was just awful, watered-down shit that didn't facilitate the process at all.

Frustrated, angry, dope sick, we ended up firing Jay Jones in the middle of the project (although he would slide in and out of our lives for years to come). For a while I was concerned that we might not even finish the record. Ellefson and I were living at the time with a man named Karat Fay, who was the sound engineer on *Killing Is My Business*. Karat was a competent enough engineer, but he was another in the long line of oddballs associated with Jay

Building up our following was going to take time, but the fans were there from the very first show.
Photograph by Brian Lew.

Singing was not my idea!
Photograph by Brian Lew.

Jones (who had hired him for the job). High on Karat's résumé was the fact that he had previously worked with KISS. Why some old dude who had spun the knobs for KISS was supposed to be right for Megadeth, I don't know. But there he was. Karat was nice enough to let me crash at his place after Sharon threw me out. That was generous, and it wasn't like I had a lot of options. But after a few days of watching Karat walk around the house naked (which was something he did far too often for my tastes), I began to wonder exactly where I was going with my life.

We wound up going to the record company and getting an extra $4,000, so the whole album cost $12,000 to make. A pittance, really. But we got it done, turned it in, and then began discussions about cover art. This, too, proved to be a disappointment.

I had already loosely conceptualized a logo for Megadeth and with the help of a friend named Peyton Tuttle had sketched out some original artwork well before the first album was recorded. I had drawn the logo myself because I had wanted to get a tattoo, one that incorporated my feelings about religion and repression and freedom of expression. The logo featured a skull and crossbones, with an additional pair of the latter placed in such a way that they looked almost like twin crucifixes. Ultimately this led to the creation of our mascot, Vic Rattlehead, a skeletal creature whose eyes, ears, and mouth are covered or clamped shut—"see no evil, speak no evil, hear no evil"—and whose mythical evolution was the centerpiece of a song called "Skull Beneath the Skin," the third track on *Killing Is My Business*. In the song, poor Vic stumbles across a black magic séance; he gets caught, captured, and . . . well, a lot of very bad things happen to him.

PREPARE THE PATIENT'S SCALP
TO PEEL AWAY
METAL CAPS HIS EARS
HE'LL HEAR NOT WHAT WE SAY
SOLID STEEL VISOR
RIVETED ACROSS HIS EYES
IRON STAPLES CLOSE HIS JAWS
SO NO ONE HEARS HIS CRIES

When I told Combat about my concept for the logo, they had no problem with it. I turned in the artwork and waited to see the finished product. Today I'd handle things much differently. I'd expect to be involved every step of the way. I'd insist upon seeing sketches and mockups. I'd work closely with the graphic artists in charge of the design. But I was a neophyte, and the record company treated me as such. To this day I don't really know what happened to the cover art I suggested—whether it was lost or ignored. I do know that when the album came back, and I saw what they had done to the cover art, I was mortified. The formidable Vic had been reduced to a caricature. Rather than a brilliant and disturbing image, the cover of *Killing Is My Business* featured what appeared to be a plastic Halloween skull and a variety of dime-store accoutrements. It looked as though someone had turned a beer can inside out and used it as a visor to cover the eyes; the blood looked like ketchup. Everything about the design smacked of amateurism. I remember holding the cover in my hands and saying, "You have got to be kidding."

Poor Vic. He deserved better. Vic had been born not so much out of my contempt for organized religion but out of my fascination with comic book lore. When I was a kid I would go down to the corner store and buy packs of baseball cards with bubblegum inside. One day they had superhero bubblegum cards, and I got one with Iron Man inside. Then I got one with Captain America, and pretty soon I was devouring comic books, immersing myself in the fantasy world of flawed but courageous heroes. I wanted to be like them. And if you think about it, Vic is very cartoonlike. Much of Megadeth's success can be traced to the popularity of certain iconic images and the way they fit into our lyrics. One of our most popular songs, for example, is "Holy Wars: The Punishment Due," the second half of which is based on *The Punisher*, a graphic novel about the great Frank Castle. Inspiration is where you find it, and mine, at least in the beginning, came from the vastly under-rated and underappreciated realm of comics and graphic novels, particularly those with a nihilistic bent.

Vic was supposed to serve as an homage. Instead, in this incarnation, he was a joke. Not exactly the way I had it planned. Years later *Killing Is My Business* was reissued with cover art more reflective of what I had in mind. But in 1985, we were stuck with a plastic skull and ketchup. And there was nothing we could do about it.

The album itself, while not exactly a masterpiece, was far from the embarrassment the cover art suggested. There was a lot to like

about *Killing Is My Business*—the energy, the speed, the storytelling. Granted, the sound was a bit muddy, but that's what you get for twelve grand. There are gems on that album that hold up to this day, especially when you listen to the digitally remastered version; all things considered, I'm proud of the way it turned out. While far from platinum, the album sold briskly, especially for an unknown band on an indie label, and was well received by critics who cared enough to take notice.

Although *Killing Is My Business* announced Megadeth as a new voice in heavy metal, it was actually an old pop standard that became one of the record's most popular tracks. The song was "These Boots Are Made for Walkin'," a bluesy little tune made famous by Nancy Sinatra in the sixties. I can still hear it coming out of the speakers of my mom's Ford Fairlane, parked by the beach at Lake Cachuma, with the doors open and the volume cranked as we splashed in the water.

"You keep saying you got something for me . . ."

I connected with that song on a visceral level, felt drawn to it in a way I'd never known. Might have just been hormonal, of course, but still . . . when that happens, you don't forget it. When we got together and started rehearsing for the first Megadeth record, the opportunity to do a cover was presented. It was an easy way to add some material to a record, to give you a little breathing room if you didn't have enough stuff; back in the day, there was only so much space you could put on each side of a vinyl LP before the grooves of the record narrowed to the point of incompatibility and the songs would begin to overlap. We didn't want to put a lot of material on those early records, out of fear that there would be bleed-through. So we kept the formula simple: four songs on each side of the record, eight songs in all. Each song would run approximately four minutes in length. We went into the studio to record *Killing Is My Business* armed with seven original songs. That meant we had room for one more. And I wanted it to be something completely different, something totally unexpected. Something you'd never expect to hear from a speed metal band.

The choice was obvious.

It wasn't hard to convince the other guys in the band that "These Boots Are Made for Walkin'" would be a great way to close the record.

"Look, we're kind of a smoky jazz band anyway, right?" I said, exaggerating just a bit (okay, maybe a lot). "It'll be perfect."

The song was good on record but great when performed live. It became a fan favorite, especially as we added drama, dragged out the bluesy intro, and turned the song into something of a showpiece. We'd have one of our roadies stand at the side of the stage and throw out a bar stool for Junior. With the lights down, he'd light up a cigarette and just sit there and play, riffing through the bass intro for as long as he felt like playing. Finally, at the end of the intro, I'd yell, "Okay!" and the guitar would kick in, and then the drums, and then the song belonged to Megadeth. And that was when Ellefson would jump to his feet and kick the bar stool off the stage.

Generally speaking, I am not a big fan of jam bands. I've seen bands that play on through extended bathroom breaks by the lead singer, or through costume changes or God only knows what else. Rarely, in my opinion, does it work. It's like that old joke popular among musicians, in which two guys are walking nervously through a jungle, listening to the rhythmic beat of drums in the distance. And suddenly the drums stop.

"Bad news," one of them says.

"Why?"

"Bass solo."

True enough. But in the case of "These Boots Are Made for Walkin'," a little jamming was appropriate. And entirely in keeping with the spirit of Megadeth.

About the only person who didn't like our version of "These Boots Are Made for Walkin'" was the song's writer, Lee Hazlewood, although, interestingly enough, he waited a very long time to voice his displeasure. I had altered some of the lyrics in an attempt to appeal to the kids who formed the core of our audience. For example, "something you call love, but confess" became, in the Megadeth version, "something you call love, but I call sex." I honestly thought the changes were so small as to be insignificant, but Lee felt otherwise and eventually asked us to take our "vile and offensive" version of the song off subsequent issues of the record.

It's worth noting here that Lee's protest came more than ten years after *Killing Is My Business* was released. A cynic might argue that Mr. Hazlewood's sensibilities were offended only after the royalty stream slowed to a trickle. I do know that he never failed to cash a check. Regardless, his protestations received some media attention, and we acquiesced. At least for a while. When we rereleased the record a few years back, "These Boots" was included, but with all of Lee Hazlewood's original lyrics rendered indecipherable. My words were audible; Lee's were beeped out.

Call it an odd compromise if you'd like. I prefer to think of it as a triumph of technology over hypocrisy.

8

FAMILIARITY BREEDS CONTEMPT

"Why the fuck is your bitch running off with the limo?"

IT WAS LIKE RIDING A ROCKET. THAT'S THE WAY I FELT IN THE EARLY DAYS OF MEGADETH. EVERYTHING HAPPENED SO QUICKLY, AND OUR RELATIONSHIPS WERE SO COMBUSTIBLE, THAT THE BEST STRATEGY WAS SIMPLY TO HANG ON AND HOPE FOR THE BEST. CHRIS POLAND ONCE SAID IT WAS LIKE BEING IN THE MOVIE FIGHT CLUB—EVERY NIGHT. THAT'S NOT A BAD ANALOGY, EITHER. UNFORTUNATELY FOR CHRIS, HE RARELY GOT TO PLAY THE ROLE OF TYLER DURDEN. THAT ONE USUALLY BELONGED TO ME.

EVERY BAND HAS ITS PROBLEMS, NOT LEAST OF WHICH IS MERELY KEEPING A LINEUP INTACT. I HAVE ADMIRATION FOR ANY BAND WHOSE CAREER STRETCHES OUT OVER

Megadeth backstage: Gar Samuelson, David Ellefson, me, and standing in the back, Mike Albert.
Photograph by William Hale.

decades, rather than years, without multiple personnel changes taking place along the way. Bands like the Rolling Stones, U2, a handful of others. Endurance of that type takes commitment, but it also takes luck, diplomacy, and common sense. About the only time it happens is when success comes early, roles are assigned and accepted, and the money piles up to such an extent that everyone realizes the folly of rocking the boat.

In most cases, though, the band undergoes seismic shifts long before anyone sees a nickel. Pretty soon you have to make a decision: do I commit to the band, or do I do something else with my life? You're sitting at home, hanging out with the old lady, and the guys are waiting for you at rehearsal. Do you leave . . . or do you stay? The old lady thinks "rehearsal" means "partying with the boys" (which it often does). The bandmates, conversely, think "hanging out with the old lady" means "I don't give a shit about the band." And so you lose either way. All bands eventually break up because of one or more of the four P's: power, property, prestige, pussy.

As Megadeth prepared for its first tour, we were an impressively wild and narcissistic collection of miscreants. We honestly believed that it was possible to drink and take drugs and fuck like Caligula every night and still be one of the most important bands in heavy metal. But there is always a price to pay. Just a few hours before we were scheduled to go out on the road—and not just for a few days, mind you, but for a legitimate tour—Chris got busted while trying to score heroin. I couldn't believe he had done something that stupid; I was livid. What were we supposed to do—cancel the whole tour? Our first tour in support of a legitimate record? The consequences would have been severe.

We had to find a new guitarist. Immediately.

"Don't worry about it, dooood," said Jay Jones. "I'll get Mike Albert."

"Who?" I'd never heard of the guy.

"Mike Albert," Jay repeated. "He played in Captain Beefheart.

Trust me, the dude shreds."

So I go meet this guy . . . and . . . Jesus. What a sight! He looked a little like Benjamin Franklin, with tufts of graying hair on the sides of his head and almost nothing on the top. A camouflage baseball cap did little to hide his age—he was probably fifteen to twenty years older than anyone else in the band. But Mike was an undeniably feisty little grandpa of a guitar player, with the cranky disposition you'd expect from someone who'd spent much of his life on the road. Mike stuttered and twitched nervously whenever he became uncomfortable, which happened a lot on that first tour.

He did the best he could, and obviously he deserves credit for stepping in on such short notice. Still, I never really warmed to Mike. For one thing, he wasn't nearly the guitar player that Chris was. Second, he had trouble keeping his mouth shut. Now, I understand this particular character flaw, as I've been accused of suffering from it myself. But you really should have the ability to back up your words with actions, a fact that seemed to have eluded Mike.

We were in Tucson one night when security guards for some reason allowed fans to enter the club while we were still doing our sound check, which proved to be disruptive and counterproductive. During the show I made some comment about how much better our performance would be if security hadn't interfered with our sound check. The audience loved that, of course—a shotgun blast of rage from the pulpit always goes over well with young metal fans; however, the club's management and security staff were not amused. Before we'd even left the stage, security guards had gone into our dressing room and removed all food and alcoholic beverages. When we finished playing and walked into the dressing room, we found only a few half-gallon containers of milk.

I had no intention of backing down. Our agreement called for specific services, including adult beverages, and I was going to hold them to the letter of the contract. I didn't get loud or angry, but neither did I cower. Diplomacy might have prevailed if not for Mike Albert's interference. He shot off his mouth, and the next thing I knew, Mike was surrounded by a tightening circle of security guards and bouncers, all of whom looked like they'd been sprinkling steroids on their Cheerios in the morning.

Oh shit . . . this is going to be ugly.

As I approached the group, I could see Mike digging through his wallet, fishing frantically for something.

"H-h-hold on," he stammered. "It's right here. I'll show you!"

The bouncers looked at him with bemusement, the way a cat might look at a mouse.

"If you take me down, I'm taking one of you with me!" Albert squealed. "I have a black belt, and I've got a card right here to prove it."

Shit came burping up out of his wallet: receipts, money, plastic. But no card. I presume there wasn't one. I mean, I hold three different black belts, but no one ever gave me a card to carry in my wallet or told me I was required to display anything before defending myself. This was an idle threat on Mike's part, a painfully embarrassing display of false bravado. I don't think any of the gorillas surrounding him were even slightly concerned that he might suddenly go all Bruce Lee on their asses. In fact, it probably had exactly the opposite effect: it just pissed them off even more.

I thought for a moment about letting them have their way with Mike—he kind of deserved it—but instead decided to calmly intervene. We ended up getting paid for that show and left with our dignity and health intact. But the entire tour, although it definitely had its high points, was less than it might have been with Chris in the lineup. Then again, considering our propensity for fighting, maybe his temporary absence was a blessing in disguise, since it delayed the inevitable fracturing of Megadeth by at least a few extra months.

Familiarity, after all, breeds contempt, especially when you're fucked-up on heroin or cocaine . . . or both.

WE RETURNED FROM the tour with no real concept of what Megadeth was onto. Things had changed—that much we knew. We'd show up at various places— clubs, parties, restaurants—and suddenly people were treating us differently. We were getting seated in places where you didn't neces- sarily get seated, places that didn't really even have seats, just the velvet rope or chain. It was, I must admit, a great feeling. Just imagine: you're at the Rainbow Lounge, where everyone is the flavor of the month, and you're hanging by the cigarette machine, at the bottom of the stairs, like every other schmuck. Wait a minute! No, no you're not. That's not you anymore. You're being whisked upstairs to a pri- vate party, with all the blow and babes you can handle. And when you get bored, you hop in a limo and find another party. And all the time you're thinking, *Wow! How did this happen?*

The second Megadeth record, *Peace Sells . . . but Who's Buying?** upped the ante by a considerable amount. The songs were better,

I loved *The Punisher* comics and wrote at least two songs that were inspired by the series: "Killing Is My Business and Business Is Good" and "Holy Wars: The Punishment Due." Photograph by William Hale.

* I got the title from an old *Reader's Digest* article.

the musicianship more accomplished, the production values more polished. When we started recording at the Music Grinder, in Los Angeles, we were still under contract with Combat Records, which had driven such a far-reaching, wartlike root into the existence of Megadeth that they owned a piece of the band for years to come. I wasn't happy about this, but I tried to focus on the music. That wasn't always easy. There were times where we would come into the studio and Poland (who had extricated himself from his legal problems) would be there in the lobby, shivering and unshaven, waiting for us to show up. When we saw him like this, we didn't even have to exchange words. We just got in the car, drove downtown, scored some heroin, and then went back to work.

You had to forgive a lot with Chris simply because he was so incredibly talented. You'd look past the shit that he pulled, forget about the fighting and the lying, just so you could get him to sit down and play guitar; he was one of the best.

Gar was a different story. He was a terrific drummer but not as indispensable as Chris, and his behavior, while not violent at all, was seriously disruptive. On those occasions when we'd have to go retrieve Gar's pawned cymbals in some shitty neighborhood just so we could commence with rehearsal, he'd invariably suggest a side trip.

"Hey, what do you say we stop by Ceres?"

Ceres was the name of the street where we typically scored dope, mainly heroin. This suggestion was usually followed by a moment of awkward silence, shrugs all around, and then laughter. The party was on.

So you see, I was not an unwilling accomplice to the debauchery. I went along for the ride, sometimes enjoyed it enormously. The truth is, I looked down on Chris and Gar even as we lay next to each other, passed out in the gutter. Why? Because I didn't see myself as an addict. Chris and Gar were hard-core drug users, shooting heroin into their veins. I hadn't yet reached—or fallen to—that level, though I was certainly on my way.

The days took on a comfortable if slightly bizarre routine: find Chris and Gar, get them well, deliver them to the studio, get their parts on tape, and get them the hell out of sight. That's how it was, or at least how it became. Ellefson and I lived together, hung out together, handled most of the mundane tasks of making Megadeth a viable creative force. As far as we were concerned, Gar and Chris were lesser partners. Not in terms of their musicianship, necessarily, but in terms of their behavior and attitude toward Megadeth. Both of them, particularly Chris, had joined the group with cynical intentions: they were jazz musicians to the core, hardly enamored of heavy metal, but saw Megadeth as an opportunity to escape the poverty and obscurity that most musicians endure. It was a decision born of practicality, not passion. I understood that from the beginning, and I accepted it, because they really did bring something unique to the process.

Junior and I pressed flesh with record company executives and publicists. Believe it or not, we were the professional face of the band. Think of it this way: if Megadeth were a military unit, Ellefson and I were the officers, and Gar and Chris were the enlisted men. It eventually became a rather sad dynamic, with lines between the two camps clearly drawn. Chris and Gar began to question the financial standing of the band. They openly suggested that we had more money than they did and wondered why income seemed not to be divided evenly. For some reason they could not grasp one of the fundamental tenets of the music business: if you write the songs, you get paid the money; if you don't write the songs, the only way you get paid is by making some kind of arrangement with somebody who does get paid the money—either by negotiation or manipulation. I know, because as the primary composer of Megadeth's music over the last twenty-five years, I have frequently been subjected to both.

I don't mean to suggest that it was all a slog or that there weren't good days. Because there were—lots of them. Even in the studio, half-baked, Megadeth was capable of extraordinary musicianship. The twin guitar attack on "The Conjuring," the guitar harmony line in "Peace Sells"—these were achieved not only through careful composition, but through the camaraderie that comes when a band is really clicking. "Peace Sells" became one of the most recognizable Megadeth songs, thanks in no small part to MTV, which, for nearly ten years, used the song's distinctive bass line as an intro to *MTV News*. Not that anyone got rich off that exposure. MTV cut the song about one note short of the point where it would have been legally obligated to pay a royalty fee.

As was the case on *Killing Is My Business*, we were given an opportunity to add a cover song on the second record. Jay Jones suggested "I Ain't Superstitious" by the legendary blues singer Willie Dixon. Not an obvious choice, by any stretch of the imagination, but an interesting one, to be sure. I liked the idea of pushing the envelope and surprising people. It had worked with "These Boots Are Made for Walkin'"; no reason it couldn't work with "I Ain't Superstitious," which was an undeniably great song.

"Picture it with really big drums," Jay said. "And at the end, you shift gears and give it that Megadeth treatment."

That's exactly what we did, and it worked beautifully. The song gave us a chance to show off Chris's guitar playing and once again challenge listeners by presenting a song that opened with a jazzy feel and closed at a breakneck, speed metal pace. Best of all, Willie Dixon gave it his stamp of approval; unlike Lee Hazlewood, he loved what we had done with his work.

IN MANY WAYS, *Peace Sells . . . but Who's Buying?* was a hit even before it was released. "Buzz" was a different thing twenty-five years ago than it is today. It relied less on technology than on old-fashioned word of mouth. Megadeth had a reputation for putting on blistering live performances, and as word of our latest studio effort began to spread, we became a hot commodity. So hot, in fact, that our contract was sold to Capitol Records, which brought in recording whiz Paul Lani to correct problems arising from Combat's sloppy engineering and minuscule recording budget. Practically speaking, this was a deal with the devil. From that moment on, Megadeth was no longer a feisty little indie band with a cult following. We were a major-label act, and with that designation came responsibility and expectations (and the implication of compromise) unlike anything we'd ever known. Not that we were concerned. We were too busy doing lines of coke at the Capitol Records Tower in Hollywood to worry about creative control. The perks outweighed almost everything.

Here's another example: the release party for *Peace Sells* was held at a place called the Firefly Bar, which was famous for,

among other things, a tradition of setting the bar afire. Really. The actual bar. Several times a night one of the bartenders would grab a bottle and squirt some sort of flammable liquid down the length of the bar top, give the patrons a quick warning, and then toss a match on the surface.

Whoosh!

Everyone would applaud reflexively and then go back to drinking. I suppose it got old if you'd seen it a few times, but I was new to the Firefly and was duly impressed.

The guests of honor were dressed in appropriately irreverent rock 'n' roll attire: formal from the waist up—black jacket, white shirt, black tie, cummerbund—and decidedly informal from the waist down—stretch denim blue jeans and high-top sneakers. The record company had also given us militant armbands with PEACE SELLS . . . BUT WHO'S BUYING? printed across them. We had arrived in full metal swagger, disgorging from a pair of stretch limos: one for the guys in the band, another for our bitches.* Somehow, even this night, which should have been nothing less than a celebration, turned ugly along the way. As we left the club at the end of the party I noticed that there was only one limo parked outside. We piled in, just the guys, and I inquired as to the location of the second limo.

"Lana took it," Chris said, referring to his girlfriend.

I could feel the anger building.

"Why the fuck is your bitch running off with the limo?" I said.

And that was all it took. Chris, never one to back down from a fight, even when he knew he was going to lose, told me to fuck

---

* Okay, hit me with the misogynist label. I am trying to use the language we would have used at the time. That was the parlance of the era, and it was particularly true in our case. They were bitches, girlfriends, companions for the evening. Sometimes they were all three things at once, since we broke up with our girlfriends at least once a week. It was what it was.

off. I responded by kicking him in the face. Gar jumped in, tried to break up the fight—and protect his buddy—by pinning my arms down, but I broke free and started whaling on him. By now the limo driver was screaming at us. These guys put up with a lot of shit, but I guess we'd managed to raise the bar. He jerked the car to the curb and put it in park.

"You want to fight? Then get the hell out of my car!" he shouted.

Hostilities instantly ceased. I think we all were more than a little embarrassed. We each apologized for our behavior and then went about the all-too-familiar task of patching things up. And how do you do that after trying to rip your friend's head off? Well, you do what any seasoned junkie would do: you go downtown and buy a bunch of heroin. I sat in the back of the limo, right next to Chris, looking at his swollen, bruised face, and got stoned out of my mind. And it just seemed like the most natural thing in the world.

PEACE SELLS . . . *but Who's Buying?* was released in November of 1986, nearly a year after we first went into the studio. The album was hailed as both a critical and commercial breakthrough, and it eventually went platinum. I think it holds up well even today; it feels raw, powerful. I'm proud of it. I still love the jacket art, which arose from a lunchtime conversation at a rib joint in New York, across the street from the United Nations. Ellefson and I were there with our agent, Andy Summers, and we just started brainstorming. By the end of that conversation, we had come up with the idea of Vic standing in front of the UN, shortly after a nuclear holocaust, trying to sell property—along with a message, of course. That became the quintessential *Peace Sells* image.

Touring in support of *Peace Sells*, however, was an exercise in self-abuse. I kept one eye on Metallica, whose third album, released just a few months before *Peace Sells*, had launched the band into superstar territory. I didn't obsess about it, but neither did I shrug it off. I can't say that I was oblivious to their success. This would be a theme throughout my career. It wasn't enough for Megadeth to do well; I wanted Metallica to fail.

While schadenfreude may be a perfectly reasonable, human response, it also tends to be loaded with the potential for karmic backlash. In September of 1986, as we were putting the finishing touches on *Peace Sells* and I was preparing to overtake Lars and James in the race for heavy metal supremacy, I got a phone call from a friend in New York whose nickname was Metal Maria, who worked for Jonny Z. I'd gotten to know her during my East Coast trip with Metallica. Over the years, we'd stayed in touch, and sometimes she'd come out to L.A. and we'd see each other. Now, though, she was on the phone, crying hysterically.

"It's Cliff," she sobbed. "He's dead."

I had no idea what she was talking about. At first I thought she meant Cliff Cultreri at Combat, but then I realized Maria didn't even know him.

"Cliff who?" I asked.

"Cliff Burton," she said. "There was an accident."

Maria told me all about it. Metallica had been on tour in Sweden, and the band's bus had tipped over after hitting a patch of ice. Cliff had been thrown through a window and crushed when the bus fell on top of him.

I had no response to any of this. I just stood there, clutching the phone, feeling like someone had punched me in the stomach. I hadn't talked to Cliff in a while but still considered him to be a friend. If I harbored some lingering anger toward Lars and James, well . . . it was impossible to work up the same degree of animus toward Cliff. He was just too decent a person.

For whatever reason—guilt, anger, sadness—I hung up the phone, got in my car, and went out and scored some heroin. I got loaded, sat around and cried for a while, then picked up my guitar and started writing. In one brief sitting I wrote an entire song: "In My Darkest Hour," which wound up on Megadeth's next album. It's an interesting song, for the lyrics were as much about the struggles within my relationship with Diana at the time as they were anything else. But the music—the sound and feel of the song—was inspired by the pain I felt upon hearing of the death of my friend. Cliff and I hadn't exactly been swapping Christmas cards or anything like that, but I still felt close to him. We had that time together in San Francisco, all those days commuting to rehearsal, and I'd never felt anything but affection for him. Cliff was transparent, and I mean that in a good way. He wasn't enigmatic; he was precisely as he appeared to be, with no pretense whatsoever.

A few months later, at a show in San Francisco, Cliff's parents showed up, and we got a chance to talk for a while. At one point I introduced them to the audience, which responded with genuine warmth and heartfelt applause. Then we performed "In My Darkest Hour."

"This one," I said, "is for Cliff."

YOU STRIKE WHILE the iron is hot, right? For a band that has just released a critically acclaimed and commercially successful record, that means one thing: hitting the road. I lived out of suitcases and hotel rooms for the better part of four years in the second half of the 1980s, and with *Peace Sells*, the grind began in earnest. Not that it was much of a burden. It was actually easier to be on the road than to be at home. I had no home; none of us did. Coming home meant finding someone to sponge off. Life on the road was simpler, if no less forgiving.

Gar had the routine down to perfection. As soon as we got into a new town, Gar would roll down a window and say to some passerby, "Hey, dude, you know where the red light district is?"

"Huh?" (This was always the initial response.)

"I'm looking for some girls," Gar would say. "Where do I go?"

It never took long to obtain the necessary information, and pretty soon Chris and Gar were on the wrong side of town, tracking down prostitutes and paying for services, but not having sex with them. The goal was not to get laid—that usually came after the show and did not require any sort of payment. Rather, the goal was to get well, and then to get fed. Always in that order. Gar did this with greater frequency than Chris, and with greater recklessness as well. We had to go into some pretty dangerous neighborhoods to pull him out. We'd be wandering around the projects, offering a detailed description of Gar that must have sounded hilarious: "He looks kind of like a locust, with a black leather vest and multicolor high-tops. You seen him?"

A substantial portion of every day was devoted to getting well and staying well.

Fighting became so commonplace that we barely gave it a thought. I don't mean harmless little bitch sessions—I mean serious, bloody, psychedelic fights, often with Chris sustaining the heaviest damage. Even Scott Menzies, who loves Chris to this day, ran out of patience on occasion. One such epic encounter began—as they always did, come to think of it—with the pursuit of drugs.

"Doood, what do you think? Two fifty? Two fifty?"

It was Jay Jones talking. We were driving along an interstate in the South, traveling from one show to another in our Winnebago, trying to stay awake, trying to kill time.

"What the fuck are you talking about, Jay?"

He smiled. "Two fifty a head. That's all it'll take."

His plan was for each of us to kick in pocket change so we could buy a twenty-dollar piece of heroin. Then Jay would melt it down, draw it up through an eyedropper, and squeeze a few drops of pure liquid smack into our noses as we drove down the highway.

It seemed like a good idea at the time. Ingenious, as a matter of fact. But we'd also been drinking and snorting cocaine, and the combination made for one hell of a magic bus. Chris, as was his tendency, began talking trash, acting up, and pretty soon Scott pulled out a knife and began stabbing furiously at the console, I guessed out of sheer frustration. The fact that he was also in the driver's seat only added to the craziness of this act, a point observed, and noted, by Poland, who began making fun of his buddy.

Scott was, for the most part, a big-hearted guy, but you provoked him at your own risk. The first time I met him he was walking across a stage, carrying a one-hundred-pound amp in each hand. With long curly hair and a barrel chest, he reminded me of Paul Bunyan. He was slow to boil, but once he was enraged . . . watch out.

Scott pulled the motor home to the side of the road and leaped on top of Poland. The two men wrestled briefly, but it wasn't long before Scott had control of the situation. He grabbed Chris by the ankles, turned him upside down, and walked him down the steps on his skull: *Bang! Bang! Bang!* Having executed one of the all-time great pile drivers, Scott concluded the match by depositing Chris in a ditch. We thought about leaving him there, just driving off and never speaking to him again. But then, we'd thought about that before. Instead, we all sat in the motor home, in various states of inebriation, and waited for the situation to defuse. After a few minutes the door of the motor home opened and Chris walked in, looking sheepish and sore.

"Sorry, man," he said to Scott.

"Yeah, okay."

And off we went.

On to McAllen, Texas, and one of our first opportunities to use pyrotechnics. McAllen is located just over the U.S. border, so naturally Chris viewed this as an opportunity to score some cheap and exotic drugs.

My response?

"You've got to be kidding."

Not that I was opposed to the score. I just thought the plan was suicidal. I envisioned Chris getting stopped at the border and ending up in a squalid Mexican prison for the next twenty years, picking roaches out of his food and squirting parasites out his ass. Chris apparently had no such concerns. He was, at that point anyway, the most reckless guy I had ever known. Sure enough, he returned a few hours later, safe and sound, armed with something known as Mandrax, which was basically a brand of methaqualone. In other words . . . Quaaludes. They came in a tin pack and appeared to be legitimate, but I was skeptical nonetheless. I've lived in Southern California all my life, and I know how they stuff the seats when they reupholster cars down by the border. The drug trade flourishes; not everything is what it's purported to be. If there were labels, the labels would say INGEST AT YOUR OWN RISK.

Chris ingested, of course. And, overcoming my initial skepticism, I did too.

On that night the drugs were comparatively safe and effective, offering a tranquilizing effect before we took the stage. The venue was kind of a shithole, and I was worried about how

Proudly displaying my Jackson King V, my first signature guitar. *Photograph by William Hale*

Top left: *Photograph by Rob Shay*. Top right: I love this Flying M guitar. Bottom left: Jimmy Page and I both received awards from *Kerrang!* *Photograph by Ross Halfin*. Bottom right: *Photograph by Rob Shay*

My daughter, Electra.

With my beautiful wife, Pam.

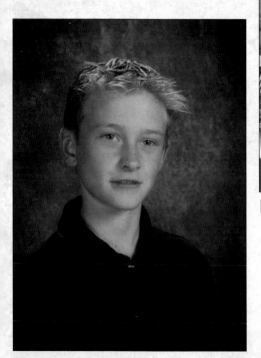

My son, Justis.

In 2004, on our first tour with pyro—*Blackmail the Universe* tour. Glen Drover is playing guitar on right and Shawn Drover is on drums. *Photograph by Rob Shay*

Partying after a show at The Whisky in L.A. with James, Lars, and Ron. *Photograph by William Hale*

Megadeth sound check with Kerry King in Berkeley, 1984. *Photograph by Brian Lew*

From the "Wake Up Dead" video shoot. *Photograph by Robert Matheu*

Me with my
B. C. Rich Bich
guitar. Playing
with Megadeth.
*Photographs by
William Hale*

This is what it looked like
before I painted it black.
Photograph by Brian Lew

The only school pictures I have. Ages ranging from three to twelve.

Photograph by Daniel Gonzalez Toriso

the performance would turn out. So when a guy who worked for the club asked if we wanted to try a little pyro, I was receptive. Anything for the fans, right?

"I've only got one," he said.

"One what? One row, one charge?"

"A single concussive charge. That's it. But it's enough, trust me."

I instructed him to hit the charge when I nodded, right before we launched into "Skull Beneath the Skin." By that point, however, we were all starting to feel the effects of the Mandrax, which was giving no quarter in its effort to render us completely wasted. Combined with what can generously be described as an unusual stage configuration, you had the potential for a disaster. Because the club was relatively small, plywood tables were used as a stage extension. No problem there, except that in an effort to be inventive, the promoter had staggered the tables; instead of being distributed evenly in front of the stage, they were assembled as something of a checkerboard, with several random gaping holes, four feet wide, eight feet long, separating the band from the audience. I admit that it looked kind of cool, but it was a spectacularly bad idea.

Just as we were about to play "Skull Beneath the Skin," I gave the signal, and the charge went off.

BOOM!

The next sound you were supposed to hear at that moment was the sound of Gar hitting his drum kit. Instead, what you heard was something like the sound of two pencils hitting the floor. I looked up at Gar; he was empty-handed.

Oh, shit! I forgot to tell him about the charge.

The explosion had so spooked Gar that he'd dropped his drumsticks. And that wasn't the worst of it. Most drummers will keep at least one extra pair of sticks near their kit while they're onstage. Sometimes two or three. But Gar had gotten so careless with his gear that he was down to his very last set of sticks. The next thing I saw was Gar scrambling down from his kit and running around to the front of the stage to retrieve his sticks.

It was that kind of night.

A few songs later I looked to my right, where Chris Poland had been standing, and saw nothing. But his guitar continued to play. All of a sudden Chris popped up in one of the holes at the front of the stage, blood streaming down his arm. Without missing a beat, he clambered back into position and continued playing, like a heavy metal version of Whack-a-Mole.

As Chris smiled, I could only shake my head in disbelief. I knew it couldn't go on like this forever. Eventually someone would overdose or die in a car wreck, or maybe even kill one of his bandmates. The potential for catastrophe was almost incalculable. The only question was, which one of us would be the first casualty?

THE END OF WESTERN CIVILIZATION

9

"You can't keep up this pace. You're going to burn out or die."

IT WAS SUPPOSED TO BE AN INTERVENTION, BUT IT FELT MORE LIKE I'D BEEN SUMMONED TO THE PRINCIPAL'S OFFICE. THIS WAS EARLY 1987, AND IN ONE OF THOSE INTERGENERATIONAL PAIRINGS THAT CAN SOMETIMES GO TERRIBLY AWRY, MEGADETH WAS SUPPORTING ALICE COOPER ON HIS CONSTRICTOR TOUR. IN THIS CASE, THOUGH, IT WAS A SHREWD MARKETING MOVE ALL THE WAY AROUND. ALICE, WHO HAD BEEN ONE OF THE MORE POPULAR ROCKERS OF THE 1970S, WAS IN THE PROCESS OF REBUILDING HIS CAREER AFTER A HANDFUL OF ARTISTIC MISCALCULATIONS AND PERSONAL TRAVAILS. ALTHOUGH PAST HIS COMMERCIAL PEAK, ALICE STILL HAD A LARGE AND FERVENT FOLLOWING AND A LOT OF RESPECT WITHIN THE INDUSTRY.

The classic *Peace Sells ... but Who's Buying* lineup: David Ellefson, me, Gar Samuelson, and Chris Poland backstage before a show (or a fistfight).
Photograph by Harald O.

Personally, I'd been a big fan of his ever since I was a kid, when *Welcome to My Nightmare* was in heavy rotation around my house, so I was excited about touring with him and his band. It was an opportunity for us to reach a bigger audience; for Alice, it was a chance to tap into a new and younger demographic. Megadeth's core audience, after all, was not unlike Alice Cooper's had been fifteen years earlier: adolescents with a taste for loud, fast, dangerous music.

Alice had been through his own challenges where drugs and alcohol were concerned but had rather famously cleaned up his act. There was no shortage of party animals in his entourage, including a snake wrangler whose job was to care for the boa constrictor that joined Alice onstage. This guy had a box of syringes that he would use to sedate the snake so that it could be handled safely, but he would sometimes skim a few off the top to use on himself. Alice, however, was sober and healthy, with a generally laid-back attitude about the whole scene, so long as it didn't get in the way of the music. In other words, he was a total pro.

After we'd been out on the road for a while, however, Alice became concerned about the antics of Megadeth. Whether he believed my behavior was worse than anyone else's, I don't know. I think he probably just liked me and saw me as the band leader, and therefore held me accountable for the craziness that surrounded Megadeth. Anyway, one night he asked me to stop by his tour bus for a little chat. He wasn't confrontational or condescending. He didn't treat me like a child, but rather like a friend.

"I've seen it all, I've done it all," Alice said. "And it just doesn't work. You can't keep up this pace. You're going to burn out or die."

I listened, nodded in all the right places, thanked him for his concern and support, and basically ignored everything he had said. I had too much respect for Alice to argue with him, but I was far too deep in denial—and having too much fun—to consider the merits of his advice. It's pretty simple, really: when you're an addict, you don't listen to people. It doesn't matter what anyone else says or does. Very rarely will you find someone with a drug or alcohol problem who is easily influenced.

Very rarely does the conversation go like this:

"Hey, man, you should stop drinking. Clean up your act."

"Really? You mean I shouldn't get high and plow through this line of Swedish bikini models? Okay, you're right. I'll stop. Thanks for looking out for me, bro."

It isn't enough for someone else to want you to change. It isn't even enough for you to want to change. You have to want to want that change.

A subtle but important distinction. At the time, I wasn't even close.

I ENJOYED THE party, but I also liked the sex, and the power that came with it. For me, standing up onstage, with a sea of guys chanting my name and their girlfriends eager to take off their clothes for me, was the ultimate vindication. After all those years of being the invisible, skinny redhead in school, I had become the coolest guy in the room. And I loved it.

I bought into every aspect of the rock 'n' roll life, drugs and alcohol being merely the most dangerous and debilitating. When Ellefson and I were living together, sometimes I'd wake up in the morning and the first thing I would see, through blurry, bloodshot eyes, was Junior sitting on the side of my bed.

"Hey, Junior."

"Hey, Dave. Want some blow?"

"Uhhh . . . sure."

And that was it. Gone, baby, gone. Two, three days at a time.

Ellefson was my buddy and running mate, but he was also shrewd. He knew if he got me loaded first thing in the morning (and let's be honest—he didn't exactly have to twist my arm), I'd pay for everything the rest of the day. I didn't really mind, since Junior was my partner in crime. Getting fucked-up and chasing chicks was a lot more fun when you were doing it together.

As for Gar and Chris, I guess I should clarify something: it was not their drug use that got them fired from Megadeth; the consequences of their drug use got them fired. For much of the band's early years, drug use was rampant in Megadeth. Each of us paid a price for the choices we made. How steep a price depended largely on how well—or how poorly—we were able to balance self-destructive behavior with the legitimate and sometimes exhausting work of being in a platinum-selling heavy metal band. I won't minimize my own contributions to the downward spiral, but the truth is this: Gar was the least equipped to deal with his own drug abuse, followed closely by Chris. Junior and I were a distant third and fourth (okay, maybe not so distant). We were also the founding members of the band, the dominant creative force, and thus burdened with a degree of responsibility not shared by Chris and Gar. I felt this more acutely than David, I'm sure, because I also wrote the vast majority of the band's material, and the pressure contributed to episodes that others have referred to as manic, but that I simply recall as drug-and-alcohol-fueled insanity.

Gar lost his spot in Megadeth slowly, and then all at once. We had picked up a new drum tech during a stopover in Detroit, before playing at a punk rock club called Blondie. While there, I was approached by a kid wearing a dirty yellow T-shirt and ridiculously tight jeans. His eyes were bloodshot, his hair long and matted.

"Hey, man, you need help setting up your drums?" he asked.

I had no idea who he was, but the truth was, yeah, we usually did need help setting up drums.

"Check with Gar," I said.

So the guy shambled off and struck up a conversation with Gar, and next thing you know he was a drum tech for Megadeth. Well, actually he didn't refer to himself as a "drum tech," but rather just as a roadie. Didn't matter—the job description was more important than the title, and it turned out that this guy, whose name was Chuck Behler, knew his way around a drum kit. He was twenty-one years old and already a veteran of a couple different punk bands. And although he had grown up in the Midwest, he had no qualms about jumping on the bus with Megadeth that very night. So if you want a job in rock 'n' roll, kids, here's a word of advice: be ready to answer when opportunity knocks.

The cool thing about Chuck was that not only could he set up Gar's drums, he could also jump right in and play. This meant that on the many nights when Gar was indisposed at or around the time of our sound check, we didn't have to wait for him to show up. As a result, we actually began to sound better when we performed. Instead of just getting to the venue and setting up on the fly because the drummer was off in the red-light district (and the guitar player was doing the breaststroke through my vomit), we were able to properly prepare for each performance—at least from a technical standpoint.

And that's how Chuck Behler became the drummer for Megadeth. Gar continued to fuck up, and Chuck was simply there, waiting in the wings. As much as his talent, it was his presence—his reliability—that earned him the job.

Gar and Chris were dismissed from the band in the same week, in the summer of 1987, right after we concluded a tour with a trip to Hawaii. I'd gone out on that last leg thinking the situation might be salvageable, but it wasn't. We got back to L.A.

and more gear went missing. And then Chris began agitating to a degree that I simply couldn't handle any longer. For a while, both he and Gar had been harmless, pawning bits of equipment to pay for their addictions. Now it had become a ceaseless, soul-sucking battle. Toward the end, it was just insane. Nothing was right, everything was wrong. Gar's addiction had stolen his ability to commit to the band, and Chris . . . well, I don't think Chris wanted to be a part of Megadeth any longer. I'm not sure he ever wanted to be in Megadeth, or any other heavy metal band. He was a jazz virtuoso who saw an opportunity to be part of something big, and I think he remained conflicted the entire time.

Regardless, Gar and Chris were now gone. They had come in as a virtual package deal, and that is the way they went out.

Filling Gar's spot was pretty seamless, since Chuck was only too eager to move from Detroit to L.A. and become a full-fledged member of the West Coast metal scene. He knew our songs, knew the personalities, and brought something different to the band: a straightforward dynamic that contrasted sharply with Gar's free-flowing style. Gar would use his kick and snare, then throw in a couple snare drum rolls for each measure. Chuck would just stay on the kick and snare, with a lot of high hat; it was more of a punk rock type of approach. Neither style was necessarily "better," but there's no question that having Chuck in the band was invigorating. It was almost a breath of fresh air to get back to straightforward, block-headed heavy metal.

I thought it would be a relief to be rid of Gar and Chris, but that proved to be a bit of a miscalculation, since I was already pretty far down the road to addiction myself. Junior and I were of the opinion that we were the best, and that no matter how sick we were, no matter how fucked-up or exhausted, we were going to get up and play. Not just go through the motions, either. We were going to outplay everybody, even if it killed us.

Chuck fit right in. He knew how to hang, he knew how to play. What more could you ask? But we still needed a new guitar player to replace Chris Poland. The first option was a guy named Jay Reynolds, who had played in a B-list metal band called Malice. For whatever reason, Malice had never quite hit the big time, but they were a legitimate band with serious, committed players. The first time I saw Jay, I thought he was fantastic, the perfect choice to play guitar for Megadeth. The guy looked great: tall and lean, with long, blond hair, boots up to his knees, playing a Flying V. Junior and I saw him at a club in Reseda, California, and my first thought was, *He's totally metal; he's the right guy.*

I knew Jay was a work in progress, that he might not have the chops to step right in and take over for Poland. But I figured we could work with him. I had taught people how to play before, and I was willing to do it again.

Unfortunately, with Jay, the package was basically empty. Jay was a well-connected drug user, which proved to be at once beneficial and detrimental to Megadeth: beneficial in the sense that Junior and I now had ridiculously easy access to a seemingly endless supply of drugs; detrimental in the sense that, well . . . Junior and I now had ridiculously easy access to a seemingly endless supply of drugs. We'd go over to Jay's apartment at least once a day. Chuck Behler ended up moving into the same building just to cut down on the commute.

"This is the smartest thing we've ever done, hiring Jay," I once said, only half-jokingly.

"Yeah . . . one-stop shopping."

I laughed. "Cut out the middleman."

We had no problems with Jay. He had a great look, great personality, always had money. Forget about the drug problem—if Jay had been a great guitar player, he might still be with Megadeth today, because that's how well we got along.

But he wasn't a great guitar player.

Jay joined Megadeth at the Music Grinder as we began writing and rehearsing, and eventually recording, our third record, *So Far, So Good . . . So What!* After two records a style had been established: I played the main rhythm tracks and the other guitarist played a single rhythm track right down the center. So I would do a rhythm track on the right, a track on the left, and the other guitar player would add a rhythm track right down the middle. We did this because it gave every song a unique sound, one that came to be Megadeth's signature, but also because I'm a better rhythm player than most of the guys who have played with the band. So we were in the studio, and it was time for Jay to start playing.

"Okay, let's hear your part," I said.

Nothing. Jay sat there on a stool, looking off into space.

"Jay?"

"Yeah . . . ummm . . . I'm gonna get my guitar teacher to come down here, if it's okay with you guys."

Guitar teacher?

"What are you talking about, man?"

"No, it's cool," Jay went on. "He'll do the solos for now, and then I'll have him teach me."

Jay smiled as innocently as a child. It was like he'd been trying to hide for weeks the fact that he was in over his head, and now he'd come up with a solution. Except it wasn't a solution at all.

I turned to Junior, whose jaw, like mine, was almost on the floor.

"We're fucked," I said.

He didn't disagree.

If we bothered to rehearse once in a while, we might have seen this coming, but with studio time already booked and paid for, and with a deadline fast approaching, we had no choice but to open our arms to Jay's guitar teacher. His name was Jeff Young, and he presented an entirely different set of challenges than did Jay Reynolds. In fact, if you had taken Jay and Jeff and cobbled together their best attributes—Jeff's playing and Jay's style—you would have had one hell of a speed metal guitarist.

Jeff, poor lad, looked like Bobby Sherman, with smooth, boyish features and perfectly layered hair that looked as though it had been subjected to a blow dryer for a half hour every morning. When he walked into the studio, he was wearing Sperry Top-Siders and Ocean Pacific board shorts that fit almost like hot pants. Remember, this is the pre-Jordan era, before kids started wearing hoop shorts down to their calves and everyone else followed suit. In some corners of the world (not mine, of course), Jeff would have been considered stylish. To me, he wasn't.

But he was willing to play Jay's stuff, and you had to admire him for that.

"Let's see what you've got," I said.

Jeff started playing, and I'll be damned if the guy wasn't good. Really good. Like . . . totally different than anything I'd heard or seen. There were a lot of talented guitar players around L.A. at the time, most of them cut from the same cloth: gunslingers all. Jeff was different, and the fact that his appearance belied such a muscular style of play really caught me off guard. After Jeff played for a little while, Junior and I excused ourselves to talk in private. Now, granted, we were both out of our minds at the time. I'm sure I was fucked-up when I saw Jeff play, so there is some question as to the validity of my assessment.

Nevertheless . . .

"He's good," Junior said. "But you know . . ."

"Yeah, we'll have to put him through Rock School 101."

Junior laughed, primarily because he was a graduate himself. He knew the curriculum, he knew the rules.

These are the clothes you will wear. These are the shoes. This is the kind of jewelry you wear in the metal community. Here's what you do with your hair (down, not up).

We took Jeff outside and chatted with him for a while, tried to get a better read on his personality, but it was just so hard, and we had so little time. I was still in a state of shock over Jay. Jeff nodded politely, answered every question with just the right amount of enthusiasm, but I was having a hard time getting to the important part. The part where I extended an offer. I couldn't get past the OP board shorts and the Top-Siders. I couldn't see his eyes through the Vuarnet sunglasses. He was such a fucking pretty boy, and I kept thinking to myself, *Am I going to regret this?*

I took a deep breath.

"Jeff, we'd like you to be in the band."

He nodded, tried to play it cool. To this day, I'm not sure whether Jeff had any idea this was coming; it's quite possible he had no aspirations beyond helping Jay learn to fit in with Megadeth. Certainly he seemed surprised.

"But there's one thing . . . ," I added.

"What's that?"

"You're going to have to change everything."

Jeff let out a little chuckle. "What do you mean *everything*?"

"I mean your hair, the way you dress, the way you walk and talk. Everything."

Jeff ran a hand through his teen-idol hair, looked down at his Sperry Top-Siders and his OP board shorts. I'm sure he thought he looked great, and in many parts of the universe, especially Southern California in the late 1980s, he probably did. But not in heavy metal. And certainly not in Megadeth. Jeff shrugged, smiled awkwardly.

"Okay, man. Whatever you need."

In retrospect, the substitution of Jeff for Jay was a personnel issue that could have been handled better. I basically called Jay up

and told him he was out—before he'd even been in. It was cold and bloody, and I regret the way I did it.* But these types of decisions just naturally fell on my shoulders; no one else wanted the responsibility. It's somewhat ironic, I know (the old pot calling the kettle black), because I wasn't exactly clear-headed and 100 percent reliable myself. But, again, it was my band. For better or worse, I had to take the reins.

HAVING REMIXED *PEACE Sells*, Paul Lani was brought in by Capitol Records to handle mixing duties on *So Far, So Good . . . So What!* Paul had some impressive credentials. It's just that, in my opinion, they were the wrong credentials. He was most famous for his work with Rod Stewart, and I didn't know that before we hired him, or I would have vetoed the

* I've since made amends to Jay and we remain friends to this day.

label's decision. Rod Stewart, especially by the late 1980s, was a decidedly pop figure; Megadeth was a thrash metal band. It's true that there are times when musical forms can be merged. Certainly there is no shortage of examples of engineers and producers from one genre cross-pollinating with another. Generally speaking, though, it's an awkward partnership. Pop and metal aren't friends. Each knows exactly where the other lives and tries to keep its distance. They choose different streets, neighborhoods, zip codes.

For those reasons and more, I was skeptical. But I was excited about the record and the songs we had assembled. Chuck had brought a new dimension to the band, and now Jeff was beginning to fit in as well. *Maybe,* I thought, *this will all work out just fine.*

By this point it had become a bit of a tradition for Megadeth to include one cover song on each album. After "These Boots Are Made for Walkin'" and "I Ain't Superstitious" we had a well-deserved reputation for making interesting choices in this regard and for putting a distinctive metal twist on songs revered within other genres. Yes, this flies in the face of my metal-vs.-pop philosophy, but a great song is a great song. I decided relatively early in the writing and recording process that I wanted to include a Sex Pistols cover on *So Far, So Good . . . So What!* I was a punk fan from way back and had long been head-over-heels in love with the Pistols. I suggested "Problems"—one of my favorite punk songs—as the perfect cover song, but Jay Jones disagreed.

"If you're going to do a Pistols song, it has to be 'Anarchy in the UK,'" he said. Jay's choice was at once philosophical and pragmatic. If there was one Sex Pistols song that everyone knew, it was "Anarchy in the UK." There would be instant identification on the part of listeners, and it could be easily marketed.

"And it makes sense because you guys are a political band," he added.

That one I didn't buy. We were writing very dark songs

containing apocalyptic images of war and death, but that did not necessarily make Megadeth a political band. Not at the time, anyway. Yes, we had touched on political themes—"Peace Sells" being the most obvious example—but we were not overtly political.

Nevertheless, after some consideration, I agreed with Jay and we decided to record "Anarchy in the UK." The coolest thing about the entire experience was getting Steve Jones from the Pistols to play guitar on the track. We didn't know how he would respond to the invitation, but he was quick to accept. He was living in Southern California at the time, and he just rode in one day on his Triumph motorcycle and strolled into the studio with a smile on his face and . . . a cast on his arm!

"What the fuck happened to you?" I asked him.

He laughed.

"Ah, I was riding my bike in Brentwood and some woman turned in front of me. I went flying right over the handlebars."

Proud man and resilient punk that he was, Jonesy wasn't about to let a little thing like a broken arm prevent him from playing. We sat around for a little bit and talked about music. I was totally enamored, of course, because I'd been such a fan of the Pistols, and it was a real treat to have him in the studio with us.

By the end of the day Steve was in the studio, playing guitar on "Anarchy in the UK," while I spit out the vocals like Johnny Rotten.

Between the time we recorded *So Far, So Good . . . So What!* and the time the record was released, a number of things transpired, some good, some not so good. Among the former was an appearance in *The Decline of Western Civilization Part II: The Metal Years*, director Penelope Spheeris's documentary about the late-1980s heavy metal scene in Los Angeles. "In My Darkest Hour" was included in the soundtrack, and I was featured on the promotional poster for the film. Remarkably enough, given our fondness for drugs and depravity, the guys in Megadeth came off as perhaps the smartest and most thoughtful artists in the film. I don't know whether that says more about us or the general state of heavy metal in the late 1980s. A little of both, I suppose. In my opinion, Penelope, who also directed the Megadeth video for "Wake Up Dead," off *Peace Sells*, is a genius; she perfectly captured the feeling of that era, in all its glorious, self-destructive decadence. *The Decline of Western Civilization Part II* was critically acclaimed and generally credited with helping to kill the glam rock* movement in Southern California. For that alone, Penelope deserves a big pat on the back.

For all our success and apparent upward trajectory, Megadeth still had its share of problems. Both Jeff Young and Chuck Behler had quickly immersed themselves in the band's culture, and I was for the most part in denial about the extent to which we were all spinning out of control. This manifested itself in ways tragic and comic, and sometimes tragicomic.

At one point in the mid 1980s, I was set up on a date with Belinda Carlisle, the former lead singer of an almost freakishly popular girl band called the Go-Gos and at that time a solo artist. In this case, I was more than happy to suspend my feelings about pop and metal making strange bedfellows. Belinda was gorgeous, and she was, at the time, ubiquitous (as well as single). I have no idea if she was a fan of Megadeth or of heavy metal in general. I know only that through an intermediary I was to meet her and we were to embark on an honest-to-goodness "date." Belinda came to the Music Grinder one day while we were starting to mix *So Far, So Good . . . So What!* Unfortunately, her timing could have been better. Moments before she arrived, I had finished snorting a balloon of heroin. As she knocked at the door I chucked the empty

* I've always maintained that "GLAM" is actually an acronym for "gay L.A. music."

balloon behind a dresser and lit up a joint—better the sweet smell of weed than the acrid odor of smack. Belinda walked in, looking positively radiant—and sober, I should add—and smiled.

"Hello," she said.

I tried to choke back a lungful of smoke, but to no avail.

"Whoo-huh!" I barked, a cloud of gray filling the air.

Belinda turned on her heel and walked right back out of the room. And that was the end of that particular love story. It was, I guess, doomed from the very beginning.

WITH SO FAR, *So Good* nearly in the can and only final mixing necessary to complete the job, Paul Lani decided that he would find greater inspiration in upstate New York than was available in Southern California.

"Let's go to Bearsville," he said.

"Where?

"Bearsville. It's near Woodstock."

Woodstock . . .

The way he said it, you'd have thought he was talking about Shangri-La. I got it, of course. Inspiration is important when you're making music or creating any type of art, and if Paul thought proximity to Woodstock or the pastoral beauty of upstate New York would result in a better record, then I was all for it.

Up to a point.

Bearsville Studios had been founded in 1969 (that's right, the year of the Woodstock music festival—hardly a coincidence) by Albert Grossman, a talent manager whose roster included Bob Dylan, Janis Joplin, and the Band. All of these artists, and many others, had called the studio home at one time or another, so the place certainly had a strong reputation. Grossman, however, had died a couple years earlier, and Bearsville Studios would soon fall into decline. Whether that process had already begun by the time we got there to mix *So Far, So Good* I can't say for sure. I do know that only a few days passed before I had seen about enough of Woodstock. My exasperation had little to do with the bucolic surroundings and everything to do with the eccentricities of Paul Lani.

I will admit that I did not bring the greatest attitude to this venture. Hell, I was a junkie, and going out on the road is a challenge for any junkie. This was a two-man job—just me and Paul—and I had only a small stash of heroin to take on the trip, so I knew I was going to run out quickly. Flying across the country and holing up in some remote locale meant facing the reality that eventually my supply would dwindle to nothing and I would get very sick. And as soon as I got sick, everything would fall apart. I'd lose my ability to focus, to concentrate, to work.

Mainly, though, I would lose my patience with Paul. Everything about the guy just rubbed me the wrong way, from his insistence on offering lessons in etiquette at mealtime ("Dave, this is the proper way to hold a spoon") to his maddeningly persnickety approach to the mixing process. Within a few days annoyance had turned to disdain, to the point that I couldn't look at the fucking guy without feeling a little bit nauseous.

As luck would have it, there was another band recording at Bearsville Studios at the same time, and it happened to be a band with a similar sensibility: Raven, another of the bands influenced by the New Wave of British Heavy Metal. We started hanging out a little bit, and when they left, for some reason that I can't quite explain, everything became crystal-clear to me: Paul Lani was the wrong guy.

Every other time that we had made changes during the production or mixing stage of the process, the decision had come from the record label. This time, however, it was up to me. I'd have to fight for what I wanted, and it wasn't going to be pleasant. But it had to be done. The very next morning—as if on fucking cue—I woke up and made myself a pot of coffee. As I stood in the kitchen, rubbing the sleep from my eyes, I looked out the window, and what I saw defies belief. There was Paul Lani, esteemed major-label record producer, traipsing through the woods in his underwear. The sight of this little Pillsbury Doughboy of a man, half-naked, hand-feeding an apple (cored and peeled, incidentally) to a deer, was more than I could take.

I need to leave. I need to leave right now. Today.

Within a few hours I was on a flight to L.A. By the end of the week we had fired Paul Lani and brought in German engineer Michael Wagener to do the mix. Michael had worked with a slew of rock and metal bands, including Metallica, but he turned in a pedestrian effort on *So Far, So Good*, burying everything under reverb and generally giving the record a muddy feel.

Although eventually it would reach platinum status, critical response to the album was mixed. I took some hits for screwing up the lyrics to "Anarchy in the UK," and in general the music press wasn't quite as complimentary as it had been following the release of our first two records. No surprise there—we weren't rookies, after all, and there is a tendency for any new band to be treated more gently than an established group. For Megadeth, the stakes were higher. As were the expectations.

It was after *So Far, So Good* that I began to develop thicker skin. I'd been king of the sound bite up to that point, and while I tried not to let a few bad reviews color my view of an entire industry or affect my attitude with regard to marketing and publicity, they certainly had an impact. I began to tune out the reviews and focus more intently on the fans of Megadeth and how they responded to our music. For me, reviews have always been a bit of a bipolar experience: "Great guitar player, but his singing sounds like two cats fucking." Even if it's true, it gets old after a while.

And anyway, I've never understood critical analysis that strives for meanness above all else.

I'm not a guy who likes to keep score when it comes to the media (talk about an unwinnable game). It is, after all, an artist's role to be judged. Ultimately, his work will rise or fall on its own merit; it speaks for itself.

10

THE TRAVELING CARNIVAL

> "This one is for the cause! Give Ireland back to the Irish!"

I LOVE THE UNITED KINGDOM. IT IS, AFTER ALL, THE BIRTHPLACE OF HEAVY METAL. FIRST TIME MEGADETH TOURED THERE WAS BACK IN 1987, FOLLOWING THE RELEASE OF PEACE SELLS. I WAS STILL FAIRLY NAÏVE AND FULL OF AMBITION, AND READY TO CONQUER THE WORLD. BUT THERE WERE A FEW THINGS I HAD YET TO LEARN. LIKE HOW TO DRINK STRONGBOW SUPER CIDER.

AFTER THROWING BACK ABOUT A DOZEN CANS OF THIS STUFF ONE NIGHT AT THE HOTEL BAR, I STAGGERED UP TO MY ROOM TO GO TO BED. ELLEFSON AND I WERE ROOMMATES ON THAT TOUR, BUT HE'D GONE OUT FOR THE EVENING TO CATCH A DEEP PURPLE SHOW. I KNEW I WAS IN TROUBLE BY THE TIME MY HEAD HIT THE PILLOW. STRONGBOW SUPER LOOKED LIKE

Opening for Dio in 1988. Listening to the crowd cheer at the Long Beach Arena—a childhood favorite of mine. Photograph by Robert Matheu.

Letting it rip during a solo from the night in Long Beach in 1988.
Photograph by Robert Matheu.

beer, tasted like sweet vinegar, and had about twice as much alcohol as beer typically sold in the States. At some point between passing out and waking up in the middle of the night, I'd become completely inebriated. Adding to my disorientation was the fact that I couldn't see a fucking thing. Hotels in England are often ancient castlelike structures, with thick, soundproof walls and heavy, floor-to-ceiling drapes that inhibit all light. So when you wake up at three A.M. with your bladder screaming for relief, you'd better be able to find your way to the bathroom in the dark.

The journey can be challenging when you're drunk off your ass.

I sat up in bed and tried unsuccessfully to find a lamp or a wall switch. Why? Because they didn't have wall switches in this hotel (or in most of England, as I discovered); instead, the lights were operated by tiny buttons that barely protruded beyond the surface of the wall. In the dark, you could spend all night running your hands along the plaster and not get lucky enough to find one. I lurched around the room, unable to see anything at all, not even my hands in front of my face. Finally, I found what seemed at the time to be a lid of some sort. Presuming it was a toilet seat (but not really caring one way or the other) I lifted it up, then dropped my shorts and began to piss.

Ahhh . . . success.

Then I stumbled back to bed and passed out. It wasn't until the next morning that I realized what had actually happened. I woke to the sight of Junior standing over my bed with a look of disgust on his face.

"Hey, man. Did you pee in my suitcase?"

A YEAR AND a half later, in August of 1988, we returned to the UK as part of the Monsters of Rock tour, which also included KISS, Iron Maiden, Guns N' Roses, and David Lee Roth. It began spectacularly, with a show in front of 114,000 fans at Castle Donington. Strongbow cider was the least of my worries by this time. Moments before going out onstage I was sitting in my dressing room, trying to make a hash pipe out of a tin can using a funky little cheese knife I'd picked up at the complimentary preshow meal. The next thing I knew, there was blood running down the back of my hand.

"Fuck me . . ."

I grabbed a towel, fashioned a tourniquet, and applied pressure for a few minutes. I'd been lucky. Could have been a lot worse. As it was, a few bandages staunched the bleeding and I was able to go out and play. The show must go on, right?

The thing is, I was pretty strung out already by the time we got to Castle Donington. I knew enough about drug use to anticipate the worst: the road, after all, was a brutal place for the cocaine and heroin addict, and there was no way around the unpleasantness. No one (well, almost no one) was crazy enough to pack a pile of smack in his baggage, so basically you just accepted the fact that when you left the country to tour, you were going to have to endure withdrawal for a few days. To ease the pain, you'd self-medicate in whatever fashion suited your needs. You drank, you smoked pot . . . you ingested hash through a tin can. Whatever worked. In time, after three or four days, maybe a week, you'd start to feel better. You could always tell the junkies on tour: they were the ones shuffling around, sniffling, hacking, looking like they were suffering from the flu. And then, miraculously, they'd all get better at once.

Or not.

If you were desperate, you could always turn to more dangerous tactics. Find out where the rough neighborhoods were, the red-light districts, and proceed accordingly. If you lacked the balls for such an adventure, you could try a more sane and subtle approach: seek out the assistance of a pliable member of the medical profession.

It was a fairly common technique employed by guys who just couldn't handle being sick on the road. And there were more than a few of them on the Monsters of Rock tour. Shit, between Megadeth and Guns N' Roses alone, you had enough drug addicts and alcoholics to open a rehab facility.

There was so much tension and excitement in the air as the tour opened, and on that very first day, at Castle Donington, the excitement turned to tragedy, as two fans were crushed to death when the crowd surged toward the stage during Guns N' Roses' performance. There is no way to put a positive or cynical spin on something like that. It was sad and horrible, and even though Megadeth was not directly involved, it took a toll on all of us. Then, just a few short hours after the concert, David Ellefson came out of the closet, so to speak, saying that he would be leaving the Monsters of Rock tour to seek treatment for a heroin addiction. Now, it would not have come as much of a shock to anyone who followed heavy metal to learn that a member of Megadeth was entering rehab. But just about everyone would have assumed that band member was me, not David Ellefson.

A number of factors contributed to the timing of this decision, including input from David's then-girlfriend, Charley, as well as a feeling of overwhelming anxiety stemming from the pressure of playing in front of more than a hundred thousand people. More than anything else, though, I think David's epiphany was sparked by a desire to end the pain of withdrawal. Simply put, he had run out of heroin and needed to get well.

As a result, Megadeth was compelled to pull out of the Monsters of Rock tour, a decision that had far-reaching implications. We had to cancel performances at seven soccer stadiums, which affected somewhere in the neighborhood of a half-million fans. We're talking about some very serious money. Everything about the scenario pissed me off—from David's issues to the public relations fiasco that ensued. Everyone on the tour knew what was happening, but for some reason our agent and manager chose to concoct some ridiculous Spinal Tap version of the truth, in which Megadeth reluctantly was forced to withdraw from the tour after the band's bass player . . . *slipped in a hotel bathtub and sprained his fucking wrist!*

"Are you kidding me?" I said. "That's the best you can do? No one will believe it. Absolutely no one."

They didn't, of course, and the fallout was instantaneous, not just in terms of revenue from our share of the gate but also record sales, exposure, and reputation. This was one of the biggest tours in the history of metal, and Megadeth had pulled its own plug. Within no time at all, the real story had trickled out and fingers were being pointed in my direction. People had long speculated about my drug use, but I hadn't spoken of it in public. I never *said* anything, and I certainly never said anything about David. So when he entered rehab, people just naturally assumed it was my fault. I'm not big on assigning blame for bad behavior, whether it's my own or someone else's. Accountability is paramount when it comes to evolving as a human being, so I'm fairly quick to cry bullshit when I hear people whining about their misfortune. It would be easy for me to say that I became a skilled heroin addict under the tutelage of Chris Poland and Gar Samuelson, but that wouldn't be fair. It's equally unfair to suggest that David Ellefson would have remained clean and sober if not for his friendship with me. We were all passengers on the same roller coaster. No one held a gun to our heads and made us get on the ride.

No one told us when to get off, either. Each of us made that decision on his own, with varying degrees of success.

I followed suit not long after David, checking in quietly and voluntarily to a little place in Van Nuys, California. To say that I was invested in the rehabilitation process would be laughable. I went in part because I knew that I had a problem, that my drug use was becoming unmanageable and more painful than fun, but mainly because others were suggesting that it would be a good idea. My girlfriend Diana had repeatedly suggested I get some help, and her intervention, such as it was, came from a place of honesty and love. Others were more pragmatic. The music industry, I had been warned, was becoming less enamored of outrageous, unpredictable behavior. If you wanted to protect your career, you supposedly had to get sober.

Supposedly.

I remember checking in at the front desk, filling out the questionnaire, and feeling mainly sadness. I was so fucked-up that all that mattered anymore was living to get loaded. And it wasn't like I was getting loaded between concerts or rehearsals; I was rehearsing between getting loaded, I was doing concerts between getting loaded. I had put myself in a very bad place. I had hurt myself and my fans. It was time to address the situation.

Except it wasn't. Not even close.

After a couple days in treatment I called up a friend and asked him if he could maybe bring something to the facility to help cut the pain and boredom.

"Sure thing," he said. "What do you need?"

"You know what I need."

"Okay, no problem."

My friend showed up the next day to visit, guitar case in hand. I told the nurses that playing music would be relaxing; it would ease the discomfort and anxiety. They smiled compassionately. As soon as they were out of sight, I ripped off the front panel of the guitar and withdrew the balloon of heroin that was hidden inside. It was no more difficult to smuggle smack into rehab than it was to smuggle pizza from Domino's (which I also did). Eight days after signing in, I walked out, no less a drug addict than I'd been when I arrived. They made me sign a release acknowledging that I was leaving "against medical advice."

I looked at the form and laughed. "You know what? If anybody should leave this place, it's me, because I was bringing drugs into this place, and you didn't even care. You're not serious about helping people."

The truth, of course, was that no one could have helped me at that time. Or for quite some time afterward.

THE MEGADETH LINEUP responsible for *So Far, So Good . . . So What!* survived for less than a year, succumbing ultimately to personality conflicts fueled primarily by drugs and alcohol. Chuck Behler's baggage included a reckless guitar tech buddy nicknamed "Gadget."

I was with Gadget one night when we went down to score heroin on Ceres. One of the hard and fast rules regarding the purchase of smack was that you never carried the shit on your

A still photo during the filming of the video "Wake Up Dead" from *Peace Sells*. It was a photo shoot inside an airplane hangar at the Burbank Airport , and the fans vandalized the planes after the shoot. Photograph by Robert Matheu.

body. You carried it *in* your body. As soon as the transaction was complete, the balloon went in your mouth. That way, if you were stopped by the police, you could swallow the evidence. But what did Gadget do? He stuffed his balloon in between the seats of my convertible Z28. We hadn't even pulled away when the guns came over the top of the car.

"Put your fucking hands up!"

I froze. There had been no lights, no sirens. I didn't even know whether these guys were law enforcement or just dealers shaking us down. But they were indeed cops. I swallowed my balloon and immediately began thinking about the consequences of what was happening. They would search the vehicle, probably impound it, and I would go to jail. Remarkably, though, that isn't what happened. Instead, they arrested Gadget, for he had been the one who was outside the vehicle, making the purchase. The cops didn't want Gadget, though. They wanted the guy who had sold us the heroin. So they let me go and took Gadget back to finger the dealer. He ended up going to jail for a few days, sharing a cell with the guy he'd ratted out. I paid more than five grand in legal fees to clear up the problem, but after that I wasn't sure we'd be able to keep Chuck in the band. There was just too much craziness, too much drama.

Chuck was rendered replaceable by the spring of 1988; in a cruel twist of irony his departure was facilitated by his own drum tech, in much the same way that Chuck had slid into Gar's job.

It's a two-day story, actually. We were playing in Antrim, in Northern Ireland, and I was backstage before the show, getting loaded on Guinness, when I heard that someone was selling bootleg Megadeth T-shirts in the crowd. This was verboten; at a Megadeth show, the only people allowed to sell T-shirts were authorized vendors. So I said, "Someone has to stop that guy and get those shirts." I will confess that the details at this point begin to get a little fuzzy. I remember a heated conversation in the dressing room, and someone trying to explain to me something about T-shirt sales raising money for "the cause," and I remember barking at the guy, "I don't give a fuck about the cause; no one is selling shirts at my concert!"

The guy went on talking, something about organized religion and oppression and bigotry. In essence, he was summarizing the ongoing dispute between Catholics and Protestants in Northern Ireland, although I didn't realize it at the time and didn't know much about the issue to begin with. And I was too drunk to give a shit. By the time I got onstage, I was completely out of control. I remember getting hit in the head by an English pound coin that some kid had tossed. I tried to find him, wanted to drag him up onstage and beat him over the head with my guitar. I was no stranger to onstage ruckus, having already kicked out a video screen during a show in New York and beaten up a fan in Minnesota after he rushed the stage. Drunk as hell both times, obviously, so when I spotted this kid trying to scale a barricade and come after me, I was eager to tangle.

Security stopped him before he got to the top of the barricade, but the mood for the evening had been established. I ended up going briefly behind the amps while order was being restored, and there I saw Chuck with his drum tech, Nick Menza, the two of them smoking pot and doing a few lines of blow.

I laughed out loud.

"Is this what you guys do back here?"

Indeed, that was exactly what they had been doing back there, for many months, in fact. I didn't give a shit. I went back to the front of the stage and resumed playing, in front an audience that by now had been whipped into a frenzy. The last thing I remember is grabbing a bottle of schnapps, which Chuck always had nearby, and taking a few big gulps. I do not remember the rest of the show, but I have been told that this is what happened. I introduced the last song of the night, "Anarchy in the UK," with the following proclamation:

"This one is for the cause! Give Ireland back to the Irish!"

I didn't know what I was doing or what I was saying. I'm sure I thought it was just something cool to say, a harmless, patriotic rallying cry. A Paul Revere kind of thing: "One if by land, two if by sea!" In other words, ignorant nonsense. Basically, though, my words created a parting of the Red Sea in front of the stage: Catholic kids on one side, Protestant kids on the other. What they had in common was drunkenness and a willingness to fight at the slightest provocation. And I'd given it to them. The show ended immediately and we were quickly escorted out of the area in a bulletproof bus.

**Young and not afraid
to take off my shirt.**
Photograph by Ross Halfin.

The carnival went on, and the next day we did a show in Nottingham, England. By the time we did our sound check, Chuck was too roasted to play.

For some time Nick had been begging for a shot at Chuck's

job. "I'm a better drummer than him," he would say. "Let me play." Now he had his chance. Nick jumped behind the drum kit and launched into the opening of a song I had written just hours earlier, a song that would later find its way onto the *Rust in Peace* album. Tentatively titled "Holy Wars," it was an outgrowth of my embarrassment over my actions the previous night. Although most people—including me—invariably laugh when they hear the story of Megadeth's Antrim show, I was mainly embarrassed at the time, so I wanted to write something thoughtful and remorseful. That's why I took a self-deprecating shot at myself in the lyrics:

> **FOOLS LIKE ME WHO CROSS THE SEA AND COME TO FOREIGN LANDS ASK THE SHEEP FOR THEIR BELIEFS DO YOU KILL ON GOD'S COMMAND?**

Nick played flawlessly. The job wasn't his yet, but it might as well have been. From that moment on, there was no need to tolerate Chuck's lapses, or even to put up with the fact that we didn't get along very well. We had a perfectly capable, affable drummer waiting in the wings.

Finding a replacement for Jeff Young would prove to be a much more daunting task, but his departure was both necessary and inevitable. Jeff had his eccentricities and insecurities, not all of which blended neatly with mine. There was, for example, the night in Florida when he threw a tantrum and threatened to quit. The reason for Jeff's anger? He had discovered an old love letter written to me by a girl named Doro Pesch, the female lead singer for a metal band called Warlock. She was a cute chick and I was flattered by the attention, and so I kept the letter, even though nothing ever came of the flirtation. But Jeff, who had unsuccessfully pursued Doro in the preceding months, was so offended that he felt he couldn't play with Megadeth any longer.

That episode was merely a false alarm. Jeff didn't quit, but his behavior had become so erratic that I was ready to show him the door and it wasn't long before we kicked him out of the band.

It's funny how time can heal these things. Not long ago we all got together—the short-lived Megadeth lineup of 1988 (including Jeff Young, now a clean and sober cancer survivor)—to work on the remix of our catalog and had a good laugh about our year of living acrimoniously. We hugged, apologized, laughed at our own depravity and the general insanity of the whole experience. But at the time, man . . . it was brutal. We wanted to kill each other, and we very nearly did.

11

AGAINST
MEDICAL ADVICE

"You are fucking blackballed in this industry! And you know whose fault it is? That mother of yours."

IF YOU'RE GOING TO PICK UP A DUI, YOU MIGHT AS WELL GET YOUR MONEY'S WORTH. I SURE DID.

IN THE SUMMER OF 1989, I WAS DRIVING DOWN VENTURA BOULEVARD, ON THE WAY BACK HOME, SO CLOSE TO HOME AND SO COMPLETELY WASTED THAT I WASN'T EVEN WORRIED ABOUT AN ENCOUNTER WITH THE COPS. I WAS ESSENTIALLY BULLETPROOF AT THIS TIME, OR SO I THOUGHT. I HAD ONE TRAFFIC SIGNAL TO GO. THAT'S IT. JUST ONE LIGHT BETWEEN ME AND ANOTHER NIGHT OF FREEDOM. I PULLED UP AND TO MY LEFT SAW SOMEONE LEANING OUT THE PASSENGER SIDE OF HIS CAR. HE WAS TRYING TO YELL TO ME, SO I ROLLED DOWN THE WINDOW TO SEE WHAT HE WANTED. HE LOOKED LIKE A NICE ENOUGH FELLOW.

Me with my Dean Angel of Death VMNT. Photograph by Robert Matheu.

"Pull over, sir," he said. I could see then that he was waving a badge.

"Okay, officer. No problem."

I remember him saying something about how they were going to take care of me, call me a taxi, and give me a ride home, and I thought that was incredibly nice of them. The next thing I knew, there were dozens of flashing lights coming at me from all directions.

Wow . . . those taxicabs look a lot like cop cars.

And then I realized they *were* cop cars.

Uh-oh . . . somebody must be in trouble.

The list of items found in my blood or in my car that night is a pretty fair indication of just how far out of control my life had spun: marijuana, Valium, cocaine, heroin, chloral hydrate (a sleeping medication), alcohol, a spoon, and a syringe. Why the last of these items was in my possession, I'm not even sure; I was not an intravenous drug user. I've shot up a handful of times in my life—once far in advance of this arrest, and a few times well afterward, when my heroin use bottomed out. There was no reason for me to have a syringe in the car. But there it was. So what the fuck? The point is, the car was like a rolling pharmacy, and I was both customer and proprietor.

The consequences of my arrest were swift and simple. I was ordered to attend ten meetings of Alcoholics Anonymous and enroll in an alcohol diversion program for a period of eighteen months. Didn't work out that way, though. After the first hour of the first AA meeting, I'd had just about enough. I didn't know enough about the program to understand that the sign-in process was optional, that I could write "Joe Blow" on the registry rather than "Dave Mustaine" and no one would have given two shits. (It's called Alcoholics *Anonymous* for a reason.) I presumed that someone was watching, waiting, keeping tabs on all the drunks facing court-ordered intervention. I came up with an idea. Because I was still writing virtually all of the band's songs, publishing fees and royalties made me the biggest earner in Megadeth. By a wide margin. So, I figured, why not strike a deal?

"Hey, Junior. What if I were to pay you to attend AA meetings for me?"

"How much?"

"I don't know. Few hundred bucks a shot, maybe."

"Okay, cool."

It was that easy.

David went to one meeting . . . then another . . . and pretty soon I was paying him to attend meetings I think he would have attended for free. Something changed. He stopped drinking, stopped doing drugs. And one night I found myself looking at him, clean and sober, and I said, "Holy fuck! I accidentally twelve-stepped Junior!"

AA worked for David. For me? Not so much. The whole idea of hanging out with a bunch of guys in bowling shirts with back hair just didn't hold much appeal. Everything about AA struck me as cynical and false. Here is a program rooted in Christianity and the healing power of God juxtaposed with the powerlessness of man, a concept that must be embraced in order to understand and overcome addiction, and yet, you're not supposed to talk about God at an AA meeting. I walked out of the first meeting saying, "You guys are so fucked-up. It's no wonder you get a hundred newcomer chips for every twenty-year chip. No one in his right mind would stick with this program."

The truth is, I didn't think I had a problem. Well, that's not quite true. I knew I had a problem. I just thought I could treat the problem on my own. I wasn't serious about getting sober. As for contrition? Yeah, I was sorry—sorry I got caught. I had no remorse about the act itself or about the reckless, self-destructive behavior that precipitated my arrest in the first place. There is a huge difference, obviously. Rehab programs and penitentiaries are filled with men who regret their misdeeds primarily because of the consequences of those misdeeds. But remorse is something else entirely. It stems from something much deeper, something purer. It stems from a desire to be a better person and to stop hurting yourself as well as those around you.

I wasn't there yet.

LIFE WENT ON, as it must, despite all of the turmoil around us. Nick Menza had stepped in to replace Chuck Behler, but the quest for a new guitar player would stretch on for several months. In the interim, I continued to write songs and continued to drink and smoke heroin and cocaine. It's twisted the way the music business works—how the machinery of a band, particularly a platinum-level band, keeps chugging along even as the various parts are rusting and creaking.

Personnel changes and personal problems notwithstanding, Megadeth remained a band with great artistic and economic potential, and so work and opportunity kept coming our way. We recorded a cover of Alice Cooper's "No More Mr. Nice Guy" for the soundtrack of the Wes Craven film *Shocker*.* Our lovely friend Penelope Spheeris was hired to direct the video for "No More Mr. Nice Guy," an experience that was both hilarious and depressing.

I have the utmost respect for Penelope, so I won't dispute her well-documented recollection that I was basically too fucked-up to play guitar at my usual level on the day of the shoot. In

* This was the first and only time Megadeth went into the studio as a three-piece band: me, David Ellefson, and Nick Menza.

Jeff Young, me, Chuck Behler, and David Ellefson (SFSGSW lineup, 1987-1989).
Photograph by Robert Matheu.

fairness, though, it should be pointed out that this was a particularly challenging job. Penelope had me standing, and playing,
on a giant rotating pedestal—like a mammoth turntable. Things
might have been easier if the pedestal had at least been flat. But it
wasn't. It was more like one of those things skateboarders use to
practice when they're hanging around the house. Like a seesaw.
So there I was, trying to play guitar as everything was spinning
and rotating and bobbing up and down.

"Keep playing, Dave!" Penelope would yell. "Keep your eye
on the camera!"

More spinning . . . more rising . . . falling.

"Turn around, Dave! Look at the camera. No! Too fast! Over
here!"

"Fuck, man! I can't do this!"

It would have been hard enough to perform and play in the
video even if I had been sober and straight. Fucked-up? Forget it.
No chance.

WE BURNED THROUGH managers almost as quickly as we burned through drummers and guitar players. Jay Jones, Keith Rawls, and then Tony Maitland, who had guided the Fine Young Cannibals to their fifteen minutes of fame. Tony was with Megadeth for about a nanosecond before turning the reins over to Doug Thaler, a former musician whose management career had taken off thanks to his work with Mötley Crüe, the Scorpions, and Bon Jovi. My first reaction upon hearing that Doug wanted to manage Megadeth was "Fuck, yeah! Now I've arrived."

It proved to be a far more complicated relationship than that. Doug's assistant manager was a woman named Julie Foley, who also happened to be David Ellefson's girlfriend. David and I were still living together and supposedly cleaning up our act. He had remained sober; I had not. So one day while I was at home, getting loaded on heroin, Julie and David stopped by. Julie was pissed and immediately called Doug, who went straight into intervention mode. He had no qualms about telling me that I needed help and that my career depended on it. Doug, after all, had been through this sort of thing with the gang from Mötley Crüe. Moreover, this was a period when it had become politically correct for drunken and drug-addled celebrities—actors, musicians, writers—to embrace sobriety in a very public (and often self-serving, cynical) manner. Twelve steps to a better career and all that.

There was, at the time, a renowned "sober cop" named Bob Timmons whose specialty was working with entertainers, primarily musicians. Doug already had a relationship with the counselor dating back to Timmons's work with Mötley Crüe. If anyone could straighten me out, Doug figured, it was Timmons.

I agreed to enter rehab and begin a relationship with Timmons, more to get people off my back than anything else. Certainly it would be a stretch to say that I was prepared to invest any emotional capital in the rehabilitation process. I just wanted to placate the folks who were nagging me to death. It all happened very quickly, which is typically the way it works with interventions:

We're going. Right now. Don't even pack. The car is on its way.

In my case, the car was a limo. As I waited for its arrival, I polished off a balloon of heroin and then rolled a joint. Last one for a while, I figured. Might as well enjoy it. A few minutes later Timmons showed up. We talked a little, got in the limo, and drove off to Scripps Memorial Hospital in La Jolla. A few blocks from the house I cracked a window and lit the joint I had rolled before leaving.

"What are you doing?" Timmons said.

"Hey, it's okay, man. I'm just going to smoke a joint on the way. You know, say good-bye to getting loaded."

I laughed, thinking a guy like Timmons had probably seen and done it all and would appreciate the joke.

He didn't. "No chance, bro."

"What do you mean?"

"I mean *no*. We're already on our way."

In a heartbeat my attitude changed from resignation—tinged with just the slightest bit of optimism—to indignation.

"Fuck you! *You're* on your way. I'm going home. Turn the fucking limo around."

"Can't do that, bro. Trip has begun."

Whatever positive energy I had brought to the proceedings (and it wasn't much, I admit) evaporated. I didn't want to be in that limo, didn't want to be anywhere near Bob Timmons, didn't want to go to rehab.

Timmons, not surprisingly, had been through this sort of thing before; he was accustomed to hard cases, and so he just talked his way through the whole thing, basically told me his life story. He said that when he was a hell-raising youngster he'd been a member of the Aryan Brotherhood. You never know about someone, I guess, but to be perfectly honest, I just couldn't see this guy in the AB. He didn't seem like he had it in him. Well, once I got sober, some years later, and started doing a little sponsorship work of my own, I got to know some recovering alcoholics and drug addicts who had done some seriously scary, heinous shit. Many of them, not surprisingly, had been in gangs, including the Aryan Brotherhood. And a few claimed to have come across Bob Timmons in their travels.

"Bad motherfucker, right?" I said.

"Uh . . . not exactly."

The way they told it, Timmons had survived his time in prison by providing sexual favors for the AB. The gang, in turn, provided protection. Was this true? I have no way of knowing, but it certainly seems plausible. Timmons died a couple years ago, and I never asked him about it. Our relationship soured rather quickly after the drive to La Jolla. Indeed, by the time we got there, I was already thinking about leaving. I lasted a little longer than I had the first time, but not much.

Easing the discomfort of my stay was a cute young lady who was covered with tattoos. We got to know each other early and discovered we had a lot in common. Well, enough, anyway.

"You like heroin? Me too!"

"You're a Megadeth fan? Holy shit! I'm in Megadeth!"

There was a patient revolt one day, with inmates running all over the place, pissed about the food, the counseling sessions, almost anything you can think of. In the chaos that ensued my little punk girlfriend sneaked out of rehab and took a cab up to Via De La Valle, near the Del Mar racetrack, a good ten miles away. There, she dashed into a restaurant, procured some heroin, and brought it back to the treatment center, where the two of us promptly got loaded.

As was the case with my first trip to rehab, I was shocked at how easy it was to smuggle in drugs. By the time I sobered up, I had lost all interest in embracing the program. I just wanted to go home. So I called the one person who would ask no questions, the one person who loved me unconditionally and would do whatever I wanted, even if it was unreasonable and not necessarily in my best interests.

My mother.

She picked me up the next day, and I checked out of the hospital—as before, "against medical advice."* When I got home there was a message from Doug Thaler on my answering machine. No surprise, really. I knew there would be a price to pay for abandoning the program. I knew Doug would be angry. I did not know that he would lose his mind.

"You are fucking blackballed in this industry!" he said. "And you know whose fault it is? That mother of yours."

Whoaaaa.

That was my first reaction.

My second reaction was, *I'm going to kill this motherfucker.*

Here's the thing about my mom. She had a hard and lonely life. She loved her kids and she would have done anything for us, and often we did not make things any easier for her. I sure didn't. But my mother was just a normal person who worked hard (cleaning other people's toilets and floors) and liked to have a beer when she got home. That's about it. She was neither a drug addict nor an alcoholic. I understand Doug's anger; I played a part in this mess. He wanted to manage me, and I was unmanageable. I was unpredictable and unreliable, and as a result I jeopardized his security and reputation. Fine. Get pissed at me. Throw a punch. But to hurl that accusation at my mother? Absolutely unconscionable.

* Meaning I was leaving against medical advice and that they were no longer responsible for what happened to my sorry ass.

Not surprisingly, that was the last day of Doug's tenure as the manager of Megadeth. While he said he would start a smear campaign, I grew some balls and made amends with him for having jeopardized his security and for not being a good client before it ever got that way. The music business is generally pretty forgiving of bad behavior—and indeed often seems to reward it—especially in those who actually have some talent and a track record of success.

OUR NEXT MANAGER was Ron Laffitte, whom I'd known, and liked, since the Metallica days. Ron was personable and smart, and we seemed to have a lot in common: his mother was German, my mother was German; his last name was French, my last name was French; he was a Virgo, I was a Virgo. Given that we both also had long, reddish-brown hair and similarly outgoing personalities, we could have passed for brothers. Indeed, Ron was more than just a manager to me at that time. He was my friend. We hung together away from the studio, training in martial arts at a dojo owned and operated by the great martial arts champion Benny "the Jet" Urquidez. We went skydiving together. In bits and pieces, I began to get healthy. It didn't happen overnight, obviously, but certainly I was in better shape, physically and emotionally, than I'd been in quite some time. It's hard to explain the trajectory of my addiction and sobriety—it was not parabolic but rather long and undulating.

As I continued to write songs for the next record, *Rust in Peace*, I tried to live like a relatively "normal" guy in his late twenties. I worked out, maintained a healthy diet, focused on my work, and tossed back the occasional adult beverage. Or two or three. I was not yet convinced that it was inadvisable for me to party like other folks. There were a lot of people in "the program," and by this I am referring primarily to AA, who were not particularly tolerant of those who weren't in the program. If you didn't have your little medallion, and you weren't going to the musicians' meetings, and you didn't walk around saying, "There but for the grace of God, dude," you weren't in the club.

I was not in the club.

At the same time, I found myself going out to bars and looking over my shoulder a bit, wondering who was watching and keeping tabs on me. Why? Because I had fear. Even though I acted like it didn't bother me, I was actually shaken by Doug Thaler's threat. It made me angry, and it motivated me to seek revenge. But I also knew that the only way I'd be able to have any credibility was to get my shit together.

To that end, I continued to search for a great guitarist, some-one who would make everyone forget Jeff Young, and maybe even make them stop pining for Chris Poland. The process was mad-deningly slow, with audition after audition after audition. One guy showed up, and he's since gone around telling anyone who will listen that he wrote the beginning of "Wake Up Dead." Now, his audition occurred at roughly the time of Megadeth's fourth record. "Wake Up Dead" was on *Peace Sells*, recorded some three years earlier. Go figure.

Then there was the guy who strolled in one morning look-ing like a session player for the Allman Brothers: long blond hair pulled back into a ponytail, square-toed boots, denim jacket, southern boogie twang to his voice.

"Awright," he drawled while plugging in. "I'm ready for y'all to show me your songs."

I was like, *Are you fucking kidding me? This is an audition! This isn't a guitar lesson.*

Junior and I had developed a system for dealing with such

inanity. We'd reach behind our backs and switch the transmitter off on the cordless packs on our guitar straps, effectively ending the audition. In this case, we just glanced at each other and performed the move simultaneously.

We're done here.

I don't even remember how many of these we endured; after a while I began to lose hope of ever finding the right player. Finally, one day in February of 1990, I walked into Ron Laffitte's office and saw an album cover on his desk. *Dragon's Kiss* was the title of the record. It was a solo effort by a guitar player named Marty Friedman, whom I vaguely knew through his work with a band called Cacophony. I picked up the record, tried not to laugh. On the cover Marty wore some sort of shimmering leather jacket (or jumpsuit; it was hard to tell) open to the waist. His hair had been styled into long, flowing two-tone curls.

"You're shittin' me, right?"

"Just listen to it, okay?" Ron said.

Less than two minutes into the first track I was sold. More than that, actually. I was shocked.

"This guy wants to join *us*?"

Ron smiled, nodded.

Marty cut an unimpressive figure on the day of his audition: holes in his jeans, five-dollar shoes, same color-challenged hair he had sported on the album cover. His equipment consisted of a budget-brand guitar, a Carvin, and a tiny piece of rack-mount gear. To haul and install this feeble setup he had enlisted the services of an incongruously large guitar tech name Tony DeLeonardo. As I watched Tony go to work, I became concerned that the equipment couldn't possibly do justice to the playing I'd heard on Marty's solo record. So I made a suggestion.

"Hey, Tony," I whispered. "When it's time for the solo, you step on this button right here, okay?"

Since I had a veritable wall of Marshalls, I had assigned one of my amps to Marty so that he could play rhythm through it. Then we set up another amp to kick in when he did the solo. The extra stack would make it abundantly clear whether Marty was up to the job or not. There would be no hiding.

Not that hiding was necessary. Marty flew through the audition flawlessly. As we had with all the other auditions, we videotaped his performance, but Marty had played so perfectly that we didn't even bother to review it. I called Ron Laffitte's office almost immediately and said, "We've got our guitar player."

Marty had the chops, and to such an extent that almost nothing else mattered. Not the bad hair or the lack of style, or the fact that his name couldn't have sounded less "metal." I figured we'd send him to Rock School, just as we had with some other members of the band, maybe get him to change his name. Marty's middle name was Adam, so I thought, *Hmmmm . . . Adam Martin. That's pretty cool.* (Marty later took my idea and named his publishing company Adam Martin.) As with David Ellefson, he didn't go for it, but I couldn't call him Junior, too. Somehow, it would all work out.

And it did. The lineup was set—Megadeth was back to being a powerhouse four-piece band, one that had the potential to surpass even the lineup that had produced our first two records. We went into the studio armed with a bunch of great songs and a commitment to playing fierce and sober like the greatest thrash metal band on the planet. Within a few weeks, though, everything began to splinter, and this time I had no one to blame but myself. I kept watching Marty play, listening to what was coming out of his guitar, and . . . well . . . I crumbled. I don't know how else to say it. He was better than me—more talented, more committed, more . . . everything. Watching Marty made me realize that I'd been slacking. I had not progressed as an artist. I had stagnated. That realization was more than I could bear, and to handle it I turned once again to the warm embrace of heroin and cocaine.

The soon-to-be famous or rather infamous Rust in Peace lineup. Left to right: David Ellefson, Marty Friedman, me and Nick Menza

I don't mean to imply that Marty was in any way responsible for my relapse. It wasn't his fault, obviously. His talent was merely a catalyst. I wanted Marty in the band, knew he was the right man to fill the void we'd had for two years. I just had to get over my own insecurity and neuroses.

Central to accomplishing that goal was a man named John Bocanegra, who was the program director at the treatment center in Beverly Hills where I spent my third stint in rehab.* On this

---

* A note on the term *rehab*. I'm using it to describe any period of inpatient treatment, but it's worth noting that the duration and intensity of these visits varied. It's not like I went to a place, got hooked up to a bunch of machines, cleared the system, and then went out and hoed rows of corn for six months with Betty Ford. That wasn't it at all.

particular trip, for whatever reason, I was ready to make a change. I wanted to get better. I wanted to *feel* better.

John was unlike any drug counselor I'd met in the past. Oh, he had some of the same swagger, the same irreverent, take-no-bullshit demeanor, but there was more beneath the surface, and I could sense it right away. I liked him and trusted him— in fact, we became so close that he ended up serving as best man at my wedding. John was a slab of a man, stood about five feet, three inches tall and weighed close to 250 pounds, with a huge, drooping mustache and dark hair parted lazily down the middle. If not for the huge gang tattoo on his neck, he could have passed for one of those fun-loving guys you see playing in mariachi bands on Saturday nights in bad Mexican restaurants.

Once you got to know John, though, you understood that there was no artifice to his toughness. This was not a man who got through prison by being a bitch. The first time he told me he'd been a gangster prior to getting sober, I kind of laughed at the term.

"Gangster? What makes you a gangster?"

John proceeded to tell me, without a trace of comic relief, about his career as a crminal. One day, he said, he had walked into a bank and shot a security guard during the commission of a burglary.

"What the fuck, man?" I said incredulously. "Why did you shoot him? What did he do?"

"First thing I said when I walked into the bank was, 'Nobody move,'" John explained. Then he paused, shrugged. "The guy moved."

Presuming this story is true, I'm not quite sure how it is that John managed to avoid spending the rest of his life in prison. He said he went through some sort of long-term lockup diversion program, eventually got sober, and earned parole. Upon release, John became a drug counselor, and I can honestly say that he played a major role in my rehabilitation. I didn't get sober for good during that trip, but with John's help I was finally able to trace the roots of my addictive behavior and to face the consequences of my own decisions. He helped me see that it was indeed possible to turn things around. John meant a lot to me, and I know he meant a lot to David Ellefson as well. You can see John's inspiration in the song "Captive Honour," with its brutal depiction of crime and punishment, for which Junior cowrote the original lyrics.

For years I'd always heard John's voice when I sang "Captive Honour," but I'd never asked Junior about it. Finally, one day, he told me that he wrote his portion of the song after hearing John relate some horror stories about prison life.

There was another side of John that I really liked, because it demonstrated the degree to which he wasn't faking his role. He once told me that he kept a syringe hidden in the dashboard of his car.

"Well, that's pretty stupid," I said. "What the hell for?"

"Just in case."

If you're not a drug addict, if you've never been a drug addict, that might sound ridiculous. But I got it. I understood the sentiment. On some level, I even admired it.

EVEN AS I started to see results, I struggled with some of the natural by-products of the twelve-step process. Anger and ambition had fueled my art, giving rise to Megadeth's disturbing and frequently nihilistic point of view. Could I write while sober? Could I generate the same sort of ferocious guitar licks without benefit of chemical assistance? Absolutely. But what would happen if I became a man of peace? Of serenity? I had spent most of my adult life provoking and prodding. Could I live without confrontation, without agitation? I had no idea, and I wasn't sure that I wanted to find out. Essentially, I had become the hole in the doughnut, trying to live my life in peace with those around me. It was a completely unnatural and foreign state of being. My popularity as a musician had sprung from my outrageousness as much as my talent. People liked Megadeth not because I sang like James Taylor—I didn't, obviously—but because of the intensity of the music. They didn't come to a Megadeth concert expecting to see the fucking Dalai Lama. They wanted to see a blistering guitar player singing about death and annihilation, pain and retribution. Could I give them that when I felt like I was turning into vanilla pudding?

You know who helped me find the answer? Alice Cooper. We hadn't talked since our last tour, when Alice had expressed concern over my drinking and drug use. I called ostensibly to discuss an idea I had for a tattoo. It would combine the images of Megadeth's logo and Alice's logo: Vic and the Billion Dollar Baby.

I wore white to try something totally different. Marty and I on tour.
Photograph by Ross Halfin.

Alice thought it sounded cool, said I didn't need his permission or anything, and then quickly steered the conversation in another direction.

"How are you doing?" he asked.

"Okay," I said. "We're going in the studio for this new record, and I'm trying to do things differently. It's hard."

"I know what you mean. If you ever need my help or anything, I want you to know that I'm here for you."

I laughed, more out of nervousness than anything else. "Really, Alice? What are you, gonna be like my godfather or something?"

He didn't hesitate. "Sure, if that's what you want."

And that's how Alice Cooper became my godfather. We don't talk a lot anymore, and I suppose our relationship has evolved to the point where it's more on paper now than anywhere else. But that's all right. He was there for me at the time, and he's been there for me since. I have a ton of respect for Alice, both as a person and as a musician, and I'll always consider him a friend. Without really even trying, he got me to say something that, frankly, I never thought I'd be able to say:

"I need help."

12

THE LIVING YEARS

"You know what? It's about time. This is the best woman on earth for you."

THE FIRST TIME I SAW MY WIFE, SHE WAS HANGING OUT WITH A FRIEND AT A CLUB IN NORTH HOLLYWOOD CALLED FM STATION, ONE OF THE EARLIER VENUES IN THE BURGEONING FILTHY MCNASTY'S EMPIRE. I WAS THERE WITH A HANDFUL OF PEOPLE, INCLUDING NICK MENZA AND HIS BUDDY JUAN. THIS WAS MAYBE LATE 1989, EARLY 1990, WHEN I WAS DRIFTING IN AND OUT OF SOBRIETY, REVAMPING THE MEGADETH LINEUP, WRITING SONGS FOR RUST IN PEACE.

AS USUAL, MY PERSONAL LIFE WAS IN A STATE OF UPHEAVAL. FOR MORE THAN SIX YEARS I'D BEEN SEEING DIANA; THOUGH OUR RELATIONSHIP WAS HARDLY MONOGAMOUS—AT LEAST ON MY PART—I HONESTLY THOUGHT FOR THE LONGEST TIME THAT SHE WAS GOING TO

David Scott Mustaine and Pamela Anne Casselberry, March 3, 1991, in Honolulu, Oahu, Hawaii. I had never seen such beauty, and I look like a stick of Doublemint gum.

be the woman I would marry. We were engaged for six years, just one year shy of becoming common-law husband and wife. Diana was beautiful and sexy, but we fought constantly, to the point where it was almost so routine you could set your watch by it. She'd come over, we'd party a bit, something would be said, we'd fight, she'd leave, I'd call her, she'd come back, we'd make up, have sex . . . and then do it all over again. Eventually I came to the conclusion that it just wasn't going to work between me and Diana. I called her during one of my stints in rehab, during one of those moments of clarity so often described luminously by addicts and alcoholics.

"I can't see you anymore," I told her. "We are simply too toxic for each other."

Predictably, she freaked out—who wants to get dumped by a guy in rehab? Talk about depressing. But I think she knew it was coming. I also think she knew that she was better off without me. As for me, well, I was making changes in my life, and withdrawing from a dysfunctional relationship was one step in the process of self-improvement. "Tornado of Souls" became my way of dealing with the end of that relationship. Really, that's all it was, an explanation of how I was feeling at the time; lyrical references aside, it was not a song about murder or death. It was about the decay that comes with being stuck in a bad relationship.

> **THIS MORNING I MADE THE CALL**
> **THE ONE THAT ENDS IT ALL**
> **HANGING UP, I WANTED TO CRY**
> **BUT DAMN IT, THIS WELL'S GONE DRY**

In all candor, though, it wasn't like I was looking for a soul mate. After breaking things off with Diana and cleaning up my act a bit, I was pretty psyched about enjoying some of the other fringe benefits associated with being a rock star. I was the lead singer, songwriter, and guitar player for Megadeth. If I wasn't exactly Brad Pitt, well, I wasn't the worst-looking guy in the world, either. Let's be honest: if you have money and can play guitar, you can get laid. God knows there have been enough ugly fuckers in heavy metal who never seem to have a shortage of ass at their disposal. I was now in a better position to partake of the buffet table.

And then Pamela Anne Casselberry came along and put a crimp in my plans.

"See that girl over there?" I said to my friend Juan.

"Which one?"

"The tall blonde."

Juan nodded approvingly. "Uh-huh. Very nice."

"Yeah. I want you to go over there and tell her I'd like to meet her."

Juan, ever the agreeable fellow, laughed and walked up to the blonde. I saw them chatting, saw Juan gesture in my direction. I held up my glass (which was filled with Coke—uppercase "C") and smiled. The blonde gave me nothing in return. Moments later Juan was back, chuckling.

"She said if you want to meet her, you should come over yourself."

Fair enough. One thing I didn't lack, when it came to women, was confidence. So I walked over and started to introduce myself. "Hi, my name is Dave."

The blonde cut me off. "Yeah, I know who you are," she said coolly. The fact that she seemed disinterested only heightened my interest. Funny how that works, huh? I cut straight to the proverbial chase.

"Look, I'm really attracted to you, and I'd like to spend some time with you. But I'm helping out a friend tonight who's trying to stay sober, and I have to hang with him.* Can we get lunch some afternoon?"

Diabolically smooth fucker that I was, I knew this would work. It implied compassion and responsibility as well as honesty and integrity. I had made it clear that I found her attractive but that I was also willing to wait for her. I did not reveal my ulterior motive: to see her in the light of day, at a sidewalk café, beneath the brilliant truth of the warm California sun. Even if you hadn't been drinking, a girl could look pretty good through the smoky haze of Filthy McNasty's at two o'clock in the morning; then you'd see her in the glare of daylight, with the pancake removed, and you'd swear she was a different person.

If that sounds shallow and inconsiderate, well, I plead guilty. I was doing the beauty pageant thing, interviewing contestants for the title of Miss Right. In reality, of course, they were all merely competing for the title of Miss Right Now. Before I'd even officially broken things off with Diana, I'd begun seeing a girl named Leslie. And while seeing Leslie, I lusted after the blonde at FM Station.

She told me her name was Pam, and we agreed to get together soon. One lunch date, then another, and pretty soon I'd begun to fall for her. Pam was one of those gorgeous California girls— long and lean, with skin that needed no spackle—who are even more beautiful in the naked light. She was just a normal suburban girl from Upland, California, with a backstory not as hard as some, but hard enough. Her father had died of cancer when Pam was growing up, and she had assumed the role of surrogate spouse to her mom and surrogate parent to her little brother. To a degree, Pam became the family breadwinner (or at least one

---

* True, actually—one of the guys in our group had indeed asked me to serve as his watchdog for the evening; incredibly enough, I was the sober cop!

of the breadwinners), which led to a distorted sense of self. Her mom eventually got married again, to a guy who seemed at first like Prince Charming but turned out to be something less. Long story short: Pam had her share of heartache before I came along, and while we fell in love rather quickly, I'm not at all sure she knew what she was getting into.

Sure, she knew about Megadeth, and she knew who I was. But she wasn't a groupie or anything like that. Pam doesn't even like heavy metal (Megadeth included). Never has. I get into my car now, and if Pam has been driving, the radio is sure to be tuned to some country station. I was put off by it, at first, because I just presumed that country was crap. But a lot of country now is really anthemic pop, and some of it's not bad at all. I mean, it's so heavily influenced by the Mutt Lange school of production that it all sounds kind of like Def Leppard. Heavy ballads, voices Auto-Tuned to perfection. Technology has made it so that anyone can sing like Mariah Carey.

Regardless, I liked Pam enough not to care in the least about her taste in music. At the same time, I was not exactly committed to this new relationship. We came back to my apartment one night after having dinner at a place called Chin Chin. I'd been wining and dining her, taking her to the most expensive restaurants I could find.

Pam wasn't feeling well and excused herself to use the bathroom, then came out looking haggard and pale. She said she needed to rest for a while. I didn't know it at the time, but she was suffering from an esophageal hernia. All of a sudden there was a sound at the door. The sound of a key entering a lock.

Oh, shit . . .

Moments later, in walked Leslie, who, of course, had a key to my apartment.

I didn't really even like Leslie very much. I'd met her through my bodyguard, and she was cute and available and into me in a big way. But we weren't exactly kindred spirits outside the bed-room. In fact, even that aspect of our relationship wasn't all that great. I would have been perfectly content to see her go. But not quite in this manner.

Leslie took two steps into the apartment, saw Pam on the couch, and turned around and walked out, slamming the door behind her.

Don't ask me why, but I ran after her. My default mechanism was to lie and cajole and try to get by on charm. And I was very good at it. In a rare moment of sanity, though, I stopped short of actually confronting Leslie and thought about Pam.

You fucking idiot! You have someone upstairs right now you actually care about. Why are you chasing this woman?

I also realized that the woman upstairs might be turning my apartment upside down, shredding my clothes, tossing stuff out the window. In my experience, women did that kind of thing when they discovered you'd been screwing around on them. So I raced back inside, ran up the stairs, and Pam was gone. In a matter of minutes, I'd managed to lose two girls. Not that I grieved for long. There were a few more phone numbers in my book, an end-less supply of one-nighters to be had on the road. Or at home, for that matter. But that's part of the sickness, isn't it? In treatment or not, I was capable of hurting people.

A strange thing happened, though. I missed Pam. While out on tour with Megadeth, I called and apologized.

"Let's try again," I suggested. "We'll take it slow."

That didn't happen—the slow part, I mean. We began dating again, and within a few months I had decided that I wanted to marry her. I hadn't voiced that sentiment, but I felt it nonethe-less. It wasn't just that I was attracted to Pam. I felt a connec-tion to her that I'd never felt with anyone else before. It helped, too, that my mother had given Pam her stamp of approval. I knew they got along pretty well, but it wasn't until Mom passed away in 1990 that I found out how much she liked Pam. Mom and I had reconnected in a really positive, grown-up kind of way during the last couple years of her life. She had always been a big supporter of mine, regardless of what I put her through, but with forays into sobriety came a desire to make her life easier. Simultaneously, Mom was warming up to the fact that I'd become successful. No matter how much her religion told her to shun me, she couldn't do it; I was her pride and glory. She used to buy everything with checks so that

During the ceremony, down by the sea. Pam was radiant. I wrote the song "The Hardest Part of Letting Go Is saying Goodbye" for her. She said she didn't like it.

people would see her last name, and they would ask her, "Is that your boy?" And she would just beam and nod.

Rust in Peace was released in October of 1990; shortly thereafter I took Mom to Europe so that she could visit the place of her birth: Essen, Germany. It was a great trip, one she'd always wanted to make, and I'm happy we were able to do it before she died. The funeral service was a little weird, in part because of tension between me and David Ellefson's girlfriend (and future wife), Julie. I was still furious over her role in my falling out with Doug Thaler; complicating matters was the fact that Julie had dated Ron Laffitte prior to his becoming our manager.

The service was memorable in other ways that were less unsettling. My sister Michelle, for example, chose this occasion to pull me aside and share something my mother had said.

"You know, David . . . Mom was very fond of Pam."

This was not a small thing, since my mother disliked almost everyone I had ever dated, including Diana. "You two are always fighting," she would say. "Why do you bother?"

A fair question, and in the end one I could not answer. Mom was smart that way. I married Pam because I loved her, of course, but also because of the resounding final endorsement I received from my mother.

I was serious about my kickboxing training and my body started to reflect that.
Photograph by Ross Halfin.

Megadeth went out on tour not long afterward. It was a lengthy tour, ending in April with several shows in Japan, followed by a pair of performances in Hawaii. This was by design. I thought it would be a cool way to end the tour: travel all over the world, work our asses off, and finish with Hawaii. Then, after the last show, spend four or five days chilling out, relaxing on the beach, having a good time. By the time we got to Hawaii, Pam was already there. She did not know that I had purchased the most perfect strand of pearls I could find while we were in Japan. Neither did she know that I had called my business manager and asked him to find a pear-shaped diamond and have it placed in a setting, surrounded by other diamonds.

Pam knew nothing except that we were going to have a nice Hawaiian vacation. Then I got on the phone and began making calls: my sisters, Pam's family, John Bocanegra, my sponsor in AA.

"Pam and I are getting married," I said. "Please come. Oh, and keep it quiet. She doesn't know yet."

When I got to our hotel room, Pam was in the shower. She walked out of the bathroom, wrapped in a towel, wearing no makeup, looking more beautiful than ever, and smiled at me.

"What are you doing next Saturday?" I asked.

Pam shrugged. "I'll be here with you. Why?"

I tried to maintain a poker face but found it impossible. I began to smile. "Well, I was just wondering if maybe you'd want to get married."

She started crying, then regained her composure enough to say yes, which was a good thing considering how many plane tickets I'd already purchased. And then we embarked on the challenging task of finding a size 1 wedding dress in Hawaii. It's true that some islanders of Asian or Filipino descent are rather petite, but it's also true that many of our Tongan and Samoan friends are not. Hawaii just happens to be one of those places with an indigenous population that is naturally large. There just aren't a lot of size 1s walking around.

But we found one, thank God, and it was actually a beautiful dress, one that fit Pam perfectly. The same could not be said of my tuxedo, which, from a distance, appeared to be cut from Reynolds Wrap. But really, who gives a shit? No one looks at the groom anyway. Nick Menza's girlfriend, Stephanie, was maid of honor. My best man was John Bocanegra. Now, one would think I would have asked David Ellefson to handle that task, but I didn't. The truth is, I was closer to John at the time. If I had gotten married when I first met David (and what a disaster that would have been), then yeah, chances are he would have been my best man. But as things took place and the band evolved, our friendship ebbed and flowed. I don't know if this hurt David or not; maybe so. I suppose it says a lot when you get passed over in favor of an ex-convict. But there you have it. I felt, at that moment in time, as though I owed a great deal to John Bocanegra. He was best-man material—in a very rock 'n' roll sort of way.

When the wedding ceremony began, I had no idea how it would turn out—we were totally flying by the seat of our pants. But the limo pulled up, and Pam got out, and she was absolutely stunning. Like nothing I had ever seen before. That may sound strange, considering we'd had many romps in the hay. I had seen Pam dressed up, and I had seen her naked. But never had I seen her like this; she was . . . angelic.

Wow! Mom was right.

Admittedly, as Pam walked across the grass, I felt a fleeting moment of anxiety. But as she took my hand and looked into my eyes, the fear faded away, and in its place I heard another voice, this one more like mine:

"You know what? It's about time. This is the best woman on earth for you."

Just for the record: it was a sober ceremony. There had been no drug use at all in Japan. I was in a clear-headed, healthy place. A place of optimism. I knew exactly what I was doing.

After the ceremony, we got in the limo and drove back to the hotel, with "The Living Years" by Mike and the Mechanics providing a soundtrack for the ride. This may not sound particularly metal, but I absolutely love that song. I love the melody and I love the sentiment. I know it's a song about fathers and sons and the damage done when the two fail to communicate. Distilled to its essence, though, it's really just a song about love. And the importance of telling those you love exactly how you feel.

That night we went to a big luau, and while there we began

talking with an elderly couple who had been married for more than fifty years. At one point I found myself chatting privately with the husband, a quiet, thoughtful man old enough to be my grandfather.

"How do you do it?" I asked. "I mean . . . half a century?"

The old man smiled. "It's simple. Never go to sleep mad at your wife."

"Never?"

"Never."

I laughed so hard I almost choked. "Come on, man. That's not possible."

He looked at his own wife, sitting just a few feet away, chatting amiably with other guests. "Sure it is. No matter what she does, no matter how mad you get, just give her a kiss before you fall asleep."

God knows, Pam and I do not have a perfect marriage. But we're still together after nearly two decades. Throw out the nights when we've been separated by work and travel, and I can count on one hand the number of nights I've fallen asleep without giving her a kiss good night.

What can I tell you? The old dude was right.

13

I PRAY THE LORD MY SOUL TO KEEP

"I'm tired of the tour, I'm tired of Megadeth, I'm not having any fun . . . and you don't want me to drink, so I'm taking Valium instead."

AT SOME POINT YOU HAVE TO TAKE OWNERSHIP OF THE THINGS PEOPLE ARE SAYING ABOUT YOU, ESPECIALLY WHEN THEY'RE ESSENTIALLY CORRECT. SUCH WAS THE CASE WITH MY ATTITUDE TOWARD MEGADETH BEING CLASSIFIED AS A "POLITICAL" BAND. I'D BEEN UNCOMFORTABLE WITH THE LABEL WHEN WE FIRST STARTED OUT, BUT WITH RUST IN PEACE AND COUNTDOWN TO EXTINCTION, IT BECAME INCREASINGLY DIFFICULT TO DENY THAT, AT THE VERY LEAST, I WAS AWARE OF WHAT WAS GOING ON IN THE WORLD; CONSEQUENTLY, OBSERVATIONS AND

During an encore I always hold my guitar above my head at the very end.
Photograph by Ross Halfin.

opinions, sometimes not very subtle ones, occasionally found their way into the lyrics of Megadeth.

The concept of *Rust in Peace*, for example, sprang from a bumper sticker I saw one day while driving on the freeway. I forget the precise wording, but it was something like "May all your nuclear weapons rust in peace," and immediately I had this image in my head of a pile of warheads sitting in a field someplace, covered with graffiti. Not exactly a hawkish sentiment, right? And yet, I've been accused at times of being a right-winger. I've also been perceived as an environmentalist, which is not exactly consistent with traditional Republican values. The truth is, I consider myself to be "political" only in the sense that I am a citizen of the United States of America and thus free (maybe even obligated) to speak out about things that pique my interest.

And so you have an album like *Rust in Peace*, which includes songs about global warming and environmental impact ("Dawn Patrol"), POWs ("Take No Prisoners"), and, of course, religion ("Holy Wars . . . the Punishment Due").

I think that most people who are familiar with Megadeth's music would say that I am a politically active artist (working for MTV as a "correspondent" during the 1992 presidential campaign probably solidified that reputation), but I'm not easy to pin down or classify, and I hope that I never am. I look at it this way: if Clint Eastwood had a party named after him, that would be my party. Okay, I know, Clint was an elected official, a Republican mayor of Carmel, California. But I'm not talking about Clint Eastwood the citizen. I'm talking about the characters he's played, from the Outlaw Josey Wales to Dirty Harry to the aging, avenging gunfighter William Munny in *Unforgiven*. The kind of man who loves his country, stands up for people who can't defend themselves, and really doesn't give a flying fuck what anyone else thinks of him. You may not always agree with this guy, but you have to respect him.

I am not a registered member of either of the two main political parties, and I suspect that will never change. I think of myself as nonpartisan: I am generally distrustful of professional politicians, so when I enter the voting booth I tend to go with whomever I perceive as the lesser of two evils. In 1990, when Bill Clinton ascended to the top of the Democratic heap and challenged Bush the elder, it was really easy for me to vote for Clinton. My feelings about Al Gore were a little more complicated. Given my sentiments on environmental protection, it was hard for me to discount the man; at the same time, I was an outspoken opponent of the Parents Music Resource Center, founded by Gore's wife, Tipper. I was a supporter, if not necessarily a fan, of George W. Bush, primarily because I admired his handling of 9/11, and I did not disagree with our involvement in Iraq. Besides, there was no way I would ever vote for John Kerry, an elitist, who had been rude and condescending when I tried to interview him for MTV. I knew he had no chance to be elected president—people see right through that smug shit.

It's pretty simple for me, really. I want to be able to carry a gun; listen to whatever music I like; eat, drink, and be merry; and not hurt anyone else (the exception, obviously, being self-defense). It's the abbreviated Sermon on the Mount: treat other people the way you want to be treated.

IF METAL FANS were put off by the lyrical themes of *Rust in Peace*, you'd never know it. The record was Megadeth's biggest success to date, selling more than a million copies and earning the band its first Grammy nomination. Not that I really give a shit (okay, maybe a little), but it also received virtually universal critical acclaim. By just about every conceivable standard, *Rust in Peace*

was a watershed event for Megadeth. Funny thing was, it didn't start out that well. We recorded at a place called Rumbo Recorders, which was owned by the Captain and Tennille, of all people. Imagine that! Megadeth tracking in the very same place where "Muskrat Love" was recorded. I was skeptical about Rumbo offering the right atmosphere, a feeling that was exacerbated one day when I walked in and saw our producer, Dave Jurdin, eating a chili dog and smoking a cigarette at the controls. The place just reeked.

Jurdin was gone within days, replaced by Mike Clink, whose credentials were strong, if not impeccable. Clink and I got off on the wrong foot as well when, early in the process, he said, "Listen, bro, if Axl calls, I may have to take off for a little while."

"What?"

"Yeah, I'm doing the Guns N' Roses album, too, so if Axl needs me . . . well, you understand."

"Yeah, I understand. You better hope he doesn't call."

He didn't. Clink made it almost to the very end, until he started bringing his new puppy to work with him, and the damn dog ate a hole in the wall and then knocked over my guitar, and we just had to let him go. But I want to be fair here. Mike Clink has always gotten credit for producing *Rust in Peace*, and I certainly wouldn't deny his contributions. It's a terrific record, start to finish.

THE TOUR TO support *Rust in Peace* stretched out over several months, beginning with our participation in the Clash of the Titans tour, which also featured Slayer and Suicidal Tendencies. I remember this as a particularly exciting and often entertaining time, as the infusion of new blood—Marty and Nick—combined with the fact that we were promoting a really strong record made touring seem far less mundane than it often did.

Of course, it helped (if that's the right word) that we had a guy like Dominick (I will not divulge his real name) on the crew.

Dom was Marty's guitar tech. He'd previously worked with Guns N' Roses—when they were functioning and we were hanging out with them, there was a lot of sharing of crews. We borrowed their sound guy, Dave Kerr; their security director, John Zucker and Dominick. Dom had a generally cavalier, disrespectful attitude toward his work.

With sharp, lizardlike features and an eighth grader's sense of humor, Dominick was not the most appealing guy in the world. But there was never any shortage of entertainment when he was around. If you spotted Dom chewing a wad of gum and asked if he had any extra, here's the way he'd respond:

"Yeah, hang on a second."

Then he would pull a testicle out of his shorts, stretch his scrotum, and add, "Just let me knock the hair off it."

Dominick clashed with everyone on Clash of the Titans, but his primary target was Marty. When Marty fell asleep in an airport, Dominick drew a swastika on his forehead, a particularly nasty prank when you consider that Marty is Jewish. Knowing of Marty's fondness for Japanese culture, Dominick had scrawled the word *Cat-eater* on Marty's Game Boy. I thought that was pretty fucking funny, actually, but Marty was so incensed that he decided to fight back. As Dominick slept one off on the plane, Marty withdrew Dominick's brushed aluminum Zero Halliburton suitcase from an overhead storage bin and wrote on the top:

DRUGS INSIDE—PLEASE CHECK!

When we landed in Australia, Dominick grabbed his suitcase, but was too drunk or hungover to notice it had been vandalized. It took him a little longer to get through customs that day; when

Me and Max Norman at the console in the studio we built in Arizona. Max also produced the first two Ozzy records: *Diary of a Madman* and *Blizzard of Oz.* Photograph by Ross Halfin.

he finally emerged, sweating and shaking, he threatened to kill Marty, who wasn't even slightly apologetic.

"That's what you get for drawing a fucking swastika on my head!"

By the end of the tour we had all started ganging up on Dominick. On the final flight home, as we boarded the plane, Dominick staggered aboard, blind drunk, and promptly passed out in his seat, which, as luck would have it, was right next to a Catholic priest. I can't imagine what this poor man was thinking as he watched us go to work on Dominick. Taking turns with a Sharpie, we blackened the tip of Dominick's nose, so that he looked like either the Scarecrow from *The Wizard of Oz* or a victim of frostbite. Then someone wrote "6 6 6" on his cheeks (I'm sure the reverend found this amusing). By the time it was over, the flight attendants had even joined in, offering the use of their lipstick to make Dominick look like the world's ugliest prostitute.

Eventually, he woke up and commenced one of those alcoholic

walks from the front of the airplane to the lavatory in the rear. Staggering, moaning, clearly in a great amount of discomfort, Dominick lurched along, and as he did so, we could hear the laughter building. By the time he got to the bathroom, having passed a couple hundred passengers, the plane was practically convulsing.

And then the laughter stopped.

All of a sudden you could hear the sound of footsteps, louder and louder, as Dominick ran from the bathroom, his face covered with red lipstick and black ink. He stopped at my seat and leaned over.

"All right, Mustaine, you fucker! Who did this?"

I shrugged, tried to stifle a laugh. "Don't ask me. I didn't see a thing."

WITH SUCCESS CAME pressure, and when we entered the studio, on January 6, 1992, to record *Countdown to Extinction*, there was no question that the bar had been raised. Once you sell a million copies, anything less is deemed a failure. That's just the reality of the music business. This was, for me, a rather extraordinary period. Pam was pregnant with our first child, and for the first time I felt as though I had achieved a degree of balance in my life. Our house was only a few blocks from Enterprise Studios in Burbank, where we were recording, so I could actually walk to work most mornings.

To produce *Countdown to Extinction*, we turned to Max Norman. Max had worked previously on the Ozzy Osbourne records *Diary of a Madman* and *Blizzard of Oz*, which in turn led to his doing the final mix of *Rust in Peace*. We hit it off, the record did great, so I figured, why not just let Max take over the controls on *Countdown*?

Less than one month after we entered the studio, on February 11, 1992, my son, Justis, was born. Pam and I had done everything we could to prepare for his arrival, but like most new parents we were thoroughly unprepared. Not for the actual birth but the aftermath. You know—the part where they let you take the kid home. Pam had gone on a ridiculously clean regimen of diet and exercise and nutritional supplements, so she was in fighting shape the day her water broke. She stubbornly refused painkillers and anesthesia for the longest time at the hospital, until, finally, I yelled, "Honey, please, take the fucking Demerol! If you don't want it, I'll use it."

Pam's stridency in this matter stemmed largely from the fact that her mother, Sally, had often bragged about how she had given birth to Pam without any anesthesia at all. She had made the whole process seem heroic. It was only after we'd been at the hospital for a while, watching Pam contorting in the throes of labor, that her mom finally admitted that maybe they had in fact given her a little something after all.

"Like what?" I said.

"I don't know, Dave. It was so long ago." She paused, reached around, and rubbed her lower back quizzically. "I do vaguely remember a little pinprick there."

"Oh, that's just great, Sally. They gave you an epidural."

Fifteen minutes later, Pam was receiving her magic needle, and not long after that, Justis slid into the world. The next day, while I was sleeping in a chair next to Pam's bed, some kid came into the hospital room to deliver a bouquet of flowers. Before leaving, I was told, he stopped by the nurse's desk and exclaimed, "Ma'am, do you know who you've got in there? *Megadeth!*"

To which the elderly nurse replied, "Oh, no, young man. This a wonderful hospital. We haven't had any deaths here in a long time."

True story . . .

WITH APRIL CAME the verdict in the Rodney King trial and subsequent rioting that set the entire city of Los Angeles on edge. It was a strange and surreal time, with tanks and national guardsmen lining the streets for days on end—you almost expected to see Sarah Connor rounding the corner at any moment, Terminator in hot pursuit. A curfew was put in place, which meant suddenly I was working banker's hours, ten A.M. to six P.M. Good for the family, especially with a new baby in the house and a wife who was enormously stressed out and suffering from postpartum depression; not so good for making a record, a process that typically involves nearly round-the-clock devotion.

Nevertheless, the record was delivered on time, and we knew before it was released that we were sitting on something special. We knew the songs were good, we knew our playing was good. We were tight, fast, loud, maybe even a little melodic in spots. And sober. Did I mention sober? For the first time in a long time, we had become a real band, with writing contributions from all four members. Nick Menza supplied the album title and most of the lyrics to the title track, ostensibly an indictment of that particularly ugly breed of "sportsman," the kind who enjoys a canned hunt. Political statements were all over this record, from "Architecture of Aggression" (about the Gulf War) to "Foreclosure of a Dream," a song about economic upheaval that includes a famous sound bite ("read my lips") from President George H. W. Bush. This was a song that grew out of David Ellefson's frustration with Reaganomics when the family farm back in Minnesota was foreclosed upon.*

---

* I ended up loaning Junior ten thousand dollars to help keep the farm in business, which didn't help our relationship when things got gnarly down the road.

Additionally, there were songs about my struggles with addiction ("Skin o' My Teeth"), the brutality of prison ("Captive Honour"), and the fallout from war ("Ashes in Your Mouth," "Symphony of Destruction").

On the eve of the record's release, in July of '92, I was about as excited as I had ever been. I knew we had a record that could alter the landscape of heavy metal.

So what happened? Well, *Countdown to Extinction* was a monster of an album, debuting at number two on the *Billboard* pop charts in July of '92. I can remember getting the phone call and sucking in a big breath of air, and thinking, *Fuck, yeah!*

And then, after all of about five seconds, saying, "Who's number one?"

"Billy Ray Cyrus."

"What?! Are you fucking kidding me? The 'Achy Breaky' guy?"

"Yeah . . . sorry."

I swear to God that's the main thing I remember about the summer of 1992: Megadeth's greatest accomplishment getting overshadowed. "Achy Breaky Heart" was everywhere (I know—remember, my wife loves country music), and the album that spawned the wretched single was nearly as ubiquitous. *Some Gave All* debuted at number one on the pop album charts and was still entrenched when *Countdown to Extinction* was released a month and a half later. It seemed to me that it would have been sufficient for Billy Ray Cyrus to settle for dominating the country charts, but the guy was obviously on a mission to rule the music world.

So befuddling was his ascendency that I actually took my eye off the Metallica ball for a moment, stopped wondering how I was going to surpass Lars and James, and simply tried to comprehend the awfulness of a system that spectacularly rewarded crap like "Achy Breaky Heart." Megadeth sold a shitload of records that summer, but nothing compared to Billy Ray Cyrus. I just couldn't figure it out. Someone once asked me if our paths ever crossed, us being chart toppers at the same time and all, and I joked, "Yeah, I told him I had this idea for a sitcom about a guy whose teenage daughter leads a double life and becomes a big pop star. Fucker stole my concept."

Truth is, we never met, and I'm sure I would not have been particularly gracious if we had. I had no respect for his music. Still don't. But I wouldn't take it quite so personally now. There is, after all, no accounting for taste.

There's also no way to adequately rationalize or explain my obsession with success, recognition, respect. It was what it was—and still is, to a degree, although I think I have a better handle on it now. With *Countdown to Extinction*, Megadeth went from being a flavor of the month to a bona fide supergroup. The album sold half a million copies (gold record status) very quickly, then a million (platinum), and it just . . . kept . . . going. Suddenly we had influence on a level we'd never known. A major tour was planned. The rock press knelt before us. Money was about to come pouring in. I had the career I'd always dreamt of and a ter-rific family as well. I should have been one of the happiest guys on the planet. But, of course, I wasn't. Instead, I was speeding toward . . . well . . . death.

By autumn we were out on the road and once again I'd become obsessive about catching Metallica. As big a hit as *Countdown to Extinction* was, it had fallen short of Me-tallica's latest release, the self-titled *Metallica* (also known as the "Black Album"), which had hit number one a year ear-lier, in the summer of 1991, and continued to spawn hit singles. Among these was "Enter Sandman," a song that nearly gave me a heart attack the first time I heard it.

A little backstory . . .

Around the time that Metallica was recording the Black

I PRAY THE LORD MY SOUL TO KEEP

Album, Megadeth was offered a chance to record a song that would be used on the soundtrack for the sequel to the film *Bill and Ted's Excellent Adventure*. We had been offered the title track, actually, and leaped at the opportunity.

"What's the movie called?" I asked.

"Bill and Ted Go to Hell."

Cool enough, I figured, and went about the job of writing a song called "Go to Hell." When I finished, Tom Whalley, an executive at Interscope Records, which was releasing the soundtrack, offered only tepid approval.

"It's not dark enough," he said.

Okay . . . so I changed some of the lyrics, made it darker, recorded the vocal track, and delivered the song. Everyone loved it. A short time later I found out that the name of the movie had been changed to *Bill and Ted's Bogus Journey*, a "creative" (i.e., marketing) decision that not only cost us the title track but also put me in the unfortunate position of having to explain why I would write a song that had the same title as a song written by Alice Cooper—my godfather, for Christ's sake. It was awful. Obviously I didn't really want anyone to go to hell. And obviously I wouldn't disrespect Alice by ripping off his title. I was simply following a Hollywood directive. Unfortunately, I got burned for it.

The song opened with the following lyric, voiced by a child:

> NOW I LAY ME DOWN TO SLEEP
> I PRAY THE LORD MY SOUL TO KEEP
> IF I SHOULD DIE BEFORE I WAKE
> I PRAY THE LORD MY SOUL TO TAKE

At the end of the song, a snarling, mutated version by yours truly is offered:

NOW I LAY ME DOWN TO SLEEP
BLAH, BLAH, BLAH MY SOUL TO KEEP
IF I DIE BEFORE I WAKE
I'LL GO TO HELL FOR HEAVEN'S SAKE!

Then the Black Album came out, and "Enter Sandman" became Metallica's biggest single. Forget for a moment that James and Lars had a history with my songs. Forget that the opening lick to "Enter Sandman" sounded eerily like the intro to a little-known song called "Tapping into the Emotional Void" (recorded by the band Excel in 1989). What really got to me was the creepy spoken interlude midway through the song:

NOW I LAY ME DOWN TO SLEEP
PRAY THE LORD MY SOUL TO KEEP
IF I DIE BEFORE I WAKE
PRAY THE LORD MY SOUL TO TAKE

Granted, it's not like I wrote the children's prayer from which it was lifted (by both of us). And maybe it was just pure coincidence. I have no way of proving otherwise. Both "Go to Hell" and "Enter Sandman" found their way into the public consciousness in the summer of 1991. I don't know which song was written first. I don't know if James or Lars heard about "Go to Hell" while they were in the recording studio. I just know that when I heard "Enter Sandman," I freaked out. The coincidence was mind-boggling and served as another reminder that I would never escape Metallica's shadow. It would always be there, looming long and dark.

I have developed at least some sense of humor about all of this in my middle age. You can tilt at windmills for only so long, after all, and with much work and assistance from those who know me best, I have learned to appreciate all that I have in my life. But at the time I was fucking enraged. I've taken a lot of verbal abuse over the years for never quite letting go of Metallica. Some of it is justified. I know some people look at me—and I include Lars and James in this camp—and say, "Why can't you just be happy with what you've achieved?" And they're right. Selling twenty million albums is no minor accomplishment. But it's about half what Metallica has sold, and I was supposed to be part of that.

You had to be there to understand what it was like, to feel like you're changing the world. And then to have it pulled out from under you and to see and hear reminders of what might have been every single day, for the rest of your life. And you know—you just fucking know—whatever you accomplish, somehow it will never be quite good enough.

That was me.

I was like the guy driving a BMW 5 Series and hating the damn thing because his neighbor went out and bought a 7. You never win those battles. You just make yourself miserable trying.

BY THE TIME we got deep into the *Countdown to Extinction* tour, I was well on my way to becoming a mess. It's never just one thing that provokes a relapse. Addiction is much more complicated than that. I can point to numerous factors that contributed to what ultimately became a near-death experience: clashes with other guys in the band, pressure to feed the gaping maw that Megadeth had become, the loneliness of life on the road, the self-loathing I'd known as a kid that periodically kicked my ass as an adult. Take your pick.

For whatever reason, or combination of reasons, I found myself cracking open a hotel minibar one night and throwing back a few beers. The rationalization was right at my fingertips: I was working hard, missed my wife and my son; I deserved a drink. And anyway, my real problem was cocaine and heroin; a few beers wouldn't hurt.

Wrong again.

Before long I was stumbling around like Mickey Rourke in *Barfly.*

"Here's to all my friends!"

Except there weren't any. Not really. It was just me and the bottle. Later in the tour I came down with a sore throat, probably should have taken some time off, but instead, at the urging of management and record company execs, I kept plugging away, aided by cough syrup laced with codeine. Codeine is an opiate, and pretty soon I was bracing for concert appearances with shots of cough syrup. When that ran out, I switched to vodka and 7 Up, with a cognac chaser. Pam and Justis joined the tour in early 1993, and Pam immediately became concerned. For one thing, she was worried about my health. For another, she found me physically repulsive.

"You stink," she said. "You smell like a drunk."

Using my astute alcoholic mind, I switched to Valium, which is really nothing more than concentrated alcohol, at least in terms of its effect on the brain. Since I was a rock star, it wasn't enough to get ten or twenty tablets; I needed five hundred, approximately enough to keep me stoned for the next couple years. Little did I know that Valium has a long half-life: it stays in your system, working its magic, long after it's been metabolized. You take one, and the next day you still have half of it in you. Take another one the day after the first, and you've got one and a half in you. And so on. It builds up to lethal levels pretty quickly. Pam became suspicious and eventually found my stash of pills, prompting a complete confession on my part.

"I'm tired of the tour, I'm tired of Megadeth, I'm not having any fun . . . and you don't want me to drink, so I'm taking Valium instead."

"You have to stop," she said. "You're going to kill yourself."

"I know."

I agreed to throw out the pills. Pam watched as I flushed them all down the toilet by the handful.

Well, almost all of them, anyway. I kept about three dozen, which I ate in a single sitting when I got back to California, an act of self-destruction and stupidity that resulted in hospitalization and a brush with death. I ended up at Beverly Hills Medical Center, under the care of a physician who shall remain nameless, but let's just say he was commonly referred to as Dr. Feelgood. We had become rather friendly after my many trips to his treatment center, but there's no question that this guy was way out there on the ethical fringe. The first time we met, the guy challenged me to an arm-wrestling match. This dude was in his seventies, but he had Jack Lalanne guns, and it took him all of about ten seconds to slap my bony junkie wrist to the table.

"Great," I responded. "Now that you've dislocated my arm, can I please get some fucking drugs?"

Believe it or not, that was not an unreasonable request in rehab. First thing they would do is hook me up to a Versed drip, then pump in some nutrients and top it off with Vistrol or Klonopin. Before long you'd be as high as you were on the street. This trip, after the Valium overdose, was not much different. To get me back on my feet, Dr. Feelgood prescribed, among other things . . . Valium! And after I was fucked-up to the point of stupefaction, the guy came into my room and talked me into buying his house.

I shit you not.

No attorney, no notary public. Nothing. Just me and the doc and an offer sheet. I don't know why I signed it. Hell—I was out of my mind at the time. A better question is, what kind of physician gets his patients loaded and then sells them real estate? Answer: a charlatan. And a drug addict. Dr. Feelgood was both. Turned out the old geezer was shooting up in his crotch at the hospital. No traffic down there anyway, so who the hell would notice? Predictably, he eventually died of an overdose himself, which in my experience is the exit chosen by a significant number of folks in the rehab business.

Anyway, while at the treatment center I began to wither away— emotionally, spiritually, physically. The last of these was the least of my concerns. Frankly, I didn't give a shit whether I lived or not, and for a while it looked like I wouldn't. One day I tripped and fell in the bathroom—just stumbled between the toilet and tub—and opened a nasty gash on my arm. I called Pam and told her that I thought I was being overmedicated and that I needed her help. By the end of the day she and Ron Laffitte had picked me up and put me on a plane. The destination was a place known as the Meadows, a rehabilitation facility located in Wickenburg, Arizona.

I'll be candid: I remember almost nothing of my first week at

Wickenburg, which is where I very nearly died. It took that long for my body to detox and recover. Once I was rid of the drugs, and beyond the risk of succumbing to a coronary event, which is not impossible in the early stages of rehab, the truly hard and painful work began. Seven weeks of intense inpatient counseling and therapy. Not just for me, either. Early in the process it was determined that Pam and I would benefit from couples counseling. If you've never visited that particular corner of psychotherapy hell, well, let me tell you—it's a real fucking treat.

I blame none of this on Pam. She expected a storybook marriage to a rock star, and instead she got . . . me: a philandering, drug-addicted, alcoholic, suicidal madman. On the bad days, anyway. And there had been far too many of those in the first two years of our marriage. The confronting of this reality, however, was tantamount to torture. Couples counseling led to a therapeutic hall of mirrors. In addition to the usual AA-style group encounters, I was sent to a men's therapy group, a sex workshop, an anger-management workshop . . . and on and on. It seemed, in their eyes, that the only compulsion I lacked was the need to gamble. Then again, it was pretty clear that I was gambling with my life and livelihood, so maybe I didn't miss that one after all. Some of it was beneficial, for sure. But a lot of it was utter bullshit. I couldn't draw a straight line between being a heroin addict (which I was) and a sex addict (which I wasn't, the occasional drunken indiscretion notwithstanding). The counselors' argument, though, was that all the behaviors were linked, and that simply by virtue of my line of work, I had been exposed to and adopted a broad spectrum of loathsome habits, all of which needed to be addressed. My poor wife was encouraged to attend Al-Anon meetings but lasted only a few minutes. All those miserable women openly fantasizing about castrating their spouses while they slept and then hugging each other in support afterward. It made Pam's skin crawl.

And then there were the two separate versions of "family week"

that I was compelled to endure. This was the highlight—or low-light—of the rehabilitation process, similar in theme to "making amends" when you're in AA. It's a rite of passage, so to speak. A post-intervention intervention. You sit down with your loved ones, and they unburden themselves of all their pent-up anger and re-sentment, confronting you with every hurtful or embarrassing act you've ever committed, sober or straight, actually. It's brutal, and I went through it twice. Once with Pam and my sisters (my blood family), and once with the guys in Megadeth (my profes-sional family). Both sessions were intense, revealing, cathartic. My bandmates at first were so angry that they didn't even want to take part in the process, but once given the green light to crap all over me, they didn't hold back. It wasn't just my drug use that bothered them but the fact that I had put their careers at risk. I understood that. I had fired previous members of Megadeth for precisely the same reason. But I don't believe they understood the depth of my problem at that point or the extent of my suffering. I wasn't even sure I wanted to continue writing songs or playing music. I sure as hell didn't know if I wanted to continue with Megadeth. What I did know, however, was that I was incapable of going out on tour at that time, an admission that deeply disturbed the other guys in the band as well as our management.

We had canceled a heavily promoted tour in Japan after I was hospitalized. Now that I seemed to be recovering, the guys wanted to resurrect that tour. Most adamant was Marty Fried-man, who by this time had basically gone off the reservation. Marty was completely enamored of Japanese culture, to the point that he eventually became like Richard Chamberlain in *Shogun*.*

---

* Indeed, Marty now lives and works full-time in Japan; we used to joke that Marty misunderstood his mother's directive: when she told him to marry a JAP, she meant Jewish American Princess.

It had been a nearly lifelong goal of Marty's to play at Budokan, and my relapse had cost him that opportunity. For that I was truly sorry. But not so sorry that I was willing to go straight from Wickenburg to Japan. The guys ultimately, if begrudgingly, accepted my apology and supported my decision. This was not the case with our agent, Andy Summers, who had rebooked the tour, which also included dates in Australia, without my permission or knowledge. We canceled a second time, further angering Japanese audiences and promoters. Then we fired Andy.

IT WOULD BE June before Megadeth performed live. We had accepted an offer to appear on the same bill as Metallica and Diamond Head at the Milton Keynes Bowl in Buckinghamshire, England. From there we would embark on a European tour. In order for this to happen, though, changes were necessary. At management's urging, an abstinence policy was put in place. I didn't disagree with the notion of running a clean and sober tour, but I had doubts about whether such behavior could be legislated. It just seemed a bit excessive and frankly impossible to enforce. We were all adults, after all. Our management was adamant, though, and I went along. Each of us was expected to sign a contract stating our intent to abstain from all alcohol and drug use while on tour; additionally, a confidentiality clause prohibited band members and crew from discussing events that occurred while on tour or in the studio. In other words, what happens in the band stays in the band. Again, a noble sentiment . . . until you demand that people accept it. At that point it stops being noble and becomes somewhat fascist.

But such was the atmosphere in Megadeth at the time. Extreme measures to deal with an extreme problem. Although I don't

Diamond Head, Megadeth, and Metallica
at Milton Keynes National Bowl, Milton
Keynes, England, on June 5, 1993.
Photograph by Ross Halfin.

think he was the only one who disagreed with the policy, Nick
Menza ultimately was the lone holdout when it came to signing
the documents. And this led to an ugly encounter between the
two of us. We had just arrived at our hotel after a transatlantic
flight, and while checking in I approached Nick and asked why he
hadn't yet complied.

"Fuck that!" he screamed. "I ain't signing a fucking thing!"

The outburst didn't really surprise me. Nick's approach to
conflict resolution was to get progressively louder and more hostile, until his opponent either surrendered or walked away out of
embarrassment. I always liked Nick; I thought he was a good kid
with a bad temper and insecurity issues. Usually I cut him slack
in these matters, but not this time. If sobriety was the mandate,

Flannel was the new black T-shirt. I hated it because the metal scene was quickly starting to look like a Pearl Jam show.
Photograph by Ross Halfin.

professionalism the goal, then we would all have to abide by the rules. Including Nick.

The argument went on for some time, until finally I backed him into a corner. "Nick, if you're going to drink and be in this band, you and I are going to have problems."

"Fuck you. I quit!"

This was less than twenty-four hours before we were scheduled to go onstage, and while I doubted Nick was crazy enough to walk away from Megadeth, I considered it a personal affront that he would even threaten to quit.

"Dude, if you quit tonight, you are fucking with my bread and butter," I said. "And if you do that, you are going to have to pay."

And then he told me to fuck off, which basically sent me into blackout mode. Using a martial arts move known as an Eagle Claw, I grabbed him by the throat, locking my left thumb against his windpipe and cocking my right arm at the elbow. By this time I had completely lost it; I was about two seconds away from crushing Nick's larynx and pummeling the shit out of his face, all at the same time. Fortunately, we had in our employ at the time a bodyguard named George who was a rather formidable man. A former Green Beret, George sprang into action, grabbing me from behind and immobilizing me until the rage subsided. We spent the rest of the night trying to heal damaged egos and come to some sort of reconciliation. Eventually the issue was resolved and we played the next night with Metallica and Diamond Head. But it wasn't what it might have been.

Obviously this was a big deal—to be appearing on the same bill as my former bandmates. But I was determined to play it cool; I wouldn't let anyone see me flinch, wouldn't appear too eager or— God forbid—starstruck. As soon as I saw James I wanted to talk to him really badly, the way you would with an old friend. Unfortunately, the nice guys in Metallica had a twisted sense of humor. They invited me into their dressing room, where a big plate of what appeared to be cocaine sat beckoning and unattended. I was really disappointed in them for that. Maybe they didn't know I was trying to stay sober, and it was like they had reached a new low by trying to leave a plate of white stuff out in their dressing room to tempt me—or to make fun of me. It just reinforced what I already knew: that Metallica could do no wrong, while Megadeth was perceived as a band that lived for the party.

We were, in fact, a broken band. Everything now was about money and drugs and power and ego. It wasn't about music and it sure as hell wasn't about camaraderie. We were having enough trouble in our band, but this should have been one of those times when everyone was willing to say, "Shit, yeah! We're playing with Diamond Head and Metallica!" Instead, we were saying, "If I want to drink a fucking beer, I'm going to drink a fucking beer!" As if that mattered. I looked at Nick and saw a man who was willing to throw everything away for a bottle of Heineken.

In reality, I was exactly the same way. Only now I was one of those insufferable, newly sober drunks whom most people despise. Shit, a few months earlier, I would have despised me.

WE GOT THROUGH the European leg of the tour, came back to the States, and then went out again, this time as the opening act for Aerosmith, in what should have been billed as the Great Sobriety Tour of 1993. Aerosmith had famously cleaned up their act after many years of leading depraved lives of rock 'n' roll excess. Bob Timmons was out on the road with them for this tour, presumably helping the band remain on the straight and narrow.

I can't say that I came away from that tour with any great admiration or respect for Aerosmith. Sure, they were pros, and I had always liked some of their music, but I was kind of surprised at the way we were treated. There were, for example, things we expected, like a chance to perform a decent sound check on the afternoon of a show; a reasonable amount of time (one hour, minimum) for our set; a place to hang our backdrop onstage. Well, after several days of not getting the things we expected— things that were supposedly stipulated in our contract—I got angry. And I started to act out. One night in Dallas, when a fan threw an Aerosmith T-shirt onstage during our set, I blew my nose into it and threw it back into the crowd. After the show, I did a radio interview.

"Dave, we love Megadeth here in Texas," the DJ said. "Why don't you guys play a little longer?"

I laughed. "We don't have a long time to play because Aerosmith don't have a long time to live."

I thought that was kind of funny. Apparently Joe Perry and Steven Tyler did not. They heard the interview while cruising in their limo to the show. The next day I was having lunch at a Taco Bell when our tour manager came up to me and said, "Hey, Dave, just want to let you know we're going home today. We got kicked off the tour."

I nearly choked on my chalupa. "What? You're kidding."

"Nope. Sorry."

I didn't ask for an explanation. Instead, for some reason, I wanted to know who would be replacing us.

"Jackyl," he said.

Oh, God.

Here we were, a multiplatinum band riding the crest of a huge hit record . . . and we got booted in favor of a cheesy, third-rate, heavy metal–southern rock hybrid.

You almost had to laugh at the insanity of it all.

Almost . . .

THE INNER WEASEL

"Jesus, man. Relax. This ain't New Jack City."

I LIKED THE ARIZONA DESERT. IT WAS STARK AND VAST, A DAILY REMINDER THAT SOMEWHERE OUT THERE WAS A COSMIC PLAN IN WHICH I PLAYED ONLY A MINOR, ALMOST IMPERCEPTIBLE ROLE. PERSPECTIVE, I GUESS YOU'D CALL IT. AND, OF COURSE, IT SEEMED LIGHT-YEARS AWAY FROM LOS ANGELES AND HOLLYWOOD, AND THE TOXIC FUMES OF FAME. SO EVEN THOUGH I HAD BEEN DISCHARGED FROM THE MEADOWS AND GIVEN A (TEMPORARY) CLEAN BILL OF HEALTH, PAM AND I HAD DECIDED THAT PHOENIX WOULD BE OUR NEW HOME. WE WOULD LIVE AND WORK THERE. TO HELP FACILITATE THIS PLAN, DAVID ELLEFSON AND MARTY FRIEDMAN MOVED TO ARIZONA AS WELL, SO THAT WE COULD COLLABORATE MORE EFFICIENTLY ON THE NEXT MEGADETH RECORD, YOUTHANASIA.

After a seriously bad haircut. The numbers on the tape were a private affair.
Photograph by Ross Halfin.

The only person in the band who refused to be uprooted was Nick Menza.

I don't believe Nick was offended by my efforts to maintain sobriety or that he was less committed to the band. In reality, while Nick may have been struggling a bit more with his own personal demons at the time, everything about Megadeth had become a bit of a grind. The bigger we got, the more we fought. We battled mainly about creative and financial issues: the types of songs we would record, who would write the songs, and how much each member of the band would be paid. To sort out these issues, as well as to address various personality conflicts, we held group therapy sessions on an almost weekly basis. These were excruciatingly painful; typically, my role was to sit at the center of the room and listen to everyone else tell me what an arrogant, egotistical, insensitive asshole I had been.

"And oh, by the way, Dave, I'd like some more money, please."

Publishing revenue became an endless source of conflict. In the beginning of Megadeth, it had all been so simple: if you wrote the song, it was yours. End of story. Then the whining began: *"Wah, wah, wah! I'm not getting enough money. It's not fair."* The problem was this: the record company wanted me to write the songs. Preferably, all of them. And those I didn't write I was expected to modify and improve through endless tweaking and tinkering. It would have been easier for me and healthier for everyone in the band if our songwriting abilities had been equal. But that simply wasn't the case, and everyone knew it.

So we adopted a new and ever-changing business model, one that divided the royalty pie into ever-smaller pieces. Here's the way it had worked in the early days. If you wrote the music, you got 50 percent. If you wrote the lyrics, you got 50 percent. If you wrote both, you received 100 percent of the royalties on that song. If you wrote the lyrics and collaborated with another band member on the music, then you would receive 75 percent of the royalties on that song; the person with whom you collaborated on the music would receive 25 percent. If you wrote nothing—if you were just a musician playing in the studio and going out on tour—well, you got nothing in the way of royalties. You received a very high salary and a cut of the gate at live events. For someone in Megadeth, at its peak, that wasn't exactly chump change, especially when endorsements and merchandising revenue were factored into the equation. For all of us, it was a better life than we could ever have imagined.

This was about as complicated as I ever wanted the formula to be. Unfortunately, each time a zero was added to the back end of a royalty statement, envy and jealousy increased accordingly, prompting further intervention and retooling of the accounting process. If one person wrote the lyrics, everyone else would have a chance to add or change a few lines, effectively creating a three-way or four-way split on the lyrics alone. The same would be true of the music. It was maddening.

"Can't one of you guys just write a fucking song by yourself?" I would say.

There was a pivotal moment while touring in support of *Youthanasia* where we discussed this subject in all its inane glory. It happened at a ramen shop in Tokyo. All four of us were there: me, Nick, Marty, David. As it usually did in those days, talk centered not on music or stage shows or anything that might have been beneficial, but rather on money.

"You know what?" Nick said. "I think we should have a collaboration fee."

"A what?" I had no idea what he was talking about, although I didn't like the sound of it.

"You know—a system for making sure everyone gets paid when we're writing music." Nick's face lit up. He was about to say something important, something that would drive his point home. "It's like Kenny G. He says he can't write unless his whole band is in there collaborating with him."

There was a long, stultifying pause. Then I erupted.

"You think I'm going to pay you to be my muse or something? That's ridiculous!"*

Lunch went on in silence after that, and we all returned to our hotel rooms. Somewhere along the way I made a mental note that Megadeth had changed forever. We were now, first and foremost, a business entity.

DESPITE THE INFIGHTING and bickering, the machinery of Megadeth chugged along. I was less concerned with healing those relationships than with trying to figure out why the hell I was so drawn to self-flagellation of one type or another. Call it a spiritual quest, a psychological walkabout that brought me in contact with an assortment of mystics, shamans, and priests, virtually all of whom had something interesting, if not downright crazy, to offer on the subject of my inner turmoil.

I went to a woman who was a spiritual healer and whose "gift" was much like that of anyone who says that they have a gift: it could have come from God, or it could have come from Satan, or she could have been full of crap and nothing would happen at all. However, when I first went to see her, she knew stuff about me and did work on me that left me feeling better. I went through

---

* No disrespect to Kenny G intended. I'm actually friendly with the dude. His kids are musicians with an interest in playing metal, so our paths have crossed on a few occasions.

every procedure she told me to do. I trusted her. Until she had a guru come work for her. This guy did acupuncture on her and stuck a needle in her vaginal area that triggered uncontrollable multiple orgasms. She left her husband for this Indian rajah, who performed a "clearing" on me using needles and cupping. So stressful was the procedure that the little fellow fainted, but not before reporting that he had seen a spectral image of a man in a silver turban who proclaimed to the rajah, "I will release him now." This, supposedly, was the beginning of my being freed from the satanic influence that had been impressed upon me as a kid. Then there was the Filipino priest whose cleansing procedure included the vision of a demonic bull's head emerging from my stomach.

Okay . . . I would be the first to admit that all of this could be bullshit, but I was willing to experiment. I was searching. For what? I didn't really know. Answers, maybe. Peace. The power to change my life. I studied Mary Ann Williamson's *A Course in Miracles*. I joined a men's group and tried to embrace all that *Iron John* nonsense. I did everything except turn to God, because, frankly, that was the last place I wanted to look.

So, for comfort, I turned to the warm familiarity of alcohol and drugs. There was a drug dealer living in our neighborhood, and the two of us got to be friendly, started hanging out, getting high once in a while. Pretty soon it became more than once in a while, and before I knew it, I was back in rehab. I wouldn't call it a full-blown relapse (yes, there are degrees of addiction, hard as that might be to comprehend). This was a period in which I was, once again, drifting in and out of sobriety; I was the newcomer to AA meetings and support groups on numerous occasions, although I was hardly a neophyte. I just kept bouncing back to the starting line.

The funny (or sad) thing was, I had begun to carve out a niche in the overpopulated, sanctimonious twelve-step universe. I would attend meetings, memorize platitudes, sponsor other

Photograph by Daniel
Gonzalez Toriso.

drunks and junkies, all the while acting as though I had something of substance to add to their lives. I'd walk into a room, stand up and tell my story, try to sound either profound or funny, or both: "Hi, I'm Dave, and I am a recovered addict and alcoholic; I mean . . . I'm more like a dope-seeking missile, and for those of you who have done inner-child work, well, I have an inner weasel." Everyone would *oooh* and *aaah* and give me a big round of applause. For a while it actually went to my head. I developed a sense of spiritual superiority (again, this is not uncommon among recovering addicts and alcoholics) that was completely unwarranted and unearned. But all that went away when I began hanging out with my neighbor—hard to do much proselytizing when you just bought an eight ball of coke and a gram of heroin.

SOMEHOW THE RECORD got made. We started at a place called Phase Four Studios in Phoenix, but technical problems necessitated a move to another venue early in the process. Logic and financial prudence dictated a return to Los Angeles, where studio time was plentiful, but there was no way I was leaving Arizona at that point. I liked the desert, and I took comfort in being some distance from the craziness of L.A.

Anyway, on the advice of Max Norman, we built our own studio in a rented Phoenix warehouse and went to work.

On October 31, 1994—Halloween, appropriately enough—*Youthanasia* was released. At the same time, the very first Megadeth website went up on the Internet, giving fans a chance to interact with band members through live chat sessions and e-mail as well as keep up with various promotional activities and band news.* With Max and I coproducing, *Youthanasia* was, in many ways, the most polished and accessible Megadeth record to date. A bit more melodic and radio-friendly. Still true to our thrash metal roots—with snarling vocals and buzz-saw riffs—but

At Milton Keynes backstage by the trucks. Photograph by Ross Halfin.

clearly inching toward a stylistic change that would soon become uncomfortably aspirational (in a mainstream sort of way). This went over well with some critics, not so well with others. Fans seemed to have no problems whatsoever. *Youthanasia* opened at number four on the album charts—basically shipping at platinum levels, it was the fastest-selling record in the band's history.

* Remember—this was 1994; I think it's fair to say we were a little ahead of the curve on this one.

The pace of life naturally quickened. For much of the next year we worked virtually nonstop, touring in the United States, Europe, Asia, and South America (twice). We contributed songs to soundtracks, put out a compilation of previously unreleased tracks and a documentary called *Evolver: The Making of* Youthanasia; we filmed the obligatory music videos. This proved to be more trouble than it was worth, since the video that accompanied the single "A Tout le Monde" was stricken from MTV's rotation, thanks to a controversy surrounding the lyrics, which supposedly advocated suicide. It didn't. I wrote it, so I should know. Here's what really happened. We had performed the song live on MTV in 1994, the day *Youthanasia* was released, at an event known as Night of the Living Megadeth. At one point I screwed up the set list and delivered a brief monologue before what I thought would be "Skin o' My Teeth."

"This next song is about how many times I've tried to kill myself!"

Only it wasn't. The next song was "A Tout le Monde," which isn't about that at all (although it is about death and dying). At that point I had two choices: do a new intro and admit my mistake, or just play "A Tout le Monde." Changing the set list and playing "Skin o' My Teeth" was not an option. We were on live television and everyone else was ready to dive into "A Tout le Monde," so that's what we did. Predictably, the shit hit the fan, and "A Tout le Monde" was dubbed a "suicide song" and Megadeth a band that advocated suicide. Didn't help, of course, that the album was called *Youthanasia*, although any idiot could figure out the title was merely a play on words, intended as a sly reference to the numbing effect of societal influences on the youth of America. Kids got it. Kids dug it. Adults flipped out. Pretty typical.

By the time we got to the Monsters of Rock festival in Brazil, in September of 1995, we were all exhausted and in a perpetual state of agitation. This should have been a highlight of the *Youthanasia*

tour—playing with Ozzy and Alice Cooper, among others—but I just wanted to go home and clear my head. Maintaining the energy and goodwill needed to sustain a tour of this magnitude is challenging under the best of circumstances; for Megadeth it was almost impossible. Sure, we had some fun, played a bunch of places we'd never played before, but it got to the point where we were going through the motions, and that's a soul-sucking experience. I was neither strung out nor sober, but rather somewhere in the middle. I do know that I was growing weary of band politics, to the point that I had begun looking for other creative outlets. I had come to detest the sight of my own bandmates because all they seemed to care about was money. I now feel differently about most of them, of course—time and sobriety will do that. In that moment, however, I had a difficult time accepting the fact that I was paying for everything and bearing the burden of responsibility for Megadeth's success or failure, and these guys were constantly complaining about money.

I needed something different—a breath of fresh air. I just wanted to be happy, to make music in a way that was simple and fulfilling. And I wasn't getting that with Megadeth at the time.

One of the first people with whom I discussed a possible side project was Jimmy DeGrasso, who was down there playing drums for Alice Cooper's band. Jimmy was open to the idea, and we agreed to talk more after the tour, when we got back to the States. It was all kind of nebulous at the time, just something I kept in my head as a necessary distraction from the routine of Megadeth. I thought about getting Flea from the Red Hot Chili Peppers to play bass, but he was unavailable, so I went after Robert Trujillo, who was then playing in Suicidal Tendencies. Robert was terrific, but he was more of a funk player, and he was too busy anyway, so he referred me to a protégé of his named Kelly LeMieux, who was barely eighteen years old but a really promising bass player. I met Kelly, heard him play, invited him to join the project. He accepted.

All that remained was to find a singer, since I wanted to focus on writing, producing, and playing guitar. My first choice was Jello Biafra of the seminal punk band the Dead Kennedys. Jello had a reputation for being a bit cranky and antagonistic, and in our first meeting he didn't disappoint.

Within the first five minutes he'd launched into an impressive, if incomprehensible, political screed about various multi-national corporations and their connections to the military-industrial complex, and nuclear warheads, and how they offer financial support to companies that produce automatic weapons that end up in the hands of white supremacists, and Corporation X does this, and Corporation Y does that . . . and on and on, until my head was spinning.

I finally cut him off. "Whoa, wait a minute, bro. I just want to do some songs. I didn't come here to get beat to death with propaganda."

We never came to terms, but I left that encounter with a healthy dose of respect for Jello, who more than lived up to his legend. He was using crutches that night, for example, and when I asked him what had happened, he explained that he had been out to a punk rock club one night recently and had gotten into a little altercation with some of the patrons. As he related the story, I laughed out loud.

Beautiful, man. The fucking grandfather of punk getting beat up by a bunch of punks! How awesome is that?

With Jello out of the picture I was left with few choices. I envisioned a band that would combine elements of punk rock, metal, and classical musicianship, and I needed a punk singer who would understand what I was after. The only other person I knew who fit the profile was Lee Ving, a soulful and talented singer for the L.A. punk band Fear. Lee signed on right away, and I began writing the songs that would appear on the record. It all came together rather quickly. The band would be called MD.45, based on a combination of our initials: MD (Mustaine, Dave) and VL (Ving, Lee), the Roman numeral for 45. Or so I thought anyway; not technically correct, as it turns out, but what the fuck? It's still a cool name for a band.

Around this same time, my drug use escalated considerably. I had problems with my band, problems with my manager and agent, problems with my wife. I had big fucking problems, and I dealt with them in the way I often had: by getting high. While we were out on tour in support of *Youthanasia*, Max Norman dismantled the Arizona studio and took everything back to California. I wanted Max to work with me on the final mix of the MD.45 record, so I began spending time in Van Nuys, where Max had reassembled the studio. While there I resurrected a friendship with my old buddies, heroin and cocaine. Very quickly my life began to spiral out of control.

Pam knew all of this was happening but felt powerless to stop it. God knows she tried. One day she called my friend and martial arts mentor, Sensei Benny "the Jet" Urquidez, and asked if he could stop in and pay me a visit at the studio. Maybe, she thought, the mere sight of Benny would shame me into submission. It didn't quite work out that way. I was ashamed, all right, but my response was one of flight rather than fight. I kept walking into different rooms, trying to avoid any contact with Sensei. He would follow me patiently, try to talk with me, and I would just ignore him. Playing it back now, in my mind's eye, I can't believe the way I acted. Here was this legendary man, at least as prominent a figure in martial arts as I was in heavy metal, reaching out to me, trying to save my life, and I was acting like a disrespectful fool: sneaking out back doors, hiding from him. Just talking about it, all these years later, still provokes a feeling of profound embarrassment.

After I left the studio that day I went straight to my dopeman's house and holed up for a while. Some guy came to the door and handed him a package. They shook hands, laughed, and then my friend opened the package and let the contents spill out onto a table. What I saw was remarkable: huge rocks of cocaine and heroin, which he immediately began breaking into smaller, more manageable pieces. Sirens should have gone off in my head, but in my twisted state of mind, all I could think was, *Holy shit. This guy delivers!*

It was easy to be friends with my dealer because there were no expectations or responsibilities. We were junkie pals, bound by a craving for numbness, and that's about it. I had a choice at this time. I could have gone back to Arizona and met with the band and with management, and confronted head-on all of the challenges we were facing. But I wasn't willing to do that, and I wasn't willing to tell them how I really felt, without fear of consequence. I couldn't deal with the possibility that they might quit and I'd be all alone, and then it would be just like when I was a kid, packing up in the middle of the night and running away from my father, leaving my friends behind and starting all over again. If you think that kind of experience doesn't have an impact on a child, you're wrong. It totally tripped me out as far as building any kind of meaningful relationships. I presumed that friendships weren't meant to last; they were meant to be ripped apart.

Some people, though, will surprise you. When you try to push them away, they don't move. And when you need help, they'll be there for you, even if you don't want them to be there.

I'd gotten to know Hadar Rahav in that way that people sometimes do as they approach middle age: through our children. Justis was attending the same school as Hadar's kids, and we'd struck up a friendship based on that simple, timeless commonality. I liked Hadar right away. I was also somewhat in awe of him, for many of the same reasons that I was in awe of Sensei. Hadar was a serious man, a tough guy not merely in appearance but in actuality.

His father, Nathan Rahav, was a national hero in Israel and that obviously left its imprint on Hadar, who grew up to become a commando in the Israeli army before eventually coming to the United States to work in private security. When Hadar and I would talk, and he'd share bloody tales of war and counterterrorism, I sometimes felt like the little kid who used to read comic books and dream about becoming a superhero. This was a guy who had actually done a lot of the things that most men only fantasize about doing.

It's not surprising that when Pam found out I wasn't in the studio working with Max Norman, but rather hiding out, she turned to Hadar for advice and assistance. Actually, that wasn't the first thing she did. Before calling Hadar, she called our business manager and instructed him to block access to any of my bank accounts. Practically speaking, this was not the most expedient manner in which to deal with my lost weekend, but she had to do something.

I had intended to make a brief visit to the dope house—just pick up enough stash to last a few days and then get back to work. Instead, I hung out for a while. And then a while longer, until eventually I lost track of time. I preferred smoking or snorting, which still seemed to me a less queasy and creepy method of delivery. But on this particular journey I was completely out of my mind: stoned, depressed, suicidal. Whatever inhibitions I might have had, they melted away in that apartment, until pretty soon I was pulling liquid heroin into a syringe and injecting it into a vein.

How long did it last? A few days, I think. Less than a week. We sat around in a perpetual state of intoxication, listening to music, eating, ignoring the outside world. At some point there was a phone call. My dealer answered. Knowing Pam would eventually figure out where I was hiding, I had told him I didn't want to talk with anyone. He stood there for a moment, phone in hand, listening. Then he cupped the mouthpiece.

"It's someone at the studio. They've got some mixes for you to approve?"

I nodded, motioned for him to hand me the phone. "Yeah, this is Dave."

"You asshole!"

Oh, shit. Pam. "Hey, baby," I cooed, trying to turn on the charm.

"Fuck you! I'm out here right now with Hadar, and we're coming up to get you."

"No, no, no. That's okay, I'll come down."

So I walked outside, where Hadar and Pam were waiting, along with a phalanx of security vehicles filled with Hadar's commando buddies, prepared, it seemed, for a firefight of epic proportions.

"Jesus, man. Relax," I said. "This ain't New Jack City."

Pam didn't laugh. "Get in the car," she said. "We're leaving. Right now."

"Yeah, okay, just let me go inside and get my stuff."

Hadar was standing next to her now. He shook his head. "You're not going anywhere. You're coming with us."

They had reasoned—correctly, I might add—that if I'd gone back inside, I would have shot up again. One for the road, as it were. Given the fact that I was already completely fucked-up, with toxic levels of heroin and cocaine coursing through my body, I'm not sure I would have walked back out of that apartment. I might have died. Frankly I didn't care one way or the other.

They put me in a car and drove to a rehabilitation facility in Santa Monica called Steps. Along the way I asked if we could stop so that I could get some candy. We pulled off the highway, and when Pam and Hadar got out of the car, I proceeded to get loaded, using a small amount of heroin wrapped in tinfoil—essentially a smack-filled joint. It's a simple method of delivery: you light the tip of the foil, the heroin begins to scald, and you inhale the smoke. Presto: instant high. By the time Pam and Hadar returned to the car, it was filled with smoke.

"Can't take it in with me," I said. "Might as well not let it go to waste."

They didn't even try to stop me at this point. They just rolled down the windows and pulled out of the parking lot. Wind quickly filled the car, threatening to extinguish the fire, so I rolled the windows back up. And so it went. They rolled the windows down, I rolled them up. Up, down . . . Up, down.

Finally, Hadar began to laugh. "Hey, Pam," he said in a thick Israeli accent. "I think I have a contact buzz."

Pam didn't even smile, just stared out at the open road. She'd been on this trip before, and it had long since lost its humor.

TO SAY I knew the rehab drill would be an understatement; by this time I could have worked the nurse's station. I checked in, went to my room, had something to eat, and then went about the business of detox. The first week or so is always the same: ridding your body of toxins and easing the sting of withdrawal. Then the unpleasant work begins: therapy.

I took some comfort in knowing that Steve C. (as they call him in AA), one of the administrators I'd gotten to know and trust at the Meadows, was now program director at Steps. At the same time, it was a little weird and demoralizing to encounter Steve again in this fashion, knowing that it signaled such a complete and utter failure on my part. That's one of the many challenges of addiction and rehab: you leave a facility, everyone pats you on the back and wishes you well, but you always kind of sense that after you're out of sight, someone says, "He'll be back." In my case, they were usually right. Moreover, my relationship with Steve had devolved since I'd been at the Meadows. For a time, we had been friends. We even went on a Mediterranean cruise together, with our wives. Unfortunately, Pam and Steve's wife, Chantelle, did not get along particularly well (I attribute this to jealousy on Chantelle's part), and the trip became something of a disaster. I had hoped that the lingering ill will wouldn't spill over into my experience at Steps, since I still had considerable respect for Steve's work, but it did.

In one of our first meetings Steve began talking shit. Now, in itself, this is not cause for concern. In fact, it's pretty common in rehab. There's a certain attitude and pose counselors adopt when they want to use a negative motivational treatment:

"Hey, hope your mortgage is paid up, asshole, because you're gonna be dead soon and it would be a shame for your wife and kids to have no place to live."

That sort of thing.

Generally speaking, the more seasoned the addict, the less likely this approach is to have any effect. It sure as hell didn't work with me. Steve tried it anyway, but it was pretty clear that his antagonism—which included several unkind references to Pam—was rooted in genuine anger. He didn't seem to me to be particularly concerned about my treatment or rehabilitation. He was just pissed.

We got past it eventually. I did my time and embraced the program to the best of my ability (which wasn't much). Rehab, for me, has always been primarily a place to heal my body rather than my psyche. It has been, quite literally, a lifesaver. But it's never done much for my spirit. Steps was supposed to be one of the best of the high-end treatment centers—the kind of place known for catering to a celebrity clientele. Really, though, it seemed pretty typical.

There's a weird dynamic in rehab—people gravitate toward like-minded folks as soon as they check in. These arrangements are not discouraged and in fact often are facilitated by program administrators. Everyone in rehab is looking for a surrogate spouse, mother, father, brother . . . whatever. Everyone is broken in some fashion, and you reflexively seek out others who have cracks in the same places so you can compare notes, try to heal each other's wounds. Experience has taught me to question whether this is the healthiest approach (especially with the sex addicts, who end up fucking each other in bathroom stalls), but it is what it is. I'd been at Steps about a week and a half when a kid showed up. He was tall and wiry, with light skin and hair and a compulsion for scrawling graffiti on the walls. It turned out he was a musician and we talked a little, got to know each other, swapped stories—all the usual shit. He was a nice enough kid and I sympathized with his problems, but still . . . the idea that we were suddenly best buddies, just because we were both junkie musicians, didn't make a whole lot of sense. And that dynamic, so common in rehab, is one of the reasons the process has never quite taken hold with me.

Although I will say this: when I left Steps, after thirty days in residence, I was clean and sober.

Again.

SOUL FOR SALE

"Are you out of your fucking mind?!"

RON LAFFITTE IS ONE OF THE MOST POLISHED AND PROFESSIONAL PEOPLE YOU'D EVER WANT TO MEET. I OFFER THAT AS BOTH COMPLIMENT AND CRITICISM, FOR IT REFLECTS RON'S ABILITY TO RISE THROUGH THE MUSIC BUSINESS, SEEMINGLY WITHOUT EFFORT, AS WELL AS HIS UNCANNY KNACK FOR A CERTAIN TYPE OF DIPLOMACY. HE IS THE TYPE OF PERSON WHO CAN LOOK STRAIGHT INTO YOUR EYE, OR INTO THE EYE OF A CAMERA, AND OFFER A LITANY OF COMPLIMENTS, EVEN IF HE REALLY THINKS YOU'RE JUST A PIECE OF SHIT.

THIS IS AN EXTRAORDINARILY VALUABLE SKILL, ESPECIALLY IF YOU'RE PLAYING IN THE UPPER LEVELS OF THE ENTERTAINMENT INDUSTRY. IT'S ALSO ONE I NEITHER POSSESS nor understand. Ron and I had our share of disagreements, some personal, some professional. In the end, the unraveling of our friendship was as inevitable as the termination of our managerial arrangement. Ron provided much of the impetus behind the group therapy sessions that nearly drove me mad while I was in rehab in Arizona. At the same time, or shortly thereafter, I noticed that he seemed to be taking a lesser role in the day-to-day activities of Megadeth. Phone calls would sometimes go unanswered; promotional opportunities would be missed. That sort of thing. While we were out on tour in support of *Youthanasia*, I found out that Ron had accepted a position with Elektra Records. He hadn't told me and I received a call from a friend who told me, rightly or not, that he had no plans to give up his position as manager of Megadeth. If that was true, then that would mean he was going to work both sides of the street. That couldn't happen, obviously. A manager has to fight for his clients; he has to be willing to kick record company executives in the balls, if that's what it takes. Hard to do that when you're taking a paycheck from a record company.

By the time we began making our next record, *Cryptic Writings*, in the fall of 1996, we had separated from Ron and hired Mike Renault of ESP Management. Mike had helped me out while I was working on the MD.45 project, and while that record (*The Craving*) did not do as well commercially as I had hoped (a fact attributable mainly to anemic promotion on the part of Capitol Records) there was much to like about it. Enough that I thought it warranted revisiting several years later. At that time we remastered *The Craving* and replaced Lee Ving's vocals with mine in an effort to entice interest from Megadeth fans who might have overlooked the original.

The late 1990s, it's fair to say, was a time of artistic and creative overhaul for Megadeth. It's also fair to say the changes produced mixed results. *Cryptic Writings* was recorded in Nashville,

with Dann Huff producing. I had first met Dann a few years earlier, around the time Marty Friedman came into the band. We
were holding auditions at a place called the Power Plant, where a
band called Giant was rehearsing in a studio down the hall. Giant
was comprised of Dann and his brother, David Huff, and two
other musicians whose names escape me. Doesn't matter. Despite
the fact that he was primarily a session player, Dann Huff owned
this band, a fact made abundantly clear the first time I heard him
play guitar. I was so impressed that I had one of my guys talk with
Dann about the possibility of sharing a lesson or two.

"Dann doesn't give lessons," I was told.

The response caught me off guard. I bristled. "Well, fuck him!
Doesn't he know who I am?"

"Yeah, he does. He still doesn't give lessons. But he'll be happy
to jam with you."

"Tell him to fuck off!"

That was my mistake, one born of equal parts arrogance and
ignorance. Session cats are a different breed. When they say, "I'll
jam with you," here's what they really mean: "Have a seat, dude,
and I'll show you everything I know." I didn't understand the
rules at the time. By the time we made *Cryptic Writings*, I'd figured it out.

Mike Renault's boss at ESP Management was Bud Prager,
whose lineup in the 1970s and 1980s included Bad Company and
Foreigner. For all practical purposes, Bud and Mike were our
co-managers, and their résumés—Bud's in particular—mitigated
any reservations I might have had that Megadeth might be com-
promising its thrash metal heritage. Under Bud's guidance Foreigner had sold eighty million records in America alone, evolving from a middling rock band to mainstream pop superstars.
You could debate endlessly the quality of the music, but there
was no questioning Foreigner's success. They dwarfed Megadeth. Hell, they dwarfed Metallica. That sounded pretty good

I am adjusting to Arizona life and the tranquillity of the desert. Photograph by Ross Halfin.

to me. And I'll admit it now: I did not go in with my eyes closed. Bud was a hit maker. He wanted us to work in Nashville, slick-city center of the country music industry (and, increasingly, pop music as well), with Dann Huff, a guy most notable for producing crystalline session pop for the likes of Reba McEntire, Michael Jackson, and Céline Dion. Shit, the dude played on "My Heart Will Go On." It doesn't get any more mainstream than that. I knew when we left for Nashville that changes would be made and that as coproducer I would be expected to nudge Megadeth in a direction it had never traveled before. I went there anyway—knowingly, willingly—because I wanted a number one hit. I wanted what Metallica had, even if it meant selling a piece of my soul to the devil.

Fuck it, I figured. It had worked for Robert Johnson, maybe

it would work for me. At the very least, I'd get that long-awaited guitar lesson from Dann Huff.

The work atmosphere in Nashville was intense and professional, if somewhat unnerving, with a constant, unwavering eye on creating something that would transcend the boundaries of thrash and heavy metal. For better or worse, *Cryptic Writings* from the outset was positioned as a record that would feature at least a few melodic, pop-friendly songs. Not an entire album's worth, though. One need only read the lyrics to "She-Wolf" and "The Disintegrators" to find some of that old Megadeth cynicism and political commentary. Granted, some of the most biting songs ("Evil That's Within" and "Bullprick") were left on the editing room floor because Bud deemed the lyrics to be offensive, and the edgier songs that remained were often bathed in shimmering melodies and sweet production, thus softening the blow. Not quite ear candy, but uncomfortably close.

The transformation occurred mostly in the studio, where Dann and Bud assuredly pushed a pop approach. The biggest song on the album, for example, was "Trust," a song that in the earlier Megadeth days might have sounded completely different. It was a hook-laden song made even more radio-friendly through repeated vocal takes. It began with my usual spit-and-snarl delivery, at a hundred miles an hour:

"Lost in a dream . . . nothing's what it seems!"

"Slow down," Dann said. "And try to stretch out the word 'nothing.'"

"Lost in a dream . . . nuuh-thing's what it seems."

Dann rubbed his chin. "Good, good. Now try dropping the G."

"What G?"

"At the end of *nothing*. And slow down just a little bit more, maybe pause after *lost*."

"Lost . . . in a dream . . . nuuh-thin's what it seems."

"Yes! That's it! Perfect!"

Whoa . . .

I realized at that moment I had delivered a vocal line that Tim McGraw would have been proud to call his own. So I took it back, retooled a bit, clipped the country twang, and settled for something that could fairly be described as pop metal. (Indeed, we went back and forth so many times on the word *nothing* that I said Dann's tombstone would read DANN "DIED FOR NUTHIN'" HUFF.)

And that's pretty much the way the entire process went.

There were times when I walked into the studio to find Bud and Dann tinkering with the controls, playing with tracks, without soliciting my input. Normally this would have provoked my spider sense to such a degree that I would have unleashed a torrent of threats and accusations. But I didn't. I suspected they were making modifications, softening the Megadeth sound, and I did nothing to stop them. There would be a payoff at the end, I reasoned.

I wasn't wrong. "Trust," a song about dishonesty, ironically enough, was the biggest hit single in Megadeth history, reaching number five on the

One of my favorite, best fitting leather pants ever, which mysteriously vanished. Photograph by Ross Halfin.

Billboard rock charts; it was also nominated for a Grammy. Three other songs also became Top 20 hits. The album almost achieved platinum status but was in some ways less than I had anticipated. Rather than introducing Megadeth to a vast new audience, it was met with a degree of ambivalence by stalwart fans, who reasonably wondered, *What the fuck is happening here? This isn't my Megadeth! This is like my dad's Megadeth or something.*

I had a little trouble accepting all of this at the time, but in retrospect I can see clearly how it happened and what it meant. Sure, it's possible to become more melodic while remaining essentially true to your metal roots. But it's a delicate dance, especially for a band like ours, which was faster and harder than just about any band that had ever come along. Megadeth was a phenomenon based on raw energy and talent, and when you take that and water it down, it's no longer phenomenal. It's ordinary. By trying to expand your audience, you risk alienating your core fans, and I think we did that with *Cryptic Writings*, and even more so with our next record, the aptly named *Risk*.

A TURNING POINT with *Cryptic Writings* involved an appearance on the Howard Stern show. We had been approached about performing live at a special birthday show for Howard. We hoped this might be a musical breakthrough between us and WXRK, the station that carried Howard's show. "K-Rock," as WXRK was commonly known, was among the most influential album-oriented rock stations in the country; it could, quite literally, make or break a band. As an established multiplatinum band, Megadeth didn't need K-Rock, but certainly its endorsement would have been beneficial in moving the band into a more mainstream position, which, admittedly, is what we were after.

Several months earlier Pam and I had gone to Europe with the twin goals of resting and reconnecting. The plan, stated quite specifically, was to conceive our second child in Paris. We stayed in the lovely Hotel Costes, and though I was not a religious man at this time, I got down on my knees and prayed with Pam for a successful conception and a healthy, happy baby. We actually knelt by the bed before making love and sought God's blessing. This was a new experience for me. I'd prayed *for* sex (*Please, God, let that blonde with the big tits in the front row be at least eighteen years old*); I'd prayed *during* sex (*Please, God, don't let her have anything contagious*); and I'd prayed *after* sex (*Please, God, get her out of here—now!*). But never right before sex.

This time I did. And right afterward, Pam began to cry. Several weeks later we found out she was pregnant. The math clearly indicated the miracle had occurred in Paris—a *French conception*, if you will.

Fast-forward to January 1997: Pam is about to have the baby, and I get this offer to play at Howard Stern's party.

"It's a great opportunity," Bud Prager said. "K-Rock determines the way the entire nation puts its pants on. If they play the single, everyone else will follow."

I made the trip, but not without serious cost to my family. Pam's due date was just a few days before the Stern appearance, so I suggested that if she hadn't delivered by then, maybe we could induce labor.

Pam graciously agreed, and everything worked out perfectly. Our daughter, Electra, was born on January 28, 1998, without complication. A seasoned dad, I actually performed the delivery. Seriously. As the labor progressed without incident and Electra poked her pretty little head out, the doctor said, "Would you like to deliver her?"

"Really? Are you kidding?"

She smiled. "No, sir."

Then she stepped aside, and I pulled my daughter into the world. I didn't just stand there and take a handful of goo; I didn't just cut the umbilical cord. It was much more than that. I was the first person in this world to touch her. I think that's part of the reason we have such a close relationship today.

Two days later we were in New York, playing at Howard's birthday bash. I was pumped. I was a new dad. I was healthy and sober. I was ready to help "Use the Man" get the boost it needed. Although I wasn't a "fan" of the show, obviously I knew about it, understood its reach and influence. I knew that Howard sometimes played Megadeth music on the air, and I appreciated that. I certainly did not look at Howard with disdain; in fact, I viewed him with affection more than anything else.

Our encounter, unfortunately, was less than inspiring. We played our song, then sat on the couch to talk, and right away Howard launched into a typically, antagonistic line of questioning.

"I hear you're a Jehovah's Witness."

"Uh, no. My parents were."

"Really? Did you kill 'em?"

Believe it or not, the conversation went downhill from there, in part because I don't think Howard was particularly interested in talking with me, but also because I wasn't a very good sport.

"I hear you beat up James Hetfield."

"Yeah, that's true."

"Are you gonna beat me up, too?"

By the time the interview ended, I wanted to grab him and say, "Howard, do you have any idea how much you just let me down?" Here was a guy with whom I hoped to perhaps build a friendship. At the very least, I hoped he would appreciate the lengths we'd gone to in order to be on his show. I mean, I had talked my wife into inducing labor! I had three band members and all the people who worked for us relying on me to make the right decision, to write the right song, to dance and move the right way onstage, so that everyone could make enough money to keep their wives happy and to pay for private school tuition and nannies and braces and, well, everything. I stood there in the dressing room afterward, thinking of what a disaster the show had been, and I felt like I had shit the bed.

I went downstairs and saw a representative from the record company, and I could tell from his demeanor that it clearly hadn't gone well. I was hoping that it certainly had nothing to do with Megadeth's performance; we were on fire. I think we kept our end of the bargain. For whatever reason, though, things didn't work out.

WHETHER LIFE IMITATES art or art imitates life, there surely is a point at which the two intersect. I don't know of a single person in the music business—especially in heavy metal—who doesn't find the movie *This Is Spinal Tap* to be both achingly funny and breathtakingly accurate. This is particularly true of Megadeth, as we've known more than our share of bickering, drug use, incompetent management, and personnel changes. Spinal Tap drummers spontaneously combusted; Megadeth's simply proved unreliable or inept or otherwise incompatible with the band's mission, whatever it might have been at a given time.

Nick Menza started out as a wide-eyed kid living a rock 'n' roll fantasy. I loved Nick when he came to the band, and I love him today, but there was a period of time, in the mid to late 1990s, when he simply was not manageable. Ours had been a tempestuous relationship for years, but it reached a breaking point when we went out on tour after *Cryptic Writings*— the road will always exacerbate interpersonal problems within a band. Nick had developed a disturbing habit of hiding gay porno in places designed to provoke the greatest embarrassment when they were discovered. He would, for example, leave mysterious manila envelopes at the front desk of a hotel, so that when the intended target checked in and asked if there were any messages, the clerk would hand him the envelope. The poor bastard would then open the envelope and be treated to some graphic depiction of dude-on-dude fellatio as the unsuspecting desk clerk stood there mortified. This sort of thing happened with alarming regularity. You'd offer a beer to a visitor on the tour bus, and when you opened the cooler, sitting on top would be a picture of some guy fucking another guy up the ass. We all grew tired of this act very quickly. It was just too perverse, even by the depraved standards of heavy metal. Our bus was our home. We were supposed to feel safe there. I didn't want to have to worry about someone opening up a jar of cookies and being exposed to porno just because Nick's comic compass had gone haywire.

But that was only part of the problem with Nick. He also developed serious health issues, some of which were surely related to his lifestyle. He became increasingly agitated and distracted. It got to the point where Nick was sleeping most of the day. He'd skip sound check, wake up maybe thirty minutes before the show, throw on his bike shorts and sneakers, and then go out and play. Predictably, his drumming suffered. There was a crescendo in "Trust" that he kept missing. Night after night. This was not the kind of thing that would have happened to Nick when he was younger and hungrier. It was embarrassing for him, and it was embarrassing for Megadeth, to fuck up the biggest hit single in the band's history.

I watched Nick's decline with a mixture of sadness and anger, but not with any great degree of shock. Megadeth had suffered from every idiosyncrasy that could affect a band. There had been problems with drugs, alcohol, women, and money. None of us emerged unscathed. It was simply Nick's turn.

The split came in the summer of 1998, during a break in the Ozzfest heavy metal tour. We were supposed to reconvene in Dallas. I flew in from my home in Arizona; Nick was supposed to be flying in from L.A. at the same time. I got to the airport—no Nick. I went outside, where our bus was waiting—no Nick. I went back inside, checked the baggage carousel, the bathrooms—no Nick. After looking around for a while, I went back out to the bus, and there was Nick, slumped in a seat, head tilted toward a window. He was wearing Ray-Bans, but I could tell he had been crying. Nick had taken to wearing makeup in an effort to hide the sores on his face, and there were now pasty streaks running down his cheeks. I sat down next to Nick and asked him what was wrong. At first he didn't respond, but eventually he began to talk. He had health issues. That much I knew. I did not expect to hear him say that he had cancer.

Nick had suffered an injury to his knee some time earlier, and the trauma had resulted in the formation of a cyst. Now, Nick told us, the cyst was cancerous. I didn't know whether Nick was diagnosing this thing himself or not, and frankly I didn't care. I just wanted him to be safe and healthy.

"You have to go home," I said. "Don't worry, we'll get somebody else to finish the tour. Our number one priority is to get you well."

There wasn't a lot of time to mourn Nick's departure or even to fret about his condition. We were out on tour, and we needed a new drummer. Immediately. The first person I thought of was Jimmy DeGrasso, who had done a good job on the MD.45 record. Jimmy is like a lot of session players: when he wants a job, he is the most cordial, professional guy under the sun. But if you ask him to be in a band, he kind of feels confined. I've only experienced this once with Jimmy, so I can't say it's a pattern, but it seemed like once he became a member of Megadeth, he changed. In the beginning, though, he was like a breath of fresh air: "Let's play! Let's play!" He was great. But that's the way session musicians are. They're accustomed to being paid by the day, so they're always eager to get right down to work. The downside is that they sometimes lack the ability to see the big picture. They're always thinking about the next paycheck, the next gig, because that's how they've been taught to live. They don't stow anything for the winter; they live for the day. That's not all session guys, of course. Some of them are shrewd and smart, but most are impulsive and short-sighted. It's just the culture.

When Jimmy joined the band, we weren't quite sure what to expect. We all knew he was talented and energetic, but whether he would be able to quickly digest the Megadeth catalog was another matter entirely. It wasn't like he had a lot of time to prepare. I still remember the first night Jimmy played live with us, in Fresno, California, and some of the guys from the other bands in Ozzfest were standing by the stage, waiting gleefully for a train wreck. But Jimmy pulled it off. And he did it without a sound check! This was an outdoor festival, with several bands in the lineup, so we all made do with nothing more than a line check—just to make sure the instruments were working properly. Then we went back to our dressing room, pulled out a big ghetto blaster, and played our songs for Jimmy, who sat there playing air drums, flailing away at nothing, and committing the moves to memory. It was a herculean feat that he pulled off an entire Megadeth set with as few mistakes as he did.

By the time Nick had surgery and got the test results back on his biopsy a couple weeks later, I had already made a decision to hire Jimmy on a full-time basis. I made the call from a hotel room in Portland, Maine, with Bud Prager on another line—I wanted an extra set of ears, because I knew it would be a difficult conversation.

"Hey, Nick, how are you?"

"Good, man. Listen, I got my test results back, and it's malignant—I mean, benign!"

It seemed odd that he would mix up the words like that, especially on something so important. But then, Nick's behavior was generally erratic in those days, his demeanor unpredictable, so you never knew what to make of him or what to believe.

"That's good," I said. "I'm glad to hear it."

"Yeah, thanks. Hey—how are things going with Jimmy?"

I took a deep breath. "Actually, that's why we're calling. Bud's on the line, too, and we want to talk to you."

"Hi, Nick," Bud said, chiming in.

A pause, like he knew something bad was about to happen. Then, "Hi, Bud."

I went on. "So here's the thing, Nick. Things are working out well with Jimmy, and we're going to stick with this lineup for now. Okay?"

Man . . . looking back on it now, I almost cringe. He evidently had lost his enthusiasm for playing in the band and seemed to want time off. Still, my handling of the situation was undeniably callous. The truth is, I'm not very good at letting people go. You trim a dog's tail quickly, right, with a single, swift cut? You don't extend the agony. I know that some people will point to the irony of my firing so many band members after I was unceremoniously dumped by Metallica, but there is a difference. I have never fired anyone without warning. I'm a firm believer in second chances. Some people even deserve a third or fourth chance. Nick had used at least that many.

I expected that Nick would accept his dismissal quietly; on some level, I thought, he wanted this to happen. He had grown tired of Megadeth—or at least he had grown tired of the work required to retain his position. But I was wrong.

"That's not going to happen, guys," he said. "This is my band, too, and I'm going to fight for it."

I thought for a moment before speaking. "Nick, you should have started fighting a long time ago."

By that, I meant that Nick should have thought about what he really wanted. He should have stopped with the jack-in-the-box porno. He should have abandoned all the side projects after we told him to narrow his focus and start taking his job more seriously.

Whenever I tried to address this subject (and others) with Nick, he responded with anger and insecurity. He should have stopped fucking with me all the time—the incessant backtalk and threats, the wiseass overtures about getting in the dojo and sparring.* He should have outgrown the sophomoric behavior and realized, after repeated warnings, that he had one of the best jobs a drummer could hope to land.

HARMONY IS A hell of a thing to chase in a band—metaphorically and literally. Jimmy's integration was nearly seamless. Everybody liked him. He picked up the songs quickly and generally brought some excitement and professionalism to the drum kit. Unfortunately, even as we patched this position, we all began to feel some distance from Marty Friedman. Marty's commitment to Megadeth had waned, primarily because of a

---

* Nick fancied himself some sort of martial arts prodigy, although I never saw any evidence of it.

disinclination to play the type of music Megadeth had become famous for playing, the type of music our fans wanted to hear. In short, I think Marty had an artistic crisis.

Like Chris Poland, I don't think Marty ever really saw himself as a thrash metal guitarist. He was good at it—hell, Marty could play anything—but I don't know that it ever really touched his heart or inspired him. Almost from the time he joined Megadeth, Marty had been unsatisfied with simply playing guitar in the band. To a degree, I tolerated his outside interests, because he was just so talented, but there was a perpetual tug of war—me trying to rein him in, and Marty always pushing, exploring other opportunities. He had done a solo record shortly after joining Megadeth, because he was still under contract to another label.

There was something weird and disconcerting about us not being able to connect on a spiritual level, and yet the guy was out there working and profiting from my art. That's not cool.

When you got right down to it, though, I think Marty's dissatisfaction with Megadeth, and his eventual departure, can be attributed primarily to the fact that he lost interest in the music. You can play the charade for a while, especially if you're as accomplished a musician as Marty. You can stand up onstage and go through the motions, hammering out blistering solos and playing the role of a heavy metal god. The money is good, the girls are good, the drugs are good. Like all of us, Marty enjoyed the fruits of his labor.

Being in a band, living on the road, leading that decadent lifestyle—it can do strange things to people. A few years earlier, when we were making *Countdown to Extinction*, there was one day when a band member brought a video to the studio. It had come to him indirectly from one of the guys in another major act.

"You have to see this," he said mischievously. Then he cued up the video and waited for our reaction.

At the studio in Arizona with my Jackson King V Anarchy model.
Photograph by Ross Halfin.

I'd been around the block a few times; there wasn't much that I found shocking. But the images that flashed across the screen nearly caused me to vomit: some dude in black leather and other bondage accoutrements getting beaten by a fat, naked chick armed with whips and what appeared to be giant knitting needles.

"Holy shit!" I yelled as she drove one of the needles through the guy's nipples, and then through his penis!

But that wasn't the worst of it. Near the end, as the guy was sitting there, beaten and bleeding, the chick took a big, steaming shit on the floor, then grabbed the guy by the back of the head and instructed him to start eating. And he did! At that point I had to leave the room. Marty freaked out as well. It's all of a piece, of course: the lifestyle, the drugs, the sex, the devaluing of human life, and the subsequent debasing of yourself. After a while you just get numb to all of it. Nothing seems too outrageous; nothing seems particularly abnormal. It's all just . . . boring.

I think Marty had reached that point by the time we recorded *Risk*. He began advocating slower, more melodic songs, encouraging a continued progression toward the pop-oriented approach displayed on *Cryptic Writings*. At the same time, he adopted a personal approach to style that reflected a changing attitude toward metal. He cut his hair, dressed differently. In retrospect, it's pretty obvious that Marty had reached the end of his rope with Megadeth. Rather than quit, however, he tried to get the band to adjust to his sensibilities. And with the assistance of Bud Prager and Dann Huff, he nearly pulled it off.

It didn't help matters any that Lars Ulrich had goaded me in the press by suggesting that I was afraid to take chances with my music. He addressed the issue cleverly, offering compliments as well as criticism, but I came away feeling like he'd thrown down the gauntlet:

I respect Dave as a musician; I just wish he'd take more risks, really push himself.

Rather than shrug it off, I let those words burn a hole in my psyche.

I could accept the challenge with our next record. And I could call it *Risk*, just in case anyone didn't get the message.

Not that I wanted it to turn out the way it did. It just sort of . . . happened. There was no intent on my part, but I will admit to some negligence. I knew something was wrong while we were writing the record. Bud stopped by my house one day and suggested we make some changes.

"You know what I want to do?" Bud said. "I want to do a record that will make the guys in Metallica say, 'Son of a bitch! Why didn't we think of that?'"

He pushed the right buttons. Even though I knew it was an unhealthy attitude—backtracking to that old head space that had caused me so much pain, trying to get even with my former bandmates—I acquiesced. Bud was already determined to keep nudging Megadeth away from metal and toward the edges of pop. The final step on this journey would be a song unlike anything we'd ever done.

"Maybe bluegrass," Bud suggested. "Or disco."

"Are you out of your fucking mind?!" I couldn't believe what I was hearing. But he wasn't kidding.

"Look, we had a Top Ten record with *Cryptic Writings*. We had a bunch of hit singles." He paused to let that sink in. "Am I right?"

"Yeah."

"Okay. Do you trust me?"

"Yeah, Bud, I trust you."

We finally settled on something that was based on a synth-pop disco sound. The song was called "Crush 'Em," and it was written as a paean to hockey and hockey fans. I love hockey, and I thought it would be cool to write something that might be played at games as a way to pump up the crowd—something to give us all a break from that inane Gary Glitter song you hear at every sporting event in the world. It wasn't like I was writing it for Megadeth fans or even for radio. I was writing it for hockey. And it got on the record.

The day we recorded the demo for "Crush 'Em" was one of the worst of my professional life. No sooner had we finished than I walked out of the studio, marched straight into a bathroom, and threw up. Basically just the dry heaves—I'd been so upset about the whole process that I hadn't been able to eat that morning. I knew I'd made a big mistake. Bud had convinced the whole band that we needed another hit, and "Crush 'Em" was going to be that song. I could have pulled the plug. But I didn't. I wanted to make everyone happy. I wanted to be a good soldier. If things went bad, at least no one could say that I had been a malcontent.

But it felt all wrong. I kept picturing KISS doing that video for "I Was Made for Lovin' You," and thinking that this was, for Megadeth, a similarly unfortunate miscalculation. I could actually hear the scissors of emasculation.

Oh, this is bad. Bad, bad, bad.

And it was. "Crush 'Em" was featured on the soundtrack of the movie *Universal Soldier: The Return* and became the NHL staple that I'd hoped it would be. Still, I took little comfort in any of that. *Risk* was rightfully rejected by Megadeth fans (who felt betrayed) and panned by critics (who were handed a gift-wrapped opportunity to crap all over us). Although there were elements of *Risk* that worked and lyrics I don't mind claiming as my own, it was largely a failure, an artistic and commercial miscalculation.

In the wake of *Risk*, I vowed to regain my artistic integrity, which meant, first and foremost, taking control of Megadeth. That meant firing Bud Prager, which was not easy, since I liked Bud and have to admit that he did for Megadeth precisely what he was hired to do.* It also meant leaving Capitol Records for a new label, Sanctuary, and convincing the other guys in the band that it was time to get back to our metal roots.

Unfortunately, not everyone agreed.

* Bud, incidentally, passed away not long ago; my condolences to his wife, Gloria, and his son, Evan.

16

SOME KIND OF GOD

"I hate my life. I hate my job. I hate my band. I hate my kids. I hate *you*. I wish I could fucking hang myself right now."

ON MY FORTIETH BIRTHDAY, SOMEWHERE BETWEEN VANCOUVER AND PHOENIX, DURING THE COURSE OF AN EIGHTEEN-HOUR BUS RIDE DOWN THE PACIFIC COAST, I FOUND MYSELF ON THE PHONE, CHATTING WITH MY OLD FRIEND AND NEMESIS LARS ULRICH. I HAD TIME ON MY HANDS, TIME TO REFLECT. TWO DAYS EARLIER WE HAD CANCELED A SHOW IN SEATTLE, IN DEFERENCE TO THE VICTIMS OF THE TRAGEDY OF 9/11. ON THE NIGHT OF SEPTEMBER 12 WE HAD PLAYED IN VANCOUVER BEFORE AN EXTRAORDINARILY GRATEFUL AND WELL-BEHAVED CROWD. SHORTLY AFTER THE SHOW, WITH AIR TRAVEL IN NORTH AMERICA AT A VIRTUAL STANDSTILL, WE BOARDED A BUS FOR THE LONG RIDE

Check out the hydraulics on the back of my right hand! Photograph by Daniel Gonzalez Toriso.

home. Pam had planned a big birthday celebration in my honor, and I didn't want to disappoint her.

But then came a conversation with Lars and an invitation to meet him in San Francisco. The idea, as I understood it, was that Metallica was undergoing some sort of group therapy session—not a bad idea—and perhaps there would be some benefit to addressing my dismissal after all these years. Lars had told me there would be a counselor present. He neglected to say that our meeting would be filmed and used as part of a documentary. I wasn't informed of that until I showed up at the Ritz-Carlton.

You might reasonably wonder why I would subject myself to such painful probing, why I would further delay arrival at the home front in order to satisfy a request from Lars, with whom I was not exactly close. Well, it's hard to explain. Maybe it had something to do with the vulnerability that followed 9/11. Maybe it was just a feeling that old wounds ought to be healed. Maybe—and it pains me to admit this—I still harbored some hope of a reunion, one in which I would share the stage with Metallica. I don't really know. Regardless, I was willing to participate in the process. I figured I'd endured enough counseling *because* of Metallica, I might as well go through counseling *with* Metallica.

When I arrived at the hotel, Lars introduced me to the counselor and said, "Hey, man, are you okay if we film this? Because it's going to be part of a movie we're doing."

I'm not stupid. Masochistic, maybe. But not stupid. I realized instantly that I'd been ambushed. That said, I thought there might be some value to taking part in the project. My only stipulation was that I be given the right to approve any scenes that included me: if I didn't like the movie or my role in it, then the producers would not use any footage involving my meeting with Lars.

So we did the interview, and it was really candid and heartfelt. I tried to be completely open, the result being that both of us ended up crying and sharing sentiments that had never been expressed. I did more talking than Lars. I unburdened myself of all the things I had wanted to say: the regret over how I had behaved in the months prior to my firing ("I . . . fucked . . . up!"); the anger over the betrayal I felt; the sadness of that long bus ride home. I wanted him to understand that even after all these years, the pain was still there—palpable and inescapable.

The interview lasted about a half hour. Lars and I said goodbye and I went home. Some time passed before I gave any thought to it again. Then, when I saw the footage—along with samples of material that would appear before and after my scene—I decided that I no longer wanted to be part of the documentary, and not merely because I didn't like the way my segment had been edited. Context is everything, of course, but what I saw felt false and manipulative. It was Lars's contention that I should reconsider— that my appearance in the documentary would actually help my career. To me that seemed cynical and wrong. I wanted nothing to do with it.

In the end, despite all this, my conversation with Lars became a pivotal scene in the documentary, which was called *Some Kind of Monster*. I have never seen the entire film, start to finish, and I don't have any desire to see it now. I will admit that the passage of time, combined with positive feedback from many people I respect, has prompted me to view my experience with the documentary in a more flattering light.

BY THE END of 2001 Megadeth had become, more than ever, my band, although I wouldn't say the autonomy was liberating or enjoyable. It was a time of tremendous flux and stress rather than freedom. Marty Friedman, burned out on heavy metal—both the lifestyle and the music—had left the band in the middle of a tour in 2000. His replacement, Al Pitrelli, was a competent musician and decent fellow who never quite fit in. Al quickly discovered that he preferred the quiet anonymity and low expectations of his previous gig with Trans-Siberian Orchestra to the fame and pressure that came with playing in Megadeth. And Jimmy DeGrasso soon brought the clichéd baggage of a girlfriend who thought she knew how to run a band—and wasn't shy about voicing her opinion.

It was not a particularly collegial atmosphere. After parting with Capitol Records in 2000, we had signed a deal with a new label, Sanctuary Records. Almost every word and note on *The World Needs a Hero* (released in 2001) was written by me, a fact that pleased the label but did nothing to encourage camaraderie among the band members. It was a lineup that simply wasn't built to endure. And it didn't.

In the fall of 2001, I was hospitalized after developing a kidney stone. While undergoing treatment, I was prescribed pain medication. For most people this wouldn't be much of an issue. You take a few pills to get through the awfulness of passing a stone, and then you go home and get on with life. For me it was highly problematic. The introduction of opiates was akin to throwing a switch; after several years of sobriety, I relapsed.

The descent was swift and humiliating. I had been attending weekly AA meetings, and it was during one of those meetings that I was introduced to the concept of purchasing pain medication through the Internet. As I said, I had no real physical need for pain meds at the time, just a powerful desire to recapture some of the buzz I'd experienced while hospitalized, which, while not quite as intense as that produced by smoking heroin, certainly was capable of leaving me comfortably numb. This went on and off for a couple months in late 2001. I'd beat back the demons temporarily, only to have them regain control. The band suffered, my marriage suffered, my family suffered. I was miserable. Finally, as another year came to a close, I decided to get cleaned up; I couldn't live this way any longer. Running Megadeth was difficult enough when I was on my feet. I couldn't do it from my knees. Really, though, I had no master plan. I knew only that I'd allowed myself to become a junkie all over again, and I hated the way it felt. I just wanted the pain to go away.

That's how I ended up in Hunt, Texas, at a treatment center called La Hacienda, nodding off in my chair and waking with a compressed radial nerve, an injury so fucking freakish that it almost defied credibility. Far worse than the injury itself was the prognosis: I'd never regain full dexterity and feeling. I'd never play guitar—at least not the way I'd played in the past. And when the doctor said those words to me—when he looked me in the eye and said, "I don't think you should count on that"—a simple, devastating thought crossed my mind.

I'm ruined.

What was my life without music? It defined me. Creatively, spiritually, emotionally—and quite literally—music had fed me. It had kept me alive.

I'd like to be able to say that I took this news with courage and perspective, but what's the point of lying? The reality is this: my life had become a frayed rope, unraveling before my eyes. As I sat in the orthopedic surgeon's office, the main thing I felt was fear. I'd known pain and sadness; I'd known loneliness and defeat. Through all of it I could always count on my ability to play music. I knew that I was a very good guitar player, and no one could take that away from me.

Until now.

I withdrew impulsively from La Hacienda, and planned to go home and get as fucked-up as humanly possible. And then I made a mistake. I let drugs talk to my wife. This was something I'd never done before. Oh, sure, I'd been high around the house, and I'd been unpleasant on occasion, but never had I let drugs completely take over my personality during an interaction with the person I loved the most. The painkillers, combined with fear and insecurity, provoked a screed of uncommon meanness.

"My arm is dead," I told Pam over the phone. "I can't play anymore."

"You'll be okay," she said in typically supportive fashion. "We'll see the best doctors. You'll have the best care. You can do it."

None of it registered. I didn't want it to register. I just wanted a place to deposit my hostility and self-pity.

"You don't understand. You're not listening. My arm is dead, my life is over."

I looked at her—the one person who least deserved my bile—and then I cut loose.

"I hate my life. I hate my job. I hate my band. I hate my kids. I hate *you*. I wish I could fucking hang myself right now."

Pam's response was a mixture of panic and self-preservation. A mother's instincts kick in at a time like this—the kids are a lot more important than the fucked-up husband. She talked with some of her close friends at church, and they suggested she consult a Christian counselor down in Tucson. This guy offered Pam some harsh advice, and the next thing I knew she'd slapped me with a restraining order and filed for legal separation. It's fair to say that in the wake of this action I was not especially enamored of the Christian community. The counselor even went so far as to suggest that I not be allowed to meet with my own children unless a representative of the church was present. I hated this man for offering such sanctimonious advice. And I was not terribly amused with my wife for listening to him.

I had only a few choices at this juncture, the most obvious being life or death. I chose life, though not in the manner you might expect. For the next four months I lived in a hotel. The majority of each day was devoted to physical therapy and rehabilitation at the Spire Institute in Scottsdale, Arizona. There was no silver bullet, no arthroscopic procedure that would magically inflate the radial nerve and pump life into my flaccid hand. There was only work and slow, painful, almost imperceptible progress.

There were days when I felt like a toddler, so mundane were the tasks I attempted to master. Imagine what it's like to spend hours on end with a pair of tweezers between your fingers, trying to rearrange a pile of carpenter's nails. I would sit at a desk and work out—literally—with a clothespin.

Squeeze . . . release.

Squeeze . . . release.

Another device looked like some weird, demented version of a dream catcher, with spokes constructed of rubber bands. My assignment was to spread my fingers through the spokes and attempt to make a fist. This was impossible at first; it also hurt like hell. The numbness in my fingers, combined with pain in the surrounding muscles of my hand and forearm, created a comic effect whenever I tried to work out on the dream catcher. Just as someone playing a video game will often contort his whole body when only the thumb and fingers are required, I would flail about in my seat, sometimes rising and moving around the room as I fought for supremacy against this simple little piece of equipment.

At the same time, I still had an issue with chemical dependency. Since I'd never completed the process of detoxing, let alone rehab and recovery, I remained addicted to painkillers. One could argue that now I actually had a legitimate excuse for obtaining prescription pain meds, but that would be twisted logic. Nerve damage doesn't respond very well to narcotics, so my injury was not a reason to be using them. Pain wasn't the primary issue; it was more a matter of inconvenience and embarrassment. There were times when I would be drinking some coffee, and I would

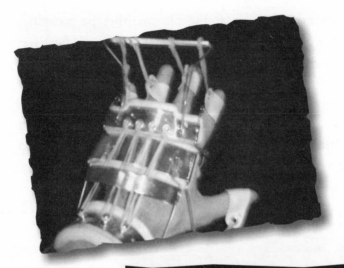

The traction device as prescribed by Dr. Raj Singh, who helped save my arm, and Nathan Koch, my physical therapist at the Spire Institute in Scottsdale, Arizona, who worked every day until I could play again. It was painful, difficult to do, and embarrassing beyond belief.

pick up the cup, forgetting momentarily about the injury, and simply drop it in my lap. At the beginning of physical therapy it was all I could do to pinch a feather between my fingers. I was that weak.

In some strange way, though, it was comforting to find that my life had taken on such a narrow focus. There is peace in simplicity; for the first time in many years I wasn't concerned with band politics or contractual obligations. I didn't think about the next tour or the next record. I thought about nothing but getting well—physically, spiritually, emotionally. The physical part came first, because that was all I had at the time. Separated from my wife, estranged from my children, I took the early steps of this journey on my own. Okay, that isn't entirely true. My neurosurgeon was the brilliant and supportive Dr. Raj Singh; my physical therapist was a man named Nathan Koch. Both were exceptionally good at their jobs, and I owe them a debt that can never be fully repaid. Still, professional support is one thing; personal support—also known as love—is quite another. I had the former. I did not have the latter.

After about a month of physical therapy I began to see significant results and realized I'd better do something about my addiction to pain meds. I decided to return to La Hacienda and finish the treatment program. There was no ulterior motive involved in this decision. Although I still loved my wife and missed my children, I was deep into the process of grieving their loss. Practically speaking, my marriage was over. Pam and I were no longer talking about reconciliation; we were working toward a settlement. So many people from Pam's church were offering her advice, and much of it was ill informed or simply mean-spirited. They wanted me to put up hundreds of thousands of dollars as some sort of dowry, so that Pam would have financial leverage as we attempted to figure out the parameters of our rapidly dissolving relationship. In other words, they wanted me to establish a legal fund for my soon-to-be ex-wife. All of this left me bewildered and frustrated.

"Pam, you know it's not about the money," I said. "The money doesn't matter. This is about you and me, and our family."

To say that Pam was reluctant would be an understatement. We'd been married for a decade, and she'd seen this movie before. So many times, in fact, that she'd probably lost count. By the time I returned to Texas to complete treatment, I'd all but given up on my marriage. I just wanted to make sure I didn't lose my kids as well. I knew I was in for a fight, since they were being fed propaganda. Once, when I was talking with Electra, she said, "Daddy, why won't you go see a psychotherapist?"

This was rather startling, coming as it did from a five-year-old. Electra was a sharp kid, but still . . .

"Honey, do you even know what a psychotherapist does?"

She smiled. "No, but Mommy's friends say you should see one."

"Really? Well, let me tell you about psychotherapists. You see, a psychotherapist is someone who tries to stay awake while Daddy talks and talks and talks. Then he takes all of Daddy's money, and Daddy feels even worse than he did before. Understand?"

"Ummm . . . please don't see a psychotherapist, Daddy."

IT'S FUNNY HOW you connect with some people and reject others, how the esteemed professional with the framed diplomas arranged neatly on the wall can turn your stomach, while a tough guy with an eye patch makes you laugh and listen. His name was Chris R., and he was my sponsor at La Hacienda. We met while I was completing detox and treatment following an encouraging prognosis on my arm. The first time we talked, I thought he was completely full of shit—like so many of the other screamers I'd gotten to know in AA and various other rehab programs. He told horror stories that stretched back to when he was a child having rock fights with his twin brother, the result being the loss of an eye. His stories were no different than most I'd heard—a litany of self-inflicted pain and suffering, all tied to alcohol and drugs. The hook for this guy was his penchant for getting in your face and lifting his patch, leaving you staring at a horrible black hole as he shouted about what the future would hold if you didn't clean up your fucking act.

"They're gonna love your bony ass in prison, boy!"

"Jesus . . . man. Get that fucking thing away from me, will you?"

That "scared straight" bullshit never did much for me. What got me, though, were the conversations we'd have late at night, when we talked about friends and family and the emptiness of the junkie's life. We talked about spirituality and the need to embrace a higher presence. I'm not talking about Christianity, specifically, but rather a general acknowledgment of forces beyond our control. An awareness that none of us is the center of the universe. We are all of us—regardless of age, race, nationality, social standing—merely tiny pieces in a vast cosmic puzzle. The millionaire rock star is no better—or worse—than the ex-con with the glass eye.

If rehab is good for anything, it's that it can, under the right circumstances, provide time and space for introspection. I knew something was different when I returned to La Hacienda. Despite all that was wrong and contorted in my life, I felt a weird sort of optimism. Granted, I was in the middle of Nowhere, Texas—the sheer isolation of which provoked a bit of perspective—surrounded by humans who weren't caught up in the hamster wheel of life. Still, something tugged at me. The anger and cynicism that had become such a prominent part of my life seemed to be melting away.

I wanted something.

I *needed* something.

Spiritually speaking, I was a creaky assemblage of broken, mismatched parts: baptized Lutheran, raised by Jehovah's Witnesses, indoctrinated into witchcraft, dabbling in Buddhism, sampling from a buffet table of new age doctrine. Nothing had worked. Nothing had "taken." For the longest time I wasn't even interested in trying. I don't know that you could have accurately described me as an atheist or even agnostic. I was more of a drastically lapsed . . . *something*. I had always believed in God. I believed in Jesus—I believed he died and rose three days later. That's the story I'd been told as a child, whether Jehovah's Witness or not. So to the extent that I believed in anything, that's what I believed. I just didn't give a shit. There was no role for religion in my life, no place for spirituality.

Until now.

I walked one freezing January night to a hilltop in Hunt, on the grounds of La Hacienda. A fire pit had been constructed, and even now, in the dead of winter, flames danced in the wind, sending sparks high into the vast desert sky. The fire pit was a popular gathering place at La Hacienda—a convenient and appropriately atmospheric spot for reflection of a private or communal nature. I sat there that evening, staring at the flames, thinking about my life . . . about the choices I'd made and the consequences of those choices, both positive and negative. Something was missing.

I can't do this anymore. This has to be the end of it.

But it wasn't the end of anything. It was the beginning.

I stood up and walked in the direction of a small A-frame structure—more like a lean-to, really, just a couple walls propped up against each other. The building, such as it was, served as an outdoor chapel. Theoretically, it was nondenominational; practically speaking, it was a Christian place of worship, as evidenced by the large cross that hung from a support beam at the front of the structure. I stood in the doorway, staring up at the cross, wondering what to make of it—whether to laugh or cry or curse at its significance. I had been brought up to believe that the cross was a fraudulent image, that Jesus Christ had died on a stake. Satanists, obviously, believed something far more malevolent. Regardless, the cross had never made much of an impact on my life. At this moment, though, something about it seemed oddly comforting and compelling.

I took a deep breath and spoke aloud. There was no one else within earshot.

"I've tried everything else. What have I got to lose?"

With those six words—*What have I got to lose?*—a burden was lifted. Not entirely, mind you. But incrementally. I stood there for a minute or so, unsure of what to say or how to act. I have heard of spiritual rebirths, of people feeling the hand of God, or something like that, reaching down to touch them on the shoulder. Or seeing an image of Christ in the darkness, sweeping toward them and taking them in a warm embrace.

My conversion—my awakening, if you will—was far less theatrical. Lacking anything more than a fundamental awareness of Christian doctrine—and frankly feeling kind of silly—I sought assistance from the center's chaplain. His name was Leroy. He was an interesting little dude who wore tiny cowboy boots and a huge cowboy hat. I don't know if there was something physically wrong with Leroy, but he had an odd way of walking, a sideways lurch and shuffle, like his toes were folded under his feet, that reminded me of John Wayne. Leroy played an interesting role at La Hacienda: he was there to support patients in their quest for holistic healing; he was not supposed to impose religious beliefs on anyone. And he didn't. He just sort of held the door for anyone who wanted to walk through.

"How do I bring God into my life?" I asked.

"Come with me."

We stood before the cross together.

"Get on your knees," Leroy said.

I shook my head. Even at this juncture, I was stubborn and prideful.

"No, I'm not going to kneel. Can't we just pray?"

And so we did. Leroy led me through something known as a Sinner's Prayer. As I recited the words, it almost seemed unnecessary. I mean, everyone knows Dave Mustaine is a sinner, right? How much more obvious could it be? Besides, I'd recited various versions of the Sinner's Prayer hundreds of times in the past—it really was no different than the Third-Step Prayer found in the Alcoholics Anonymous Handbook:

> **God, I offer myself to Thee—
> To build with me
> and to do with me as Thou wilt.
> Relieve me of the bondage of self,
> that I may better do Thy will.**

Here's the truth: I could have recited these words in my sleep. I had let them pour from my mouth so many times, in so many settings, without ever really thinking about the truth behind them. I'd been brainwashed to recite the mantra in AA, but I never truly understood the meaning, never gave myself over to it. I just responded reflexively.

Sure, I'll turn my life over to you. Why not? My life sucks anyway.

To a degree, nothing had changed. I mean, my life was about as bad as it could be on the day Leroy and I held hands and recited the Sinner's Prayer. My wife had filed a restraining order against me. I rarely saw my children. My arm was getting better, but I still doubted that I would ever resurrect my music career—and frankly I didn't care. And yet . . .

There was hope. I don't know where it came from or why it came. But it was there nonetheless.

It wasn't long afterward that I fell to my knees and said all the prayers and accepted Jesus Christ into my life. It didn't happen without some resistance on my part, and God knows that in the years since I have been at times inconsistent in following a Christian way of life. I am not an extremist. I am not a fundamentalist. I have lapsed in ways large and small. I curse. I do not always exercise the patience and tolerance I should. But I believe in God and I believe that Jesus is my savior, and those are the overriding principles that guide my life.

When I called Pam to tell her of my conversion, I expected a skeptical response. What I got was something else entirely.

She laughed.

"This isn't funny!" I said.

"I know," she said. "But all my friends told me this would happen. They knew you'd come around. That's why I'm laughing."

"But you're happy, right?"

"Yes, of course."

The reconciliation was far from painless. There were more meetings, just as there had been in Arizona during my previous stint in rehab. We did the big family gathering and intervention, during which I was again confronted with all of my transgressions. I deserved it, of course; I had brought it on myself. But that didn't make it any less uncomfortable. In order to salvage our marriage, Pam and I talked through all of our problems and issues, most of which were really my problems and issues. The majority of those stemmed not just from my drug use but from my work. I don't want to make excuses, but the truth is, the Megadeth lifestyle simply was not conducive to family life. The music business really is sex, drugs, and rock 'n' roll, and if you are married and want to be monogamous, and you want to lead a coherent life, it's a struggle. It's a terrible environment if you have a history of promiscuity and drug addiction, which, obviously, I did. There had been times when I'd been out on the road, and for no apparent reason Pam and I would have a long-distance fight. The fight would give me an excuse to go from *Hmmm* . . . to *Oops!*; from merely *looking* to allowing myself to be *pawed*; from having a drink to having one too many. All of these moral transgressions I blamed on things happening at home: problems with the kids, problems with money, problems with my wife. The reality is that I had to take responsibility for these issues and behave differently. I had to be a better person.

Here's the thing, though: it's not all about conviction and sturdiness. Sometimes it's about being smart enough to avoid temptation. If you're a weekend warrior you can probably balance work and family without too much trouble. At my level? Much more difficult. Drugs are accessible and affordable. As are the groupies. The best way to stay married when you're a famous rock star? The best way to be a faithful husband and devoted father?

Quit. Just walk away and do something else.

That's the way it's always been and the way it always will be.

But it's easier said than done. There was a time when I would see people taking time off for their kids—people who had serious clout and prestige within the entertainment industry—and I would wonder what was wrong with them.

Why are you being so stupid and soft?

I see things differently now. Life really is about family and kids. I've worked my ass off so that I can spend more time with my children, but Justis is eighteen now, and soon he'll be out on his own. I worry that maybe I missed the best years of his life, and that saddens me to an extent you can't imagine. It's that song, man. It's that fucking Harry Chapin song, "Cat's in the Cradle." You hear it when you're a cynical teenager, or a hard-partying, childless, heavy metal guitar player, and you think, *What a fucking wimp!* Then you get to be my age, pushing fifty, and you look at your kids, grown in the blink of an eye, and suddenly the song takes on a whole different meaning.

THERE WERE PLANES TO CATCH
AND BILLS TO PAY.
HE LEARNED TO WALK WHILE I WAS AWAY.

I hear that song now and I don't laugh or sneer. I want to cry. Same thing with Cat Stevens's "Father and Son," or even John Mayer's "Daughters." These are songs that tug at the heartstrings, that speak to parents. And that's what I am above all else:

a father. Thing is, when you are driven to succeed, as I certainly was, and start working to the degree where nothing else matters, you totally lose sight of what's important. That's what happened to me. And in the end, if you care enough, you find yourself in rehab, spouting the Serenity Prayer over and over. Or some version of it, anyway, which, at its core, is simply this:

"Fuck it."

SO I WENT home to Arizona, back to my wife and kids, and tried to rebuild my life—a happier, healthy version of my life, anyway. Among the people I met who helped in this journey was Darian Bennett, a former marine and NFL linebacker. Darian also was an accomplished martial arts instructor as well as a Christian, and soon we were training together and hanging out. I felt like we had a lot in common, except for the part about him being a marine and a former professional football player, and me being a rock star and recovering drug addict. Fundamentally, we were both fighters, and we connected on that level. Although our backgrounds were vastly different, we shared a warrior's mentality. It helped, too, that Darian was several years older than I was and far more entrenched in the Christian lifestyle. I needed a mentor at this time—a father figure, even—and Darian filled that role. We've grown apart in recent years, especially since I moved back to California, but for a while I considered him one of my closest friends, and I will always appreciate his guidance and companionship.

Part of the problem, I discovered, was that I had very few male friends. Oh, I had "buddies," partners in crime . . . but no true friends. The friends I did have were either unhealthy relics of an earlier life—a life I was trying to escape—or professionals with

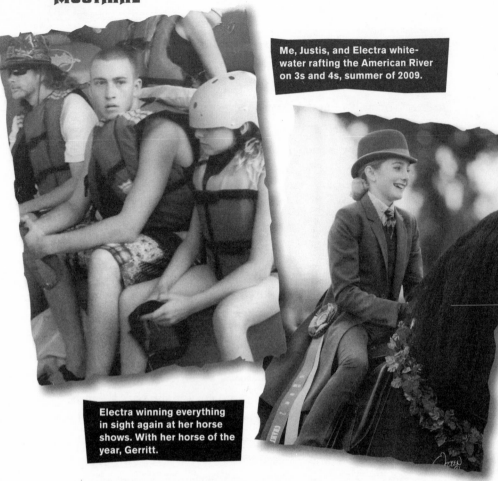

Me, Justis, and Electra white-water rafting the American River on 3s and 4s, summer of 2009.

Electra winning everything in sight again at her horse shows. With her horse of the year, Gerritt.

little time to invest in friendships. Such is the burden of being a successful man in today's society. Again, it comes down to setting priorities. You work endlessly to achieve success and provide for your family, and then you wake up one day to discover you have few people with whom to share that success. Moreover, it was a struggle for me to break out of the artifice of adolescent male relationships. I was good at getting drunk or stoned and chasing women or getting in fights. Grown-up male bonding? I didn't know anything about it.

In the interest of enlightenment, I tried (again) to join a men's group, this time bringing a better attitude and a clearer head.

What I sought was a life outside Megadeth, a life that would supplement my family in a healthy, positive way. Through all of this I continued to tiptoe down the path of Christianity and enlightenment, trying simultaneously to understand that most of my problems could be traced back to issues of abandonment in my childhood while also accepting responsibility for my misdeeds; simply put, a shitty upbringing does not relieve you of the burden of accountability.

Life goes on. Deal with it.

I had allowed myself to become a victim, and in many ways I hated myself for it.

There were things I recognized about my own addictive behavior that didn't necessarily dovetail neatly with twelve-step protocol. For example, I recognized that I wasn't the kind of guy who couldn't stop after one or two beers. For me it was more a matter of understanding that I'd have one or two beers, and then someone would say, "Hey, let's do a line of coke!" And then I'd be off to the races. I understood the domino effect. If I didn't drink heavily, I didn't get in trouble. Consequently, now I hardly drink at all.

Come again?

Right . . . here's the controversial part.

When I speak of sobriety, I am not referring to abstinence in the strictest sense of the word. I haven't done cocaine or heroin in many years. There have been a couple minor slips since 2002 involving pain medication related to a serious and ongoing degenerative disc condition in my neck, but I place that in a different category. Eventually, that problem will require surgical intervention—all those years of headbanging take their toll! But I do enjoy a glass of wine occasionally. And that's about it: a single glass, an hour or so before I go onstage or when I go out to dinner with my wife. Rarely does one glass become two. The first few times I did this, an army of people cried bullshit. Everybody said it wouldn't work: abstinence, they said, was the only strategy for someone like me. I understand the sentiment. Alice Cooper did the same thing: got saved through Christ's intervention and simply stopped drinking on his own. No meetings, no twelve-step programs. Know what I said when I heard that?

"Bullshit! Doesn't work."

But then I looked at the commitment I made, and I realized that faith can inspire miracles. Those dudes who walk on burning coals? Or the guys who use their bellies as chopping blocks (on which some machete-wielding ninja hacks a watermelon in half)? How do they do that?

Faith.

For me it's faith in God. Faith in Jesus Christ.

I don't want to paint with too broad a brush. If rehab has taught me anything, it's that every situation, every person and experience, is unique. All addicts are not the same. What works for most people might not work for me. (Shit, after seventeen trips to rehab, that's screamingly obvious, wouldn't you say?) For me, only one thing worked: establishing a relationship with God. That changed everything.

See, there are three different types of drinkers: the moderate drinker, the heavy drinker, and the alcoholic. If you are not an alcoholic, given sufficient reason, you can get sober. I think I was an alcoholic because of the cocaine. You take that out of the mix, and things are different. Really, though, it comes down to this: I no longer wake up in the morning with drugs or alcohol on my mind. For a long time, I couldn't say that. I lived for the next drink, the next line of cocaine, the next balloon of heroin. No more. I can't explain it, and I know that there is no shortage of critics who will call me delusional or, worse, a liar. I don't care. I know how I feel. I don't walk around during the day thinking, *God, I can't wait until five o'clock so I can uncork that bottle of wine.* The craving is just . . . gone.

They say God sends people to AA, and AA sends them back to God. If you really have a spiritual awakening, why put a limitation on that? My experience has been extraordinary. I know that, and I don't expect everyone to buy into it. You fuck up seventeen times, well, there's bound to be some skepticism. The thing is, it's been a great ride. I love my life; I love what I've accomplished and created. I've seen the error of my ways and what drinking and drug use has done to me and my family, and what it's done to my career and my body. Drinking and doing drugs, for me, makes about as much sense as pissing my pants on a winter's day: it'll feel good for a little while . . . until that cold wind begins to blow. And then it won't feel so great.

But you know what? I also wouldn't want to have missed out on the experience I've had, so long as the outcome remained positive: going from being someone who was brought up in a stifling atmosphere of perverse religiosity to hating God and then coming full circle and believing in God again. It's been rewarding and fulfilling in ways that are hard to fathom, unless you've been through a similar experience. I went from being a homeless kid to a self-made man, to a self-made millionaire, to . . . someone who now realizes that there is no such thing as "self-made."

Anything about me that's good is a result of some higher power. Now that I recognize that, it's like I finally fit into the picture—without having to hammer the edges into the frame.

17

MEGADETH:
REBORN

"We will be back!"

WHEN I WALKED OUT OF LA HACIENDA, I WAS CONVINCED THAT MEGADETH WAS FINISHED. I HAD NEITHER THE ENERGY NOR THE INCLINATION TO RESURRECT THE BAND IN SOME NEW SHAPE OR FORM. IT WAS, ONCE AGAIN, JUST ME AND ELLEFSON. AND FRANKLY, MY FOCUS WAS ELSEWHERE: ON MY HEALTH, MY FAMILY, MY SPIRITUALITY. I HAD NO IDEA WHETHER I'D EVER BE ABLE TO PLAY GUITAR AGAIN AT A LEVEL THAT WOULD MAKE PERFORMING A VIABLE OPTION. SURE, I WAS GETTING BETTER, IMPROVING EVERY DAY THROUGH EXERCISE AND PHYSICAL THERAPY. BUT TO PLAY THE SORT OF BLISTERING SOLOS THAT HAD BECOME A TRADEMARK OF MEGADETH? THE KIND OF DANCING FRETWORK THAT HAD MADE ME FAMOUS? MAN, THAT WAS A LONG WAY OFF.

Shawn Drover, James MacDonough, me, and Glen saying good night.

Rather than put everything and everyone on hold until I figured out what I wanted to do with the rest of my life, I called David and suggested we get together. We met at a Starbucks in Phoenix. There was a tone of finality to the discussion, but it was completely amicable. David was like my littler brother, and even though we had drifted apart in recent years—I wanted to do something for him.

"I'm quitting," I told him. "And I want to turn everything over to you. I want you to be executive producer of the archives. I want you to oversee the estate."

I don't think David was surprised by my decision to leave the band. Certainly, he seemed genuinely appreciative of my candor. I believe he felt this was a generous offer. I also think he understood exactly what it meant. I was not giving David permission to add new band members; nor was this tacit approval of touring and recording under the Megadeth brand. That could not happen without me. Megadeth was my band, and even though I no longer wanted to be part of it, I wasn't about to let it evolve into something I never imagined, something I could not control. I simply wanted Junior to have something to do on a day-to-day basis, something that would generate a tidy income and other opportunities.

"Thanks, man," he said. "I love you."

"I love you, too."

We had another cup of coffee and talked about old times for a little while. Then we stood up, hugged, and went our separate ways. I figured it would be weeks, maybe months, before our paths crossed again.

Wrong.

Five hours later, I was confronted by David in a public parking garage. I was completely shocked by this encounter, and I have no idea what provoked David's anger. Regardless, his behavior was wildly inappropriate for the public place.

"If you're moving on with your career, then I'm moving on with mine!" he shouted, tossing in a few F-bombs and other epithets for good measure.

I tried to reason with him. I wanted to just defuse the situation and get him out of there.

"That's it," I said calmly, trying very hard to resist the urge to hit him. "We're done."

I got in my car, turned the ignition, backed out, and drove away, leaving him in the rearview mirror.

ON APRIL 9, 2003, I played guitar in public for the first time in seventeen months. The occasion was a benefit show at a place called Nita's Hideaway in Phoenix, to raise money for the family of a former Megadeth roadie named John Calleo. John had also been my personal assistant during the *Youthanasia* tour, but we had sort of lost contact over the years. He was a sweet and fun-loving guy who never really gave up the rock 'n' roll lifestyle; the heart disease and kidney failure that ultimately took his life probably had as much to do with continued self-abuse as it did with any congenital abnormalities. Still, it was hard not to like John, and it was impossible not to feel for the wife and eight-year-old daughter he left behind.

I'd been making slow, steady progress with my hand, which, as it turned out, had also sustained some ligament damage related to years of ferocious guitar playing. But that felt better now, too. The sabbatical that had been forced upon me, it seemed, generally had been a good thing, leaving me healthier than I'd been in years. When I was invited to play at John's benefit show, I didn't hesitate to accept the offer.

I won't deny a bit of anxiety. Hell, when you haven't performed in nearly a year and a half, there's bound to be some rust. I didn't know what to expect. Didn't know how I'd play or how I'd feel about playing. And this was an unusual sort of gig: an acoustic set of just four songs in a very intimate setting, before just a couple hundred people (including my godfather, Alice Cooper). The set list was carefully chosen, though I can't say for sure how many people understood what I was trying to say. I opened with "Symphony of Destruction," primarily to give my fingers an appropriate workout and to demonstrate to myself and the audience that I was up to the task. Then came "Use the Man" and "Promises," the former because it so clearly spoke to John's drug use and demise, and the latter because I wanted to let his wife and daughter know that if John could promise anything, it would be to meet them in the afterlife. Finally, I closed with "A Tout le Monde."

A TOUT LE MONDE (TO ALL THE WORLD)
A TOUS MES AMIS (TO ALL MY FRIENDS)
JE VOUS AIME (I LOVE YOU)
JE DOIS PARTIR (I MUST LEAVE)

After singing the last line, I stood up; walked offstage; offered my condolences to John's wife, Tracy; and headed for the back door. To my surprise, I ran into David Ellefson on the way out. We hadn't talked in many months—specifically, not since that night in the parking garage—so there was a bit of awkwardness in the encounter. Circumstances, however, dictated politeness above all else. Shit, we had gathered to honor and support a former member of the Megadeth family. A bit of perspective was in order. So we shook hands, chatted very briefly, and went our separate ways.

It was almost like the argument had never happened, perhaps because it seemed so surreal. David has neither the disposition nor the tools to be a fighter; it goes against his nature. He is fundamentally a laid-back, nonconfrontational sort of fellow, which is why his outburst had been so startling. When we were kids, just starting out, David was not the kind of guy you wanted in your foxhole. A great partier and musician. But a fighter? I once watched an asshole in a UCLA letterman's jacket shove a slice of hot pizza into David's face following a dispute over a parking space. David didn't even react, just stood there as the cheese scalded his cheeks like molten lava. It took me all of about two minutes to kick that guy's privileged ass all over the asphalt. That was the difference between me and David.

The inevitable bolt of lightning didn't strike until a few days after the benefit show, when I picked up my guitar and started playing a little bit and thinking about how much I had enjoyed being back onstage, playing my music. The more I thought about it, the more I wanted to get that feeling back. This was no simple task. My retirement had not been a minor matter. I hadn't just slipped quietly away with a promise to return when I felt better. Oh, no. I had *quit*. And because I wanted to leave honorably, I had called a lot of the people with whom I enjoyed endorsement contracts and told them of my intentions. I didn't have to do that. I could have just kept all the gear and let the money continue to trickle in. But I didn't. Instead, I sold a ton of equipment to pay off my debts. I didn't want to be one of those musicians who leaves vendors holding the bag. I had people who had shipped stuff for me and who believed in me: lighting companies, sound companies. Everything was gone now, so when I decided to come out of retirement, I was pretty much starting from scratch.

Fortunately, since I hadn't destroyed any of those relationships, there was no shortage of companies eager to support my comeback. Pretty soon I had all the equipment I needed, a fistful of new endorsement deals, and a rehearsal space in Phoenix.

All I needed was a band.

The initial plan was to record a solo album. I hired some studio musicians—including the well-traveled drummer Vinnie Colaiuta, most notable for his tenure with Frank Zappa and the Mothers of Invention—and went to work in the fall of 2003. Business, however, always gets in the way of the music. The solo record was interrupted while I helped remaster the entire Megadeth back catalog. By the time I got back to the solo project, in the spring of 2004, EMI had begun seriously pressuring me to put out another album under the Megadeth brand. It was the label's contention that I was contractually bound to release another Megadeth record before turning to solo ventures. Rather than get embroiled in an endless, expensive, and ultimately futile legal dispute, I decided to simply take the songs I had written and recorded and release them as the latest, and probably last, Megadeth record, the aptly titled *The System Has Failed*.

But then I had an idea. If Megadeth was going to be reborn, with a new record and even a tour in support of that record, then why not reconvene the most successful Megadeth lineup? Commercially and creatively speaking, I thought this was a great idea.

The first person I called was Nick Menza, who jumped at the opportunity.

Okay, we're off to a good start. One down, two to go.

The next call went to Marty Friedman. I'd always liked Marty, admired his playing ability, and even though I was extremely disappointed by his departure and the manner in which he tried to exercise undue creative control during the recording of *Risk*, I harbored no personal animosity toward him. On some level you had to admire Marty. He had the guts to live out his fantasy. The guy had always said he wanted to live in Japan, play more mainstream music, and teach others how to play the guitar. And that is precisely what he had done. More power to him. I didn't want to drag Marty away from all that for any great length of time. My plan was to reunite the *Rust in Peace*–era Megadeth for a very specific window. I'd give these guys the opportunity to go into a studio and retrack *The System Has Failed*, replacing and hopefully improving stuff already done by session players. We'd sell a bunch of records, go out on tour, and then everyone could go back to their previous lives. For me, that meant focusing on solo work.

Unfortunately, this idea didn't generate the excitement and enthusiasm I had anticipated; instead, it mainly opened old wounds and provoked prickly discussions about money and control. In other words, the same old story.

My initial conversation with Marty went something like this:

"Hi, Marty."

"Hi, Dave."

"Hey, I'm sorry about everything."

"Yeah, me too."

Small talk, blah-blah-blah.

I told Marty about the new record and the proposed tour, and then I asked if he had any interest in getting together. Marty hesitated, then fired a series of questions that I wasn't prepared to answer.

What was the marketing budget? The touring budget? The recording budget? How much money would he get paid? Did I have the specific dates?

My head was spinning.

Whoa, dude. Slow down.

I couldn't believe he was asking me this shit less than two minutes into our first conversation. I was like, you know what, Marty? This is stuff you don't need to know. You don't need to know what the recording fund is because you didn't record the record. You don't need to know the touring fund because you're going to be a hired gun.

So it started to sour with Marty right away. Then I called up Ellefson. Basically, here was my pitch:

Hey, Junior. I just want to let you know that I've decided I want to play again, and I'm going to be going out on the road. And I want to talk to you about going out with me. I've written a new record, it's almost done, so you don't have to worry about any of that shit. It'll be coming out soon. If you're interested, we're mixing it in Nashville; you can go out there and try to beat what we already have. If you can, we'll use it. If not, no big deal; you can still go out on tour.

And just like Marty, David launched into a litany of inquiries. Without delving too deeply into the mind-numbing minutiae of Megadeth's accounting practices, let's just say that David sought something akin to a full partnership in this venture. Well, that just wasn't going to happen. I'd put together the entire project. I'd written every song, produced the record, conceptualized the tour. I needed a backup band, and I thought it would be nice to assemble the old Megadeth gang. But it was all much more complicated than I had expected.

"Junior, I don't have the answers to any of this stuff yet," I explained. "And frankly, if I did know, I wouldn't be comfortable telling you all of it. That's a lot of information to give the bass player for a single tour."

And that's all it was: one record, one tour. It was not a *reunion.* I tried to make that as clear as possible.

As quickly as my hopes had risen, they were dashed. It took only a few more phone calls and uncomfortable conversations to reach the obvious conclusion: there would be no reconvening of the old Megadeth; it was time to move on. I thought that was the end of it. Imagine my shock when, in early July of 2004, Ellefson filed an $18.5 million lawsuit against me in Manhattan federal court.

The lawsuit claimed, among other things, that I had cheated David out of publishing and merchandising royalties and failed to make good on a promise to turn over control of Megadeth to him following my retirement. I had never made such a claim, and the agreement David signed—a legally binding contract—spelled out the terms of our separation in great detail. In his lawsuit, however, David claimed that he had changed his mind shortly after signing the separation agreement, and therefore the contract was invalid.

When I heard about Junior's lawsuit I was so pissed I could barely see straight. It wasn't just the money; it was the fact that I had been publicly and unfairly attacked by someone I had supported and defended for so many years. The entire lawsuit—the actual document—somehow found its way to the Internet, where it was posted in all its salacious detail. The battle then naturally leaked into the wider universe of heavy metal fandom, with factions forming along these lines:

1) Mustaine is a greedy, egomaniacal asshole.

2) Ellefson is a pathetic, ungrateful asshole.

Among those who took the time to do their homework, the resounding verdict was: number two.

Vindication came not only in the court of public opinion but in the courtroom of Federal Judge Naomi Buchwald, who in January of 2005 dismissed Ellefson's lawsuit in its entirety. In so doing, she basically declared that the suit had been groundless. Which it was. In the end, David was the person who had to write a check. A big check. My attorney said it was the first time in his twenty-seven years in the business that one of his clients got sued and ended up making money off the lawsuit.

By that time I'd already put together a new version of Megadeth, released *The System Has Failed*, and gone out on tour. For a while when I was trying to put a lineup together, it looked like at least one member of the old Megadeth would be on board for this adventure. Even as negotiations with Marty and Junior fell apart, Nick continued to express a desire to return to the band. He showed up one day in Phoenix in the summer of 2004 with a U-Haul full of equipment and a drum tech named Sticks. This guy dropped Nick off, then fell asleep in the truck while sitting in the parking lot of a Frey's Electronics store. This was Arizona, in the middle of the summer, where the temperature routinely soars into the triple digits. Eight hours later Sticks woke up, baked and dehydrated but luckily still alive. I knew then that Sticks wasn't long for the job. We sent him home shortly thereafter.

Over the next few weeks two more drum techs came and went, and pretty soon I came to the realization that the problem wasn't with the drum techs; the problem was Nick. There's no place to hide under those conditions. The new bass player, James Mc-Donough, was solid, if not particularly enthusiastic. And former King Diamond guitarist Glen Drover was a pro. Nick, however, was the same old Nick. He'd play a song or two, jump down from his kit—"Give me a few minutes, guys; I gotta run down to the AM PM mini-market to get something"—then ride off on his bike, leaving the rest of us standing there, shaking our heads in disbelief. Sometimes he'd return quickly, while other times, "a few minutes" would turn into a few hours. He was so unreliable.

One day Glen suggested that we contact his brother, Shawn Drover, to see if he'd be interested in the once-again-vacant drum tech's job. Shawn had played drums in a band with his brother and had teched for the drummer in King Diamond, so he knew his way around a kit.

Within minutes we had Shawn on speakerphone, conducting a conference call. I was in the control room with Glen and James; Nick was nearby, laying on a couch, shades covering his eyes, trying to look the part of a bored, disaffected rock star.

"Hey, Shawn," I said. "How are you?"

"Good, man. How's everyone there?"

Before I could answer, Nick jumped in. "Who is this fucking guy? I don't even want to know him."

It went downhill from there, with everyone trying to hide their anger and embarrassment. I apologized to Shawn, told him we'd call back later, and then went outside to talk with Glen, who was understandably offended.

"I can't play with that asshole," he said. "If he stays in the band, I'm quitting."

What could I say? There was no defending or rationalizing Nick's behavior. I talked to our manager, and by the end of the day Nick was gone. Now we needed not just a drum tech but a drummer as well. And there wasn't a lot of time—we were scheduled to go out on tour in five days.

"How about Shawn?" Glen suggested. "He already knows all the songs."

The last time I had heard someone make such a ludicrous proclamation, it was Al Pitrelli. I had called him from Denver in the middle of a tour, just hours after Marty Friedman had quit.

"Yeah, I'll be there in two days," Al had said. "I'll know all them songs, back and front, and I'll play 'em with a cigarette hangin' outta my mouth."

"We don't smoke in this band, Al."

"Well, Nicorette gum, then."

He was there in two days, all right, but he couldn't play all the songs. Not even close. There were just too many idiosyncrasies. Granted, drumming was substantially less complex than playing guitar. You could flail about, capture the timing and spirit, hide the mistakes from all but the most discriminating ears. Nevertheless, it seemed a long shot that Shawn would be able to fill Nick's shoes on such short notice.

But he did. The guy knew all the songs he would be expected to play on tour. Not perfectly, but at least as well as Nick had been playing. *The System Has Failed* was released in September of 2004, to a generally favorable critical and commercial response. Considering all that had preceded its release, I was pleased with the way the record turned out. And then we went out and played.

The first show of the Blackmail the Universe tour was in Reno, Nevada, in October of 2004. Unfortunately no one had arranged for a barricade to be erected between band and crowd. If you think this seems like a small thing, well, it's not. If you don't have a line of demarcation at a Megadeth show, you'll be chasing kids off the stage all night. And that's exactly what happened. I spent two hours playing guitar with one hand and swatting people with my other hand. By the end of the concert, the entire stage was covered with security guards.

We got through it safely enough, but afterward, in the dressing room, I noticed that Shawn seemed disoriented. He was dizzy and having trouble breathing. When his condition failed to improve, we had him transported to a local hospital. The diagnosis: vertigo.

"Has this ever happened before?" I asked Glen.

"I don't know. I don't think so."

"What do you mean, *you don't think so?*"

Glen shrugged. "Well, he's only played a couple times before. I mean, in front of people."

"What the fuck?!"

I didn't know a lot about Shawn. I had presumed that he'd been playing in various bands for years. You didn't get to be that polished simply by hanging out and playing in your basement. But that's mainly what Shawn had done. The guy was completely self-taught and utterly devoid of onstage experience. I later learned that Shawn and Glen had grown up in a broken home, and to deal with the pain, they had immersed themselves in music. In the process they'd not only become accomplished musicians but had grown incredibly close. Glen had progressed beyond the basement into the world of professional music. He'd done rather well, too. Shawn, for the most part, had remained offstage, in the shadows, satisfied with jamming and working as a drum tech while occasionally playing with Glen in the Canadian studio band Eidolon.

And we'd taken this poor guy—overweight, unhealthy, inexperienced—and thrown him out in front of thousands of ravenous, headbanging metalheads?

We're lucky he didn't die.

But here's the completely improbable happy ending. Shawn has turned out to be one of the most reliable and resilient musicians I've known. Five years after that baptism by fire in Reno, he is still Megadeth's drummer; only Nick Menza sat at the kit longer. You never know what someone has inside. Talent is only one of the traits required for success, and it's often overrated. Shawn is a terrific musician. He is a drummer by trade but can also play guitar, just as Glen is a guitar player by trade but also an accomplished drummer. More than anything else, though, Shawn is a survivor, a characteristic that is of no small significance in my eyes. The guy just kept plugging and working, getting better and better, learning on the job, until one day he looked exactly like the person he was supposed to be: the drummer for one of the biggest bands in heavy metal. How can you not respect that?

In all honesty, though, I had mixed feelings after that first show. I didn't know whether this particular lineup would last a week, let alone the many months required to complete a world tour. But Shawn jumped right back on the horse, and it became instantly clear that he was not only talented but a fighter as well. Glen was good, too. And so was James. For the first time in . . . well . . . a long time, playing music was fun again. Being in Megadeth was *fun*. We toured the U.S. with Exodus, selling out shows almost everywhere we went. Then, after taking a break for the Christmas holiday, we went to Europe and toured with Diamond Head and Dungeon. Everything was going smoothly until May of 2005, when we were scheduled to play shows in Greece and Israel with Rotting Christ and Dissection, both of which had been labeled, accurately or not, as "satanic" bands.

Glen and older brother Shawn Drover. They can switch instruments and we did, several times.

Now, this obviously presented something of a dilemma for me. When I first embraced Christianity, I felt like I needed to protect myself from being in the wrong environment. Some people get saved and blend into the background, leading quietly dignified, meaningful lives. I couldn't do that. Too many people knew who I was and how I had lived previously. Fame can be a terrific thing; it can also be a bitch. When Dave Mustaine announces his conversion to Christianity, there's no shortage of people eager to find hypocrisy in the decision.

"Oh, yeah, right . . . Mustaine is a Christian. The guy is a fucking drunk and a drug addict."

Well, as a matter of fact, that's exactly what I was. And what better reason to let God into my life than to atone for all of the horrible things I'd done? I couldn't change people's opinions, and frankly I didn't care to try, but I could exercise a degree of control over my life. I could be a better person. And I could be careful.

One thing I could do to maintain a healthy lifestyle was avoid playing with bands whose philosophical outlook was an affront to my beliefs. There are degrees to all of this, of course. I have never been the type of Christian who gets in your face and tells you how to live your life. I don't do any recruiting in the name of Jesus. To each his own, man. But at this point in my life—newly saved—it just didn't feel healthy to share a stage with a band called Rotting Christ. A band that a few years earlier had been part of a black metal festival known as the Fuck Christ tour.

I didn't even know much, if anything, about the music of either of these bands. But I did know that if there was a line in the sand to be drawn, this was it. I wasn't comfortable playing with a band called Rotting Christ. The name was simply too offensive. Here's the way I saw it. I'd been around for two decades, sold more than twenty million records. I had earned the right to play with whomever I liked.

As for Dissection, well, that was a bit more complicated. I checked out their website and discovered that they were from Sweden and one of the founding band members, Jon Nödtveidt, was a bona fide Satanist. Then I found out that he had been trashing me on the Internet in the wake of my religious conversion. I was, he said, his "sworn enemy." I couldn't believe it. I didn't even know this guy and he was declaring war against me. At first I brushed it off as good old-fashioned Swedish insanity. Then I did a little more research, and what I unearthed was disturbing, to say the least. This crazy motherfucker had recently spent several years in prison after being convicted as an accessory to murder.

Regardless of motive or degree of involvement, this was clearly a bad and disturbed guy, and I didn't take his threats lightly. I voiced my concern to my agent, who in turn voiced concern to the show's promoter . . . who promptly booted Dissection off the shows. But that wasn't the end of it. Two weeks later we were supposed to play at a festival in France with some two dozen bands on the bill—including Dissection. I had no control over this engagement. If we're headlining a tour and some promoter schedules Rotting Christ or Dissection to open for us, then I certainly have the right to veto that decision. But festivals are sprawling, multilayered events designed to appeal to a broader demographic, and it's not at all unusual for bands of disparate backgrounds to occupy the same space. I suppose we could have withdrawn from the festival, but I didn't think that was necessary. At least not until Nödtveidt started spewing nonsense into cyberspace again, this time promising that when Megadeth arrived in France, he would be waiting for me.

This got my attention. Here was a guy who had already served time in prison, so it was unlikely that the prospect of punishment would serve as much of a deterrent. In this case, my usual arsenal of intimidation—fame, money, power, martial arts expertise—didn't mean shit. This guy knew what it was like to snuff out a human life. I didn't. Was I scared? Yeah, somewhat. More than that, though, I was pissed that my agent had gotten me into a predicament where not only was my safety in jeopardy, but I was in the middle of a huge online schism: Dave and his supposed Christian fanaticism (which isn't fanatical because I don't push it on anybody) vs. this poor, harmless devil worshipper and the little band he fronted.

Except, of course, he wasn't harmless. He was a murderer.

So we went to France, and I got all prayed up and ready to go. The promoter of the festival hired extra security for the day, and we arrived not knowing what to expect. The first person I ran into was John Dee, who was my manager at the time. John had gotten there early in the day, in time to see Dissection's performance, and then immediately sought out Nödtveidt. Without identifying himself, John had bumped into the guy, sort of gave him the bully shoulder, just to see how he'd react. Nödtveidt, according to John, was small and unimpressive, and the bump nearly knocked him off his feet. His only response was to look at John and say, "Excuse me, sir."

Then he walked away.

"Where is he now?" I asked.

"Gone. Took off right after their set."

I threw my hands into the air, at once relieved and disappointed. "Are you kidding me? All that worry, all that hassle. And the guy is a pussy?"

John laughed. "Apparently so."

I never did meet Nödtveidt in person. Never got an explanation for his online aggression. Which is probably for the best— it's pretty clear to me now that the guy was seriously fucked-up. By the summer of 2006 he'd removed himself from the human race, shooting himself in the head during what was rumored to be a ritual suicide. Strange, isn't it, the way some of my enemies end up? Meanwhile, I'm still here.

Over the years, more than a few people have leveled charges of hypocrisy at me in regard to the issue of playing with so-called satanic bands. As I've tried to explain, this is an area shaded with gray. First of all, I am much more secure in my own faith now than I was in 2002, when I first welcomed God back into my life. My spirituality is largely a personal matter, and one that I generally do not feel compelled to defend or explain. But I figure if you're going to write a book, you might as well be as candid as possible—you owe the reader that much. So here it is. I never said I wouldn't play with satanic bands. I'm not stupid enough to deal in sweeping generalities. What I said was this: I wouldn't *tour* with satanic bands. A tour is a business arrangement, in which I am an active and willing partner. A festival or single show involving a multitude of acts is completely different.

Moreover, there is the challenge of defining your terms. "Satanic" is a blanket label applied to almost any metal band with darker overtones. And sometimes the label is misapplied. Slayer is a great example. People might wonder, "How can Dave say one year he won't tour with any satanic bands and the next year go out with Slayer?" Well, the truth is, when I first got saved, there were things I didn't know. And it's like that old saying about when you're cooking: "When in doubt, leave it out." There were opportunities for Megadeth to do shows with some other bands, but some of their lyrics and stuff made me uncomfortable. I just wanted to make sure I took my time before I went out and started playing with certain bands. I have a long and sometimes acrimonious history with Slayer and Kerry King. We've both hurled our share of insults, dating back to a time when I was anything but a faithful Christian. But Kerry is not a Satanist, and Slayer is not a satanic band. It took time for me to get comfortable with the shadings of these terms and to not necessarily feel threatened by associating with any band with dark sensibilities.

Now I make my decisions on a case-by-case basis. It's as simple as that.

I realize that sometimes religion—or the renunciation of religion—can be a front. I know people who play in satanic bands who really don't believe in what they are doing. Maybe they're cynical. Maybe they're just lost. Sometimes I feel a need to be around the darker bands, if only briefly, just for my own reassurance and edification—so I can be happy I'm not going down that path anymore. I was there, man. I can tell the people who are real and the people who aren't, and it's a great for me to be able to say, "Hey, I'm lucky. I got out. I found a better way." The thing is, most people who become Christians do it the way the dudes do it on TV. Not the radicals, like me—people who really go out on a limb and embrace their spirituality in a different way. You know, there's a whole movement of kids who are tattooed up and wear black and play heavy music, and they have great bands . . . and they believe in God. And there is nothing wrong with that. In fact, one of the things I'd like to do with the rest of my career is help kids find a safe place to rock out. I wish I had that when I was younger.

Here's the thing, though. I spent a lot of time as a new Christian trying to get comfortable in my own skin. There were times when it felt smooth and right; there were also times when it felt like I was suffocating. It wasn't until the summer of 2005 that I began to sense harmony between my spiritual and artistic lives. It really kicked in with Gigantour, the annual six-week traveling heavy metal festival I conceived in response to the plethora of festivals that were springing up all over the musical landscape. Gigantour allowed me to stretch as an artist and a businessman. That was my baby, and I loved it. During one memorable show in Dallas, on August 2, a bunch of guys from different acts jammed together on the Pantera song "Cemetery Gates," in honor of the band's late guitarist "Dimebag" Darrell Abbott. Over the years I'd had my share of unpleasant encounters with the guys from Pantera. What can I say? I was an arrogant alcoholic and drug addict. It wasn't hard to push my buttons, and when Phil Anselmo would walk up to the microphone and say, "Fuck Mustaine," while opening for Megadeth during the *Countdown to Extinction* tour, well, that hit a button or two. I said some unflattering things about Pantera's music, and the war was on. But when Dimebag was murdered onstage by a crazy fan in late 2004, it seemed time to put aside all the petty bullshit. I contributed to a eulogy on MTV and later acknowledged Dimebag's incredible guitar chops and gentle spirit in an open letter on my website. That went a long way toward thawing relations with the rest of Pantera, and playing Dimebag's solo on "Cemetery Gates" remains one of my fondest Gigantour memories.

Life is too short to fight meaningless battles. I'd rather just play music and spend time with the people I love and respect. That was the thought that occurred to me as I stood on a stage at Obras Stadium in Buenos Aires, Argentina, on October 9, 2005, at the Pepsi Music Festival. What a night, what a crowd. We hadn't played in Argentina in several years, and yet here they were, out in force, cheering madly, reciting every word of every song—chanting the fucking guitar parts, for God's sake! It was like having twenty-five thousand backup singers. I felt like a kid again, like I wanted to do this forever. And so, before leaving the stage and heading home, I leaned into the mike and made a promise:

"I want to thank you again for coming down here and joining us tonight. I hope you had a great time, because we sure did! And we *will* be back!"

I meant it, too. Megadeth, in one form or another, would endure. And so would I.

EPILOGUE: THREE BOATS AND A HELICOPTER

'M SITTING IN A SCREENING ROOM AT FOX STUDIOS IN HOLLYWOOD, WATCHING A ROUGH CUT OF A WILL FERRELL MOVIE. I'M PRETTY PUMPED ABOUT BEING HERE, SINCE IT REPRESENTS ANOTHER CREATIVE AVENUE TO EXPLORE. I'VE BEEN ASKED TO PROVIDE SOME ORIGINAL MUSIC FOR THE SCORE, SO MY JOB IS TO WATCH THE MOVIE AND ENVISION PRECISELY THE RIGHT TYPE OF GUITAR WORK FOR TWO SPECIFIC SCENES. IT'S A TRIP, HONESTLY, TO BE INVITED INTO THIS WORLD. I'M A THRASH METAL GUITAR PLAYER, AND WE AREN'T OFTEN WELCOME IN THE MAINSTREAM. BUT A BIG-BUDGET SUMMER MOVIE STARRING WILL FERRELL IS ABOUT AS MAINSTREAM AS IT GETS, SO I CAN'T HELP BUT FEEL A SURGE OF EXCITEMENT.

One of my favorite shots. We had never used fire until this tour.
Photograph by Rob Shay.

The movie rolls along, and I'm watching it less for entertainment than inspiration—an odd sensation, to be sure.

"Right here," someone says. "This is where we need you."

I lean forward in my seat. Talk about a long, strange, remarkable trip. How on earth did I get here?

Suddenly my attention is diverted. Music floods the screening room, overwhelming the dialogue on-screen—or maybe it just seems that way to me, because I recognize it instantly. They call it a "placeholder" in the movie business, music that will never make it onto the score or soundtrack but is intended to merely fill a spot, to give the actual composer an idea of what is needed. It serves as both inspiration and guidance.

Or, in my case, annoyance.

I turn to my assistant manager, Isaac. Neither of us says a word. But I can tell we're thinking the same thing:

Metallica? Are you fucking kidding me?!

Isaac has worked with me for a few years now, long enough to know that nothing is more likely to trigger a Mustaine meltdown than an unexpected dose of Metallica. And this is about as unexpected as it could be.

Hear that, Dave? That's what we're after! Something that sounds like Metallica but isn't Metallica. Can you do that? Please?

I let my head hang for a moment, and then I smile. And Isaac smiles. And then we begin to laugh. Sometimes the world is too perverse to be met with anything other than a sense of humor. I realize at this very moment that it'll never end.

It will never . . . fucking . . . end.

Someday they'll be lowering my casket into the ground, and they'll be ready to play me off one last time ("A Tout le Monde" would be great), and someone will have left a Metallica disc in the CD player.

I'M HONESTLY TRYING to be better about all this shit. You can hold a grudge for only so long. It's just not healthy. Unfortunately, it seems sometimes that the most efficient way to bury a hatchet is to drive it into the back of your enemy's skull. That's the way I felt a few months earlier, when I got an e-mail from Scott Ian of Anthrax, which ended with the words, "See you in Cleveland, on April 3, right?"

I had no idea what he was talking about.

"What's going on in Cleveland?"

Another e-mail soon landed in my mailbox.

"Sorry, my bad. I thought you knew. Metallica is getting inducted into the Hall of Fame, and I thought you would be there."

"Sorry," I responded. "I haven't heard anything. Say hello to everyone for me, okay?"

Now, here's what really happened. I knew, of course, that Metallica was being inducted into the Rock and Roll Hall of Fame. That news had been announced in the fall of 2008. I tried to put it out of my mind as quickly as possible, reasoning that even though, if you want to distill it to its essence, it had everything to do with me . . . it really had nothing to do with me.

But Scott's e-mail, coming as it did near the end of Megadeth's most recent European tour (with Judas Priest), presented a dilemma. I knew what was coming. Metallica was going to be inducted into the Hall of Fame, and I was going to be invited to attend the ceremony.

As a spectator.

Sure enough, a few days later my manager, Mark Adelman, told me the offer had been extended. The band would pay for

Pam and me to fly out to Cleveland and attend a big party on the night of Friday, April 3. The next night we'd sit in the audience, along with the rest of Metallica's extended "family"—office staff, tour managers, fan club administrators, roadies, whatever—and applaud warmly as Lars and James and the boys were officially enshrined.

"What do you think?" Mark asked.

"You know what I think. The question is, how do we handle this?"

I had a graceful exit: I was incredibly busy. I'd be home in the States for a few days after the Priest tour, then I was supposed to go back to Germany to do some promotional work for Marshall Amplification, and then I had to prepare for a performance at the upcoming Golden Gods Awards. All while recording a Megadeth album. In order to attend the Hall of Fame induction, something else would have to give. Frankly, it wasn't worth it.

So I bit my tongue and wrote a letter—a press release, really—thanking Metallica for thinking of me, and congratulating them for being inducted, but ultimately expressing regrets that I could not attend.

And that was it.

No venom, no anger.

Not publicly, anyway.

I was walking a balance beam, for sure. I knew that if I revealed my true feelings—that there was no way I was going to sit in the fucking audience when I belonged up onstage with the band I helped create—everyone would just shake their heads and say, "Yup, same old bitter Dave."

And if I tried to act nonchalant, an equal number of people would say, "Ah, bullshit. He's not busy. He just doesn't want to be there."

A lose-lose proposition, as it's often been with me in regard to Metallica.

And yet, I couldn't compromise my principles on this one; I couldn't deny what was in my heart. Better to just stay away and keep my mouth shut. Take the proverbial high road.

But I couldn't quite let it go at that. So I reached out to Lars one last time. I sent him an e-mail, asking if we could talk sometime soon. He texted me back.

"Hey, man, it's a nutty suburban afternoon and I'm out with the kids. Can I get back to you in a couple days?"

Two weeks later he texted me again. Typical rock star timing: one week for each day. So I hit him back: "Yeah, I'm here now. We can talk."

A few seconds later, my cell phone rang. I was sitting in the kitchen of my house, on the outskirts of San Diego, on a perfect sunny morning. Pam sat across the table so that I could focus on something positive. The conversation was neither heated nor healing. There was no catharsis of any kind. It was almost banal, like neither of us had the energy to work up much emotion. We were both closer to fifty than forty now, on the downslope of life in every measurable way. If it wasn't quite possible to embrace like the brothers we once were, neither was it worth the effort to fight like warriors.

"I'd like you to be there, man," Lars said at one point, after launching into the same old tired explanation: that everyone who had been part of the Metallica experience had been invited to the ceremony, but that only those band members who had played "on record" could be inducted into the Hall of Fame.

In my head I could hear the voice of Sir John Gielgud, a graceful butler chastising the self-possessed alcoholic millionaire played by Dudley Moore in *Arthur*.

"Why, you little prick!"

I'd been on record with Metallica, of course. I'd been on DVD. I had songwriting credits. I had history. But what was the point of flogging that rotted horse? I understand Lars now. Or at least,

I understand that he has a purpose in my life, and that purpose is to challenge my humility, to keep me humble and hungry.

"I'd like to be there, too," I said. "But I can't. Not like this. We have different ideas about stuff. And since I can't be there the way I want to, it's probably best if I just support you guys from the sideline."

I took a deep breath.

"But I want you to know that I'm proud of you, man, and I really wish you the best."

"Thanks," Lars said. "You, too. And I hope you change your mind."

"If I do, you'll be the first to know."

I DIDN'T DWELL on that conversation for long. There was too much work to be done, too many other things to occupy my time. I had to get right back in the studio and put the finishing touches on the twelfth Megadeth album, *Endgame*. Whether this is an ironically titled project remains to be seen. Creatively and professionally speaking, there are some other things I'd like to do with my life at this point: more film scoring, teaching, solo albums. And I'd like to spend more time with my family, catch up with my kids after all these years. Justis has his own musical interests, and I'd like to help in whatever way I can; Electra, so charming and wise beyond her years, has a burgeoning television career. I've missed enough. I don't want to miss anything else.

But it's been this way for some time now. Every Megadeth album for the past decade has felt like it might be the last, like I'm wrung out and there is nothing else left to say. The process is utterly exhausting. Then the album is released, and we get to perform . . . and it all seems worth it.

I had no idea what to expect in the spring of 2007, when *United Abominations* was released. The lineup had been revamped again, with James LoMenzo replacing James MacDonough on bass. Didn't seem to matter. The songs were strong, the playing tight, and the album took off, selling more briskly than any Megadeth record since *Youthanasia*. Fifty thousand copies in the first week alone.

Maybe it'll be the same with *Endgame*. I like the record (please permit my anachronistic terminology—I am, after all, a child of the vinyl era). A lot. I like the new band, too. Yup, that's right. More personnel changes, with the awesome Chris Broderick stepping in for Glen Drover on guitar. If you're keeping track, that's eighteen musicians who have been a part of the heavy metal warhorse known as Megadeth.

Seventeen who have come and gone. Or stayed.

And me.

I have no animosity toward anyone who played in Megadeth; in fact, I've tried to make amends with just about everyone I might have hurt along the way, and I've tried to forgive everyone who fucked me over—there is no shortage of either. A couple years ago I flew out to Phoenix to meet with David Ellefson. We hadn't talked in a while, probably not since his lawsuit was tossed out of court. We went out to dinner, talked about old times and new opportunities, about wives and friends and kids.

"I gotta tell you," Junior said. "Leaving Megadeth was the dumbest thing I ever did."

I laughed. "Yeah, I know."

We all do stupid things. The trick is to recognize your mistakes and do better the next time around. I could have been the biggest guitar player in the world, if only I had been able to handle my fists—and my thirst. But I was incapable of doing those things. All the trips to rehab, the drinking problem, the drug problem, band problems, fighting with people in and out of the music business, problems with my fidelity, my children—I look at all this and I think, *I'm capable of so much more.*

I've had this feeling for a while now that there is something important to be done with the years I have left, and I don't think it's limited to going out onstage and banging my head for Megadeth—not that I don't enjoy it. I think opportunities will be placed in my path, and if I don't pay attention, I'm going to miss them.

You know that old joke about the guy stranded in the flood, perched atop the roof of his house, waiting for God to save him? He repeatedly turns away rescue efforts based on the belief that God will personally take care of him. The floodwaters ultimately sweep him away and he winds up at heaven's gate, wondering why God has forsaken him. St. Peter looks at the poor guy and laughs.

"What are you talking about? We sent three boats and a helicopter."

I feel like the boat has come by for me more than a few times. Whether I deserved it or not, I had success with Metallica. I had success with Megadeth. I had success with Megadeth again after my arm was wrecked. I have a wife who has stayed with me through some very hard times. And I have two healthy, happy children. So at some point you have to wonder: how many times does God have to say, "Dude, I love you," before I straighten up for good?

I've got everything a man could want, and then some.

It's time.